BISHOP OLIVER

LETTERS
&
REMINISCENCES

Compiled by his Brother

John Green-Wilkinson

Published 1998

by

WILTON 65
Flat Top House, Bishop Wilton, York. YO4 1RY

Copyright © John Green-Wilkinson

ISBN 0 947828 56 7

Printed
in
Great Britain

CONTENTS

ILLUSTRATIONS

OLIVER

OLIVER AND THE AUTHOR
SETTING OUT TO RIDE IN THE NEW FOREST

FOREWORD

Twenty five years after my brother Oliver died, I realised that I must put together a history of his life, as I have numbers of letters, photograph albums, and news cuttings about him. They needed sorting out, so what better way of doing this, than by putting it all on paper.

He had a unique life, with his army and ecclesiastical work, plus a rapid escalation to Bishop, and could claim to have had three double barrelled names in his life: Oliver Green-Wilkinson, Oliver Northern Rhodesia, and Oliver Central Africa! He also signed himself Oliver Zambia, which he said had the distinction of being the last name in the local telephone book!

At school he was sometimes called FOG-Wilkinson, from his initials for Francis Oliver (I was tempted to add Michael to our second son's names, so that his Simon Oliver might give the more up to date nickname, at that time, of SMOG-Wilkinson!) At university, Oliver was often known as OLLIE.

Oliver had a distinguished life at school, at university, and in the war time army. Then, after the war he rose from priest to bishop in five years, with a further eleven years to archbishop; all this happening at a time of chaos and change in Europe and Africa.

His great sense of humour prompted me to collect some of his anecdotes, which he used to love to tell us on his visits from Africa. I discussed with James Robertson, who was one of Oliver's priests in Africa, the idea of writing a history of Oliver's life, and he was very enthusiastic. He gave me the names of a number of Oliver's colleagues and from there it snowballed, so I have stories to tell. I also received many tributes, which I have to record in his honour.

He had such a promising life, only to be cut short at the early age of fifty seven, when his car burst a tyre and turned on its side, giving a fatal blow to his head. He died shortly

3

afterwards at St. Francis Hospital, Katete, without regaining consciousness.

Oliver had been fully prepared for unexpected death and left a list of special wishes, in addition to his Will. At the end of this book, you are find the tributes which were recorded at his funeral and the memorial services in Lusaka and in Westminster Abbey.

His sister, Prudence, who gave him support as companion and hostess at Bishop's Lodge in Lusaka died at Epiphany 1990, at the age of seventy two. Prudence developed Parkinson's Disease, while out in Zambia, which was of great concern to Oliver before he died. For her last two years she lay motionless in a Freeland Nursing Home, unable to speak except the occasional word which showed she knew everything that was said to her. The nurses were amazed at the way she ,never complained. The way she bore her illness was an example to us all.

I am most grateful to all of you who have contributed to this book. In particular Canon James Robertson and Canon John Houghton, while Lord Holderness has not only contributed with his memories of Oliver, but is instrumental in printing this book with his wife, Diana. Without their help, the book would never have been completed.

As well as my thanks to all the contributors, I am particularly indebted to my daughter-in-law, Anne, who has spent many hours typing much of this book.

When I embarked on the project I had no idea of the quantity and quality of the letters Oliver had written, which I was holding. These would never have been available if my father had not kept all the letters so carefully, even making pencilled copies, when the original had to be passed to another member of the family. Perhaps he was made aware of the need to keep letters, by the two folders containing all the letters his father had written from the Crimean War and Indian Mutiny. All who read this book must thank him for his foresight and care in keeping Oliver's letters.

4

I am also indebted to my mother for the family photographs she took and carefully preserved.

John Green-Wilkinson

December 1997

[Note. Throughout the book, the Editor's comments are in square brackets].

POEM WRITTEN AT OLIVER'S BIRTH
BY HIS GRANDFATHER, SIR FRANCIS EDWARDS

O livi: young life doth flow
Like to a rippling stream:
Into his thoughts come & go
Visions of hope's bright dream.
Endless delight & love crown all his days
Rich with the promise of numberless Mays!

7 May 1918.

OLIVER'S PARENTS

LUMLEY

MYFANWY

6

CHAPTER 1

FAMILY AND YOUTH

Oliver was born on 7th May 1913 at Aston Tirrold Rectory. His father had been made Rector of the parish the previous year, and Deborah, his sister, was by then 18 months old. Lumley, his father, was the younger son of Lieutenant General Frederick Green-Wilkinson C.B., Colonel of the Oxfordshire and Buckinghamshire Light Infantry at the turn of the century. The General had served with the 42nd Highland Regiment, The Black Watch in the Crimea and Indian Mutiny.

The name Wilkinson had been added in 1808, when Mr. Wilkinson left his inheritance and name to Mr. Green. As Captain Gronow writes in his *Reminiscences of Regency Life*, a friendship had developed when elderly Mr. Wilkinson entered St. Marylebone church late for a Service and could not find a seat. Young Mr. Green, who had arrived early to hear a special preacher, nobly gave Mr. Wilkinson his seat. A great friendship developed from this meeting, and when Mr. Wilkinson died, he left Mr. Green his small fortune plus his name. 'A civility rewarded,' as Captain Gronow describes the occasion in his book.

Lumley had volunteered, as a young man at Magdalen College Oxford, to join the City Imperial Volunteers (C.I.V.) to fight in the Boer War in 1900. It may have been from this visit to South Africa that a love of the country and people developed and was passed on to his son Oliver. Lumley and his friends were all privates in the C.I.V. and he acted as a dispatch rider, using the recently invented bicycle as a form of transport. He had to buy the bicycle himself from Harrods, and sold it back to them after the war, for display in the shop window, to advertise this new form of transport, even though it had no brakes and relied on back pedalling to stop. He actually paid for his extra year at Magdalen from the money

OLIVER'S PATERNAL GRANDPARENTS

GRANDFATHER
LT. GENERAL FREDERICK GREEN-WILKINSON

GRANDMOTHER 'GIBBIE' WITH OLIVER AND DEBORAH

8

he received from Harrods, plus the sale of photographs of crews rowing on the river. The coaches liked to buy the photographs to check on the exact action of each member of the crew. Until then photography had been restricted to photographs of the crew seated in chairs with crossed arms. Action photography was a new idea.

After getting his degree at Oxford, Lumley went to Cuddesdon Theological College and was ordained Priest in 1903. His first job was Curate at Holy Innocents, Hammersmith. From 1907 to 1908 he was Chaplain to the Bishop of Stepney, Dr. Cosmo Lang, a Magdalen man. He then founded the Magdalen College Mission in Somers Town Euston, and worked there until 1912, when he moved to Aston Tirrold. In 1910 he married Myfanwy Edwards, the daughter of Sir Francis Edwards, who had been the Liberal member of Parliament for Radnorshire. The Edwards family is descended from Rhodi Mawr, King of Wales, who was killed by the Saxons in 877. Myfanwy had an uncle by marriage, the Right Reverend Alfred Edwards, Bishop of St. Asaph, who became the first Archbishop of Wales.

While they were at Aston Tirrold the First World War was being fought, so Lumley felt that he should volunteer to act as a temporary Army Chaplain. He joined the 41st Infantry Brigade, part of the 14th Division, on 29th Sept 1914 at Aldershot. The Division sailed for France on 19th May 1915 and were at Ypres soon afterwards. He was Chaplain to the 7th and 8th Battalion of the Kings Royal Rifle Corps (60th) and 8th Battalion of the Rifle Brigade. From Lumley's Anniversary Book it is noted that the 41st Brigade attacked with 'Liquid fire' at Hooge on 30th July [presumably an early flame thrower!]

After Lumley returned from the army to his Parish at Aston Tirrold, Prudence Anne was born in April 1917. She was nearly 4 years younger than Oliver and was the sister who became his companion many years later in Lusaka.

Soon after Prudence was born, the family moved from

9

Aston Tirrold to Ascot Heath. Lumley had his first Sunday at All Saints on 10th June 1917, but was not instituted Rector until 29th September. They lived in a rented house, Englemere Wood, as the Rectory was too small. Hilaré was born in May 1918 and Felicity in February 1920.

On 1st June 1920 Alfred Edwards, Bishop of St. Asaph was enthroned as the first Archbishop of Wales. Cosmo Lang who was at that time Archbishop of York, attended the enthronement and invited Lumley to act as his Chaplain and Oliver to be one of his pages. Oliver was then 7 years old.

Myfanwy, his mother, wrote on 2nd June to her father, who had been unable to attend the enthronement. It was a very long letter describing all the event, and extracts are given below.

'Dear Fuz, [her name for her father] Lumley met Ebor [Cosmo Lang] at Chester and motored with him to the Henry Gladstones. Blanche, [Branston, a cousin] Oliver and I went on to St. Asaph arriving at 6.12 ... Oliver having a bath and going to bed ... Dinner at 8. Canterbury took in Peggy, Uncle Alfred, Mrs. Davidson; St. Davids [Bishop of] took me. St. Davids was full of enquiries about you and was quite nice and lively, which was something ... Uncle Alfred and Peggy stayed up to receive the Lloyd Georges, who were arriving by car at 10.30.

'Blanche and I were coming down the top flight of stairs, when the car arrived and were just at the top of the main stairs, when they came up! Lloyd George exclaimed with pleasure, when he saw me and said "Where is Frank?" He was so disappointed not to see you. Later, when in my dressing gown, we heard singing, so crept along to the top of the stairs and stood behind the curtain and heard *Jesu Lover of my Soul* sung in Welsh by an enthusiastic crowd in the drive. Uncle Alfred spoke to them and explained that Lloyd George was too tired to do so. So they went off.

'Oliver was awfully good. He was quite by himself all the time, but didn't mind a bit, and was fast asleep, when I

OLIVER'S MATERNAL GRANDPARENTS

SIR FRANCIS EDWARDS

KATHERINE EDWARDS
SKETCHES BY JOHN SINGER SARGENT

BISHOPTHORPE,
YORK.
12 June 1920.

My dear Oliver,

Here is a photograph of the Archbishop whose train you carried at St. Asaph on June 1st. He is not much to look at but he is an old friend of your father's, and he is very grateful to you for your attendance upon him and for your going through your duties without any mistake and with so much solemnity. When you grow up perhaps you may like to remember that you attended one of the Archbishops who were present at a great day in the history of the old Church in Wales, and this photograph may remind you of that day.

Yours affectionately,

LETTER OF THANKS FROM THE ARCHBISHOP OF YORK

12

peeped in after dinner. It was rather wonderful for him having breakfast with Canterbury and the Prime Minister, not to mention the new Archbishop of Wales!! ... Lloyd George and Mrs. Lloyd George were at the Celebration at 8.15 and communicated. They were really far more reverent than the Bishop of St. Davids.

'After breakfast I spent a good deal of time getting Oliver's collar fixed comfortably on his cassock. Dr. Allan had turned up for breakfast and was much amused at the arrangements and Canterbury said he would stop the whole proceedings if Oliver's collar got crooked in any way!

'By 11, Peggy and Lady Dundonald, Eily, Sylvia, Blanche and I went to the Cathedral and were cinematographed as we walked along the top path. Eily and I were both given seat 16 and when we got there, we found a 3rd person in possession (there was only one seat for four of the rest of the party!). They brought extra chairs and we eventually got settled.

'Lloyd George was led in by the High Sheriff and Prince Arthur [Duke of Connaught] came in with the Lord Lieutenant Henry Gladstone. The Service was very impressive. It was a thrilling moment for me when the procession began, and I kept my eyes on the aisle and not the hymn - I am afraid! Oliver was carrying Ebor's train, so I could concentrate on Ebor for my 'belongings'. He came one of the last and I had jimjams up and down my spine, when I suddenly saw Lumley carrying the cross and looking really splendid. He was doing a proper military step and carrying the heavy cross well up and out. Ebor next, then Oliver and a little Lloyd boy - both looking most reverent, but Oliver extra so. Mrs. Davidson said afterwards, that she thought the look on Oliver's face, as he gazed straight ahead, was one of the most impressive and beautiful parts of the day, and the Prince sent his Equerry to congratulate Lumley on his splendid dignity and good marching!

'After luncheon I saw Lumley for the first time to speak

13

to and heard about his time with the Gladstones. Prince Arthur was there and on Lumley being introduced to him said, 'Is it a brother of yours in the Rifle Brigade?' and made him sit next to him after dinner [his brother Louis had been A.D.C. to the Prince].

'The Prince and Lloyd George went off by special train to London directly after lunch. So we saw no more of them.'

By 1921 the family were moving once more. This time Lumley became vicar of St. Peter's Church, Bournemouth. When plans were being made for the move, Oliver was asked "Would you like to stay to see the new baby, or go to the seaside?" His reply was "Oh, lets go the seaside, we see a new baby every year!" So he went to the seaside and John was born in March. When they all arrived at Bournemouth, Myfanwy had four children under four years of age for a few months! On 7th April Lumley was instituted Vicar of Bournemouth.

CHAPTER 2

PREPARATORY AND PUBLIC SCHOOL 1922

FARNBOROUGH

Oliver went to Farnborough Preparatory School on 12th April 1922, and on 21st June he had his first visit from his parents and was able to tell them that he had just passed his swimming test [which was to prove useful when in Zambia many years later.] He visited a specialist in July and had his tonsils removed in October.

Nothing much can be said about these schooldays. We know that he did not like the school and he was not an athletic type of boy.

During this period, on 24th June 1923 his father was asked to preach the University Sermon from the stone pulpit at Magdalen. It is interesting that Oliver was to preach also the University Sermon from the same pulpit, while in England for the Lambeth Conference in 1958.

At the start of 1925, St Peters Church, Bournemouth, held a New Year's Party in the Hall, attended by a record 400 guests. The local paper records that Deborah, Oliver, Prudence, Hilaré and Felicity presented a charming little play *The Blue Prince*. Little John (aged 3) gave a rendering of *Wee Willie Wimble*. John also recalls joining his 3 older sisters in singing *Felix kept on Walking* disguised as cats. They had to process round the stage and end up in a row at the front of the stage. Unfortunately the flower, marking where John was to end up, got kicked to the back of the stage, so that was where John firmly stood, all on his own.

Oliver writes from school, on 22nd February, to his father, 'The roofs were white this morning, so I think it must have come down hard in the night. There is a sermon tonight by Rev. Keymer and a collection for the Parish Funds. In work at last I have got 1st in classics, but I will not be able to keep there, I am afraid.' Then his letter of 1st March to his father ends ' ... What book shall I read in the Bible next; I will finish Kings II in one or two days. I started it this term.'

Later that year the family rented Corrie Fodley at the Bridge of Cally, near Blairgowrie in Perthshire, for August and part of September. It was here that Oliver showed his brotherly love. He was twelve and his brother four, when one evening they went out to shoot rabbits with their father. Two had shotguns, while John was armed with his cap pistol. It was not long before Oliver saw and shot a rabbit. Then on the way home, when no more rabbits had been seen, Oliver suggested to John that they should go into the nearby wood, to look for a rabbit. When they were in the wood Oliver said "Stop John, do you see the rabbit at the foot of that tree?" John was doubtful, but being trustful of his older brother, he did what he was told and fired his pistol. Whereupon, Oliver leapt forward and came back carrying a dead rabbit. John was then made to arrive home carrying the one and only kill of the evening!

'THE GUNS' - LUMLEY, OLIVER AND JOHN

16

Oliver had been confirmed at Farnborough school earlier in 1926, by the Bishop of Guildford, and had his first communion at St Peters, Bournemouth in April. By September he had passed his Common Entrance Exam and went to Eton College. He was a boarder at Sheepshanks' House. 'Sheep', as the family knew him, had served in the Rifle Brigade during the 1914 war, so Lumley had met him when he was Chaplain at Ypres with the 41st Brigade. Arthur Sheepshanks (A.C.S.) was a great character, with a good sense of humour and had a considerable influence on Oliver. He was a bachelor and a cricketer (dry bob). However, Oliver preferred to row and learnt skills which were to be valuable to him at University. Academically he showed greater promise, as we shall see from his school reports. He ended his time at Eton under Robert Birley as his History Tutor. Their paths were to cross after the war, when Birley was teaching in South Africa, before becoming Headmaster of Eton.

At the end of Oliver's first 'half' (term) at Eton, Sheep wrote in his report, 'In trials he did excellent work, and had it not been for a lapse in science, he would have been top of his 'remove' instead of third. A most satisfying pupil, because he is so thorough in all his work, and is not contented with anything but the best.

'I am afraid I rather shock him with my frivolity now and then, but one cannot always be too serious.'

Then in March 1927, Sheep wrote, 'It was bad luck missing so much of the 'half', though he probably enjoyed his time in the Sanatorium.' This was probably when he had measles and had to start wearing glasses. He wore glasses until his eyesight improved, while in Zambia after the War. Sheep continued, 'He is beginning to be mildly impertinent to me, when egged on. This is as it should be, for without it, he might run the risk of being too good and of being lacking in spirit. So I shall continue to encourage him to answer me back ... He did well to win a prize in the Rhodes Geography Paper. I am so sorry to hear that you have to take a rest.' This refers to Lumley having to retire from St. Peters, Bournemouth, due to his throat troubles, which made it impossible for him to preach. He frequently had 'come overs' as he called them, when his voice would give up and tears would pour down one side of his face. This made preaching sermons difficult and in February he told the Parish that he would have to retire. Lord Dawson of Penn advised him to rest his throat for 6 months or more. In May his father-in-law died, so it was decided to take the family to Europe for 10 months.

Oliver wrote to his mother on 5th June 1927, 'I have had the most marvellous day of my life. There was no early school, so after breakfast at 8.15 I went out to get food for tea and supper, and a white carnation button-hole. Then came Chapel after which I changed into my full glory! My waistcoat was a great success. Then in my full dress I paraded the street [this was for the 4th June Celebrations]. My first draw was the Stuart-Mendith girl that we met riding at Bournemouth, but I didn't dare speak to her, as difficult to explain myself ... [Sir Francis Edwards had died on 10th May 1927, so that is why his parents were not present on the 4th. Dodo, his aunt, came down from London instead, and was suitably fed in Oliver's room]. Then we went back to my room for supper of chicken and another 2lbs. of strawberries etc. At 9 o'clock we started to go to the fireworks. It was mercifully dry during this, but the fireworks were wet ... occasional 'duds' went on till the Boats arrived. But the men were so demoralized by their failures to make Brocks fireworks a success, that they completely 'boshed' this part. The boats usually saluted in darkness and a blaze of light came, when nothing was happening and a wonderful cock-fight set-piece was put on while one of the Boats came down! One boy fell in ... and had to be pulled out of the water by a punt. Dodo got a taxi at about 11.10 and I hope got home by midnight. I *do* wish you had been there.'

In July Sheep wrote, 'He is learning to manage his House Tutor rather well. When I start in my bullying way to browbeat him, he becomes most impertinent and I collapse like a pricked bubble! But I can absolutely rely on his judgement, to tell me frankly what he thinks of me, on the proper occasions! He is a very good boy, whom I like very much.'

On 11th December Oliver wrote to his mother, 'I have a nice surprise for you. Since about a week before 'Leave' I have been reading a book on the Crusades and last Thursday we had an exam on it, the Lower Boy History Prize and *I* won it! 79%. I believe the prize is worth about £5. I have bought my Christmas present. I was told I must get fur lined gloves, for chilblains, so I thought you would like me to have some. They are lovely. My chilblains are, touch wood, *gone* as the result of one treatment. Perfectly marvellous.'

Then at the end of the Michaelmas Half, his report said, 'Oliver has done terribly well this Half in his work. It is a great achievement to be second and have time to read a book on the Crusades, so carefully and thoroughly that he has won the Lower Boy Rosebery History Prize ... I hope he will do well in Trials. He will enjoy Rome.' In fact, in the Trials, he got a distinction, a science prize and the Brinkman Divinity Prize.

The reference to Rome in his Tutor's Report, was because his parents plus five children, a governess, nanny and lady's maid set off for a tour of Europe that summer and they moved from Portofino to Rome in December. Oliver had been taken back to Eton from Glion on Lake Geneva by his parents on 20th September. Then in December he came out to Rome for the Christmas holidays. He travelled out with his Uncle Louis. While he was in Rome his father arranged an audience with Pope Pius XI, on 20th January 1928. His brother John was horrified to have to wear velvet shorts and his sisters were covered in veils. Even worse, the taxi taking them to the Vatican broke down in Via del Corso, the main shopping street of Rome, and they had to stand on the pavement in full view

THE FAMILY NEAR THEIR HOTEL IN ROME

DRESSED TO SEE THE POPE

20

while the wheel was repaired. When they eventually arrived at the Vatican, Myfanwy told them to remember to say 'Your Holiness' if they were spoken to by the Pope. They were ushered into a room with a red cord forming a circle, round which they and others stood. The Pope came in, circled the room before blessing them, and spoke to Myfanwy. Pointing at John, he said, "What age has he?" Myfanwy replied, "Six," forgetting to say 'Your Holiness,' to the family's great amusement.

Oliver returned to school from Rome accompanied again by his uncle, who reported on the journey to Lumley on 26 January, 'We had a capital journey in the greatest comfort, and saw Elba from the train and a good view of the Tower of Pisa. Oliver seemed amused at the ancient story of the conversational old lady who asked her fellow traveller, "Have you been to Pisa," to which he replied, "I only got out to get a bath bun" ... train absolutely punctual everywhere. We got deck chairs facing East and the fierce SW wind drove us across at a great pace. Roughest sea I had been in, in a small ship. At one moment I thought Oliver and I *and* his basin would land in the lee scuppers, which were flooded, but we just hung on. Oliver took this bravely and tried to sleep. He stuck it out well and was not ill. I think he probably never will be now.' When Oliver was back at Eton, early in 1928, Lumley wrote a postcard to him from Rome, which said, 'This morning we had a distant view from the Quirinal Hill, of General Diaz's State Funeral. Yesterday we went to see his coffin resting above the 'unknown soldier' and crowds filing past. I raised my hand like a real Roman, as I went by!' He does not say that as he neared the coffin he heard something being said, as the Fascist Salute was given. So, when it was his turn to be 'like a Roman,' he raised his arm and said "Passa Avanti" which had a good ring to it, but not realising that he had heard the officials calling out, "Pass along, please."

The family had arrived in Rome by train, and the story goes that as the large party passed the ticket collector, he raised

WALKING IN THE ALPS NEAR CHAMONIX

FAMILY LUGGAGE ON THE WAY
FROM ROME TO CADENABBIA ON LAKE COMO

22

his eyebrows and said "La Caravana!" There was an occasion a few years later when the family travelled to Tabley near Knutsford, for theatricals with the Leicester-Warrens, Lumley found it cheaper to book the family on the train as a football team. When they arrived at Crewe Station, a top hatted station master was there to meet the eleven, and was surprised to find a family.

Sheep wrote in his report, March 1928, ' ... he is a glutton for work and the only fear is that he may over do it. So far he has only got one prize this Half, a Holiday Task prize. He continues to be a most satisfactory boy, extremely conscientious and trustworthy. He is, of course, very serious minded, but he does condescend to frivol occasionally, when encouraged to do so.'

Then in July 1928, Sheep wrote, ' ... It is hard to keep pace with the number of prizes he gains, but I know there has been at least one during the course of the Half. He is sure to do well in Trials [he got a distinction]. I hope he does not work too hard. I have found him asleep in his chair at 10.30 pm with his light burning [lights had to be out by 10 pm] but I do not think this happened very often.'

In August, while he was at home from school, he won 3rd prize on his horse, Spindles, at the Knighton Show. The family had moved to the Cottage Knighton, from Bournemouth, on the death of Sir Francis Edwards, while looking for a home nearer to London. Then in September, Oliver had his first cub hunt with the local Teme Valley Fox Hounds. A year later when he went out hunting with an attractive companion, the Tatler photographer was at the meet. Oliver was photographed alongside his companion, but he was rather indignant when the photograph appeared showing the attractive young girl with only the hindquarters of his horse! He had a good laugh at that.

By December, Sheep was reporting, 'He went in for the English Literature Prize and naturally won it, but only by a short head from Morrice his stable companion, roughly speaking. He is no high flyer at Classics, but obviously has a gift for writing his own language, and for retaining History in his memory.'

On 24th March 1929, Oliver wrote to his father, 'The steeplechase was much harder than I thought it was going to be. There were about two hundred and twenty starters. We started off across a newly ploughed field, and I managed to sprint up to about 4th over the first field, and so got out of the crowd.

'We then crossed two fields with hedges, and ditches, and when we got out on to open country again, I was just at the end of the 'select band' of about ten, who were leading.

'About a mile from the start I began to feel incredibly ill, but half a mile further on, I had got to such a point that I was running automatically, and was far less painful. I went up one place here, and then we had four broad ditches full of water, ending with the 'school jump', which you must have seen in the newspapers. I was too dead to do much of a sprint at the end, so lost one place, but I was given a good cheer by the admiring crowd!' Lumley would have been very interested in his progress in the steeplechase since, when Lumley was at Radley, he was leading at the finish of his steeplechase; he thought the great cheers were for him and failed to look round and see the boy overtaking him at the finishing line!

Oliver ends his letter, 'I think that the photographs of Cymro and Brennyn are awfully good.' These were two Welsh ponies who had been bought at Knighton to replace Spindleshanks, Oliver's earlier mount.

On 28th July, Oliver wrote 'I was elected to the Debating Society [in his House]. I can now fag other boys! Morrice also got in.

'It is thrilling to think that in another two days I shall be at Tidworth [with the Officers Training Corps in camp] doing real soldiering ...

'You can imagine that I am feeling a bit weary from Trials, since I have been up at half past five every morning since Monday bar one! Since Morrice has done the same, I haven't even the satisfaction of feeling that I deserve to beat him, which I certainly shan't do. Still, that won't, if all is well, hinder my getting into Sixth Form, as he leaves a year before me.'

His Report at the end of the Summer Half said, 'He is obviously a promising historian and should become a History Specialist after Christmas. I am extremely glad that he was successful in the Birchall Prize. He deserved it. My only fear is that he does too much work. But he does not seem to wilt under the burden.'

His Classical Report added, 'He did some of the best Sunday Questions in the division.' These were religious essays written on a Sunday.

On 14th August all the family went for a holiday in North Wales, and stayed at Beddgelert. On Sunday they went to church in a Welsh Chapel. As the hymns were in Welsh, Oliver sang heartily, using the only Welsh words that he had been taught by Dosia, his mother's Welsh maid. He discovered after the service that he had been singing 'Go to the cow shed'!

In December 1929, Sheep wrote, ' ... He has managed to keep his head above water in spite of the floods' and ended, 'I hope you have recovered from your indisposition and will be able to cope with your son two days before the advertised time.' Floods had sent the boys home early.

HISTORY SPECIALIST

Then on 23rd January 1930, he became a History Specialist and wrote, 'I have been to see my new Tutor, Birley, and am frightfully excited with the prospect of my new work. He is very nice, young, very tall and fair.' Robert Birley was to be his History Tutor and became a life long friend.

On 23rd February, Oliver wrote home, 'How thrilling that we have really got the prospect of a home in April. It sounds very much what we want.' He was referring to Lovel Hill in Windsor Forest, which was to be their home until 1949.

25

LOVEL HILL IN WINDSOR FOREST
AFTER SNOW HAD FALLEN

THE 'FOURTH OF JUNE' CELEBRATIONS
OLIVER ENTERTAINS HIS BROTHER AND SISTERS
(LUMLEY IN THE BACKGROUND WITH GOVERNESS)

26

Then he reported on a visit to Burlington House to see Italian Pictures, which he simply loved. Five boys were taken up to the exhibition, by Robert Birley, 'All at his expense!'

He continued, 'I had a terrible time to start with in the Debate [House Debating Society] as all except Morrice were strongly against 'Home Rule' (only eight were present). All the five speeches simply riddled me, and I had to spend an hour, after the 'house was opened' answering masses of questions and cross questions entirely on my own, except for two speeches by Morrice. It was rather a triumph to end by carrying the motion by four to two, with Graham abstaining!'

In March 1930, Robert Birley wrote in his Report, 'He has done a few historical essays for me, and they have been thorough and not at all badly written. His general subjects have not been so good. He is too unadventurous. Until he begins to take risks, he simply will not get ideas of his own. The more he reads the better, and as widely as possible ... on Italian Painting he had something to say, and has become quite communicative.'

In June the family moved from their temporary home in Bracknell to Lovel Hill, Cranbourne. This enabled Lumley to travel to London twice a week by train from Windsor to Lambeth Palace, for his new unpaid work, as Private Chaplain to Cosmo Lang, his old friend from Stepney days.

In July Robert Birley spoke of improvements, ' ... his work has improved immensely. His answers to historical questions were among the best in a good division. He showed a flair for new ideas. His Sunday Questions were generally about the best and he has shown a new readiness to take a risk. He has been most 'talkative' in a very forthcoming Division, and what he has said has been well worth while.'

On 26th July 1930 Sheep wrote, 'His experience in the House Four on the river will, I hope, be useful to him next year. I gather that he has improved a lot.' This is interesting since up until then Sheep had expressed the wish that he might excel at sport, to balance his academic skills; as success could not be found on the football field, it was now found on the river.

On 8th August Oliver set out alone to stay with a French family in Paris. On his return he went up to Scotland to stay with Victor Balfour-Brown, an old friend of his father from Magdalen. B.B., as the family called him, was a successful barrister who owned Glen Kinglas, a deer forest. He was a famous painter of wild life and, in particular, of deer. He was a skilled stalker and in his later years enjoyed stalking the deer to touch them, rather than shoot them.

Lumley had visited B.B. in 1926. To reach Glen Kinglas you drove from Tyndrum to Taynuilt past Loch Awe. You then travelled by boat up Loch Etive to Ardmaddy. From there you had to walk up Glen Kinglas to the Lodge in the Black Mountains, a distance of nearly 10 miles. When Lumley got to the Lodge, his feet were in such a poor state that he had to give up any idea of stalking. This was considered a poor show by B.B., who wanted to reach his quota of 'head' shot! Luckily Oliver did better and shot a stag weighing 14st. 2lbs. on 2nd September, as recorded in the Anniversary Book.

Next year, on 22nd January, the book records that his sisters, Prudence, Hilaré and Felicity had their first day at Eton. Until then, they had been taught by a governess at home. Now their parents heard of a day school, being run in Eton by Miss Scott, for the benefit of Eton masters' children. The school met in Mr Lyttleton's House (the son Humphrey was already showing his skills on the drums - later to take to the trumpet). Poor Oliver had to face his sisters in the streets of Eton occasionally, to his embarrassment.

ELECTED TO LIBRARY

During March, Oliver was elected to the Library, which meant that he was now a House Prefect. Sheep reported, 'by September [he] will be fully qualified to take over the running

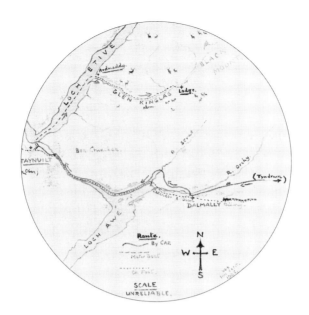

MAP OF GLEN KINGLAS
PAINTED BY VICTOR BALFOUR-BROWN FOR HIS GUEST

ANNUAL FAMILY LINE UP
DEBORAH, OLIVER, PRUDENCE, HILARÉ, FELICITY AND JOHN
(SOMETIMES KNOWN AS FAITH, HOPE AND CHARITY: AND MAHJONG!)

29

of the House, with all its responsibilities.' He was to be, in September, Captain of the House. Robert Birley then said, 'I have found his weekly essays a great deal more interesting to read ... He must take more risks in putting down his own ideas.' Alington, the Headmaster said, 'Sunday Questions have always been well done.'

On 4th June, Oliver received his 'Lower Boats' and rowed in the St. George boat in the Procession of Boats.

At the end of the Summer Half, Birley was able to write, 'He has done a great deal of work, which is usual with him, but the improvement in his essays is something new. He has at last got the feel of writing an essay, less wooden and he is getting ideas of his own. I should say that they are certainly up to scholarship standard ... I shall be interested to see how he does in the July Examination.' The Headmaster ended his Report, 'I have nothing but praise for him either as a member of the Division, or as a member of Society.'

When Oliver came top of the History Specialists in the December Trials, Birley reported, 'I must congratulate him in particular on three excellent pieces of work - an essay on India for which he was 'sent up for good,' a long essay which he wrote in the School Library and a paper on Medieval Architecture for the Essay Society.'

The Spring of 1932 must have been severe, as there is a lovely report on Oliver from Lieutenant Colonel J.D. Hills M.C. (as Sheep describes him), 'When there is too much East Wind, when the heating apparatus fails to function, when it is stuffy, when everybody coughs or sneezes, or is gloomy, when in fact the usual bleakness of the Easter School time takes charge, then I am glad of Green-Wilkinson. Alone, unaffected by the English February, or by temperamental companions, he is invariably fresh, cheerful, almost gay. He asks questions, pulls legs, (very decorously of course) continues to make Magna Carta seem interesting to him, as well as to me, in fact saves the situation. If only the President of Magdalen College could have realised this, he could scarcely have failed to give him at least an Exhibition.' Sheep added, 'Oliver the sunbeam, your heart will be filled with joy' and ended, 'under Oliver's beneficent rule, we have been a cheerful community ... The Library seems happy, the middle of the House are well behaved and the Lower Boys well kept in order. Oliver is very sure of himself and behaves with dignity and judgement ... Oliver is proving a worthy successor to Southby, Whitaker, Huntley and Graham. This is, in my opinion, high praise.'

Finally Birley remarked, 'He is a boy with real taste for History. The bare, unvarnished and unromantic little fact brings a glint into his eye, which is the sign of the true historian.'

During the April holidays Oliver went with his sister, Deborah, and his parents to stay at Tabley House, Knutsford, where Cuthbert Leicester-Warren had converted the stables into a small theatre. *The Middle Watch* written by Ian Hay (Major Beith) was produced by the author at this theatre for four performances and Oliver took a small part, alongside his father.

Later that month, all the family stayed two nights in the Old Palace at Canterbury, while the Archbishop was away.

When Oliver returned to Eton for his last Half, he rowed in the Thetis Boat on the 4th June. This was still a Lower Boat, but it was all good training for his rowing at Oxford, later.

In his final Report, Sheep said, 'You know already my very high opinion of Oliver's character, and you can guess what a pillar of strength he has been in the House.' Robert Birley said, 'While it is true that he is not a 'flier,' he is not so very far off it, and his essays and answers now are not those of a worthy plodder, but someone who is interested himself, and can make himself interesting ... He has had a great deal of influence, and this has been very much for the good. I am sorry to lose him as a pupil, and I hope I shall see him again.' Prophetic words, as they were to meet often after the war.

CHAPTER 3

UNIVERSITY 1932

His time at Eton came to an end in July, and on 8th August 1932, he went with his father to see his rooms at Magdalen College, Oxford. They were in Longwall III, and on 6th October he went up to Oxford for his first term.

On 7th, he wrote to his sister Prudence, 'So far I have been having a very thrilling and happy time. After Daddy and Mummy left, I went to lunch with Morris, the boy who sat near us at Lords. [Malcolm Morris was later the heavy weight Number 5 in Oliver's successful crew and later still, a prominent Judge]. After I had unpacked I saw a lot of people I know including Kenneth Crawley, Pat Koppel, and Alan Wigan. He was in very good form, but rather timid ... By the way, 'Wormot' Thesiger is here.'

Five days later he wrote to his eldest sister Deborah, 'I dined with Charlie [Mott-Ratclyffe] on Monday evening at the 'Grid', and enjoyed it very much. He had quite enjoyed his attachment to the R.B. [Rifle Brigade].

'Alan [Wigan] and I went to dine at the Carlton with Chris Huntley last night and saw the *Shanghai Express*. It really is streets above the average film.

'Angus Macdonald of Largie called on me this afternoon, and was very kind. They are still 'tubbing' freshmen who have never rowed before on the river; Malcolm Morris was tried in the 2nd VIII yesterday. Poor Rick (Rickards) has lost his place in the Christchurch IV. [Later a successful oar].

Soon, Oliver was to join the 2nd VIII himself as stroke with Malcolm Morris as Number 5. Then in the Spring of 1933, he showed his skill as an oar. In the Torpid races, which are bumping races, he led his crew to great success. On the first day, 16th February, his boat made an 'over bump.' That is to say, the two boats ahead of them bumped and fell out of the race. His crew then went on to bump the boat in front of the two which had stopped. This meant that the next day Magdalen moved up three places in the order of starting, instead of one place. The following five afternoons they made a bump, so their total bumps were eight, and they moved up into the 1st Division.

The crew were; J.H. Townsend Bow, L.H.P. van der Goes, E.J.S. Clarke, R.G. Etherington-Smith, M.J. Morris (15 stone), P.H. Macmillan, R.M. Beck and F.O. Green-Wilkinson Stroke, the Cox was J.A. Watt.

In the summer he rowed at Henley Regatta in the Magdalen B. Crew and was a substitute listed for the A. Crew. From photographs, it looks as if he may have been called upon to row in the A. Crew as well as the B. boat. Anyhow all this energetic rowing, especially as Stroke, who has to lead the crew to greater efforts, was too much for his heart and he had to give up rowing.

When he was recovering, a charming poem was written, probably by Bill Baillieu:

> Your heart is getting stronger
> It cheers the heart of men
> O live a little longer
> O live to stroke again.
>
> For many a Magdalen Crew, Sir
> You used to set the time.
> Now we demand that you, Sir
> Commit a timely crime,
>
>
> And take the time from others
> A very patent folly -
> But fellow oars and brothers
> The toast, the toast, is OLLY.

In addition to his rowing and academic work, he enjoyed acting, like his father. He had taken the part of 'Aunt Emily' in *The Boy Comes Home* by A.A.Milne at Eton in July 1932 and had taken a small part in *The Middle Watch* at Tabley. Now at Magdalen he took the part of Colonel Jeffery of the Indian Army in *Sweeny Todd* in November 1933 and a small part in *Ticket of Leave Man* in December the following year.

It is not known with whom he went into 'digs,' but we do know that many of his friends such as Mark Meynell, Kenneth Crawley, John Elphinstone, John Verney, and Alan Wigan, were at 51 The High.

Alan was particularly fond of the steak and kidney pie produced for him at Lovel Hill, when visiting the family with Oliver. Myfanwy was not only a superb host, but also a practical joker, who was very good at keeping a straight face on those occasions. So on one visit she produced a steak and kidney pie stuffed with brown paper for Alan's enjoyment!

Another trick of hers was to have pancakes cooked around calico. Every other pancake would be real, so her guests would see their neighbour eating happily, while they struggled with the one on their plate. When John returned from school one holiday, he asked his mother at lunch, "When are you going to tell me about that joke you played on Alan?" He happened, at that very moment, to be struggling with his favourite pancake! Such was the life at Lovel Hill!

Mark Meynell, who was later to be ordained a priest, writes of those days, 'I suppose it was because I was reading Zoology - the Church not having entered my consciousness at that point - that Oliver asked me suddenly "Evolution isn't going on now is it?" That seemed like Canute stopping the tides! So I said "Yes of course it is." I understand what he was wrestling with, at that moment; I don't think my own wrestling with that was ever the same, for thought for me began with Science, and Religion had to fight its way to get a look in. With Oliver it was the reverse. I thought that little question illuminated our respective upbringings very clearly.'

It is interesting to note that John had a godfather who was a Magdalen friend of Lumley's, Dr. Henry Wynyard Kaye, a Wykehamist, who had done wonderful work in organising field hospitals in the First War. When he died of pneumonia at the early age of forty eight, no doubt due to the strain of war, his obituary stated, 'He secured the highest college honour a Magdalen undergraduate can aspire to, when elected President of the Junior Common Room.' It was this same honour that Oliver was granted for his last year at Magdalen.

CHAPTER 4

FARMING IN AFRICA - THE VOYAGE 1936

After University Oliver decided to gain some experience of the world, and give himself time to confirm that he had a calling to follow his father into the priesthood. So he found a farming job for five months in Northern Rhodesia.

It had not been easy to find somewhere to go, as the Triggs wrote at the last minute to say that they had left their farm and were now living in Fort Jamieson. Oliver was stalking in Scotland at Dundreggan, Glenmoriston with B.B. [Victor Balfour-Brown] who suggested that Lumley should write to another Magdalen man, Sir Randolph Baker. This he did on 26th August, and by 29th, Sir Randolph had agreed to Oliver working on his farm at Makeni, 10 miles south west of Lusaka, the capital of Northern Rhodesia, providing the manager, Alan Hewitt, agreed. He added, 'Our farm is 20,000 acres and we grow wheat under irrigation, maize, and we have a lot of cattle and do some dairying. We should want £5 a month to cover everything but drinks and smokes.'

On 21st September Sir Randolph had heard that Alan Hewitt had approved the plan, so Oliver was able to take up his reservation to sail on 1st October 1936.

Oliver was abroad for ten months, and from his fifty two letters written over that period, we can follow his fascinating journey to a place which was later to be of great significance in his life. After farming at Makeni, the remainder of his time abroad would be spent visiting friends in Southern Rhodesia and South Africa, before sailing home.

He departed from Tilbury on the Union Castle line ship, *Llandaff Castle* and wrote of his companions, 'I sat opposite the Scot going to Beira and his friend with a broken hand. Both friendly. I sat next to the toughest looking man I have ever seen, who turned out to be the servant of the Spanish Jew family. He could not speak a word of English and seemed unaware of my ignorance of Spanish! The man we liked at St Pancras [Station] has a family party and two nice looking daughters!'

On the 4th October he wrote, 'I have recovered from the Bay of Biscay which was very bad. For just over 24 hours I felt awful, though I was able to get up and was not actually sick, only ghastly attacks, when I thought I would be ... Tomorrow we land at Tangier and Gib. I see that there might be fighting in the Straits! The passengers are a *very* good lot. There are only 2 in my cabin. A Toc H parson named Harper returning to Natal. Very friendly and helpful. He held celebration this morning, which I attended. The other is a Scotch Engineer named Hendry, whom I like very much. He has a friend named Quinn and both are travelling to Beira.

Then there is a sort of 'Jolly party' to which, when not sick, I roughly belong. A Captain Hughes, very amusing, a real thruster, who always gets what he wants and is going to Tanganyika for the government, as Surveyor and Engineer. A young bearded coffee planter going to Mombasa - amusing and interesting. A ridiculous youth going to gold mine in Kenya and a nice public school boy going to farm there. The females of the party consist of a very nice girl called Pakenham-Walsh going to Beira to visit a brother. A very trying girl going to Kenya and a very charming French girl returning from six months in Gloucestershire who unfortunately leaves the boat at Tangier!'

On 7th October he described his visit to Tangier and Gibraltar, 'I went ashore at Tangier and spent about an hour wandering round the town. There were some lovely mosques and a good market place and of course filthy smells! Masses of French, Portuguese and Italian sailors from battleships in port. The hills in Spanish Morocco were magnificent and come right down to the sea.

'We arrived at Gibraltar at the most thrilling moment. The sun was setting over the Spanish mountains and over Gibraltar there were some fierce looking clouds and a most vivid rainbow. In port were H.M.S. *Barham* (battleship) and the American flagship in Europe, the *Raleigh*.

'I went ashore from 7.30 to 11 with Captain Hughes and an old Harrovian of about 35, who runs a Gold mining firm in Kenya and a man from Glasgow. We visited two cabarets full of British and American sailors and of course Spanish girls. At the first one the senorita, who sat herself down at our table, behaved all right till she became convinced that we were supporters of Franco, produced a pen-knife and showed us what she would like to do to Franco with the blade! An anxious moment. At the next place everyone agreed that Franco was splendid, because he ruled well, allowed bull-fights and played football. ... We sailed about 11 o'clock on a lovely moonlight night.

'Now we are at Palma. We are not allowed to land, as the island is in rebel hands. The men are repairing the central turret of the Cathedral, which the government ships knocked down. A rebel officer said that the enthusiasm in the rebel provinces for Franco was enormous. He thought the Catalonians would give in the moment Madrid falls.

'I continue to like the other passengers more and more. There are some very interesting men among the settlers, business men or engineers. The women are on the whole, less pleasant. Some very nice poorer married women, but otherwise the only ones I should not avoid with pleasure are the twin daughters of a man named Dudgeon, a Kenya settler. They are very nice, but I never remember to which one I have spoken!'

On 9th October Oliver wrote from off Nice, 'We had a *very* rough passage from Palma to Marseille. We were 12 hours late. You can judge what it was like, when I say that 3 stewards had to leave duty! Our arrival at Marseille was very lovely, at sunset. After dinner on board I went off with Armytage the bearded settler, Lilian Pakenham-Walsh and another girl and had some good dancing at the cost of 3/-! Next morning Armytage and I took a taxi up to Notre Dame de la Garde, a wonderful church very high up on a rocky hill above the town, and walked back to the Port. I found I could speak quite fluently - a great asset as hardly anyone else on board could do so. Also, I now have a Frenchwoman (very safe) travelling to Mombasa sitting next to me in the saloon, who cannot speak any English. Very good for my French.

'The deck sports are a nuisance, except the quoit tennis, which is a good game. The chairman of the Sports Committee is so tough the chief steward said he thought he shaved with a blow lamp!

'I continue to like the Dudgeon family and have made greater friends with the Harrovian Engineer and his wife, whom I have just discovered are Onslows. I must ask if they know Dick Onslow.' [Cousin].

13th October, off Crete, 'We had 12 hours at Genoa and went by bus to Portofino. Well worth the 15/- including lunch, to see Portofino again. It was looking really lovely. The church tower was being mended, otherwise no change. The hills above Rapallo already had snow on them this boiling-hot day. In the evening I wandered round Genoa, which is the most impressive port and town now. Italians were very friendly and pleased to see British tourists again. We saw some soldiers in tropical uniform just returned from Abyssinia.

'For three days we have been sailing in a calm sea with sun and a fresh breeze. We saw Corsica, Elba, Stromboli (rather quiet) and the straits of Messina which thrilled me, especially the entrance to them between Scylla and Charybdis!

'My principal friends now are Capt Hughes, the Onslows and Dudgeons. The Onslows are cousins of Richard's. He is very interesting and she is Irish and fond of horses. They have pressed me to stay in Kenya, unfortunately impossible. Dudgeon is a very charming Major in the Army, a gold miner and a 'First' at Cambridge. The twins, aged 21 and looking about 14, are full of life, quite good-looking, plump, and fairly short. I asked one of them to be my 'horse' in the Landaff Derby, the principal event of the sports. It was not till after I had asked her, that I discovered that I did not know which I had asked and that one was engaged!! I had luckily asked the unattached one, but they had discovered that I could not tell them apart. I can now do so by their hair from behind.

'It is a delightfully friendly atmosphere. There is a particularly nice Welshman named Llewelyn who knows the Walford Davies' and Bishop Paget very well.'

20th October, 'Port Said and the Canal were very thrilling. John Armytage and I walked round Port Said. We bought one box of Turkish Delight offered at 2/-, for 4d! The bargaining is really tremendous fun and done with great good humour. In the evening Capt Hughes, John Armytage and I took the Dudgeon twins and a girl called Kathleen Howard to the Eastern Exchange Cabaret plus dancing. Not very expensive and very great fun dancing on a tile floor in the open air. The boat sailed at midnight and we waited up some time to see the canal at night. Up early next morning to see desert and lots of camels! Terribly hot. Capt Hughes can hardly contain himself with excitement at the sight of the desert. He speaks Arabic fluently. We had to tie up for an hour to let boats pass south of the Great Bitter Lakes. The view over the desert and patches of maize along the sweet water canal to the high hills west of the canal is superb. We sailed from Suez about five. The chief feature of the Red Sea is the marvellous light at sunset. The red glow over the Sudanese hills (very high) is wonderful and the light after the sun has set, when the moon and planets are brilliant in a yellow and green sky is quite unlike anything I have seen before.

'At Port Sudan I had my 5th pleasant bathe at the Red Sea Swimming Club. A really lovely pool with water warm enough even for me. We went in a glass bottomed boat to see the submarine coral gardens. The most lovely corals with splendid little coloured fish swimming among them.

'Last night was the Llandaff Derby. The girls, dressed in Jockey clothes, have to cut a thin tape with curved scissors holding it in two fingers only, beyond the scissors. The ship runs a Tote on it. Jean Dudgeon in my colours of Red and Yellow won the heat in great style and was second in the Final. This triumph involved me in the joke race of winning owners. I cannot say I was well backed on the Tote as one of the least of my opponents was a haberdasher, but carried (and lost for them) the money of some loyal friends.

'The Dudgeons are great fun. Very much of the Trafford Verney style. Major Dudgeon says his nearest neighbour in Kenya is a Woodbridge-Whitmore. I suppose it is Daddy's friend.'

Also on 20th October he wrote to his uncle Louis, who had been in the Sudanese Camel Corps at the Relief of Khartoum, 'I thought of you when I saw the fine Sudanese soldiers. ... I think you underrated the females in telling Mummy they were safe [he had seen Oliver off at Tilbury]. The Salvation Army - yes; but there are others.

'My particular friends are two twins, absolutely indistinguishable, a great difficulty as one of them is engaged to be married.' Uncle Louis was always trying to find brides for his nephews, usually looking in prams, as he was a firm believer in a large difference of age - all done as a leg pull.

26th October from Mombasa, 'We reach Mombasa tomorrow. We are probably at this very moment crossing the Equator. The sea is glassy, the morning very hot, with a strong swell. Mercifully there are no line crossing celebrations, as I am the only tourist who has not crossed it before.

'When going through the Straits of Bab-el-Mandeb (Gate of Tears at south end of Red Sea) we were all searching every inch of Perim Island with glasses, when the ship slowed down and reversed. Consternation on board till it was discovered that a 20 ft shark had impaled itself on our bows (poor thing) and in no other way could we get rid of it.

'Aden is a most impressive rocky promontory and looked very thrilling, but entirely desolate. Great fun watching camels drawing carts through the streets. Since Aden we have only seen land at Gardafin (Italian Somaliland) which looked desolate and is inhabited by man-eating tribes.

'The great event on board has been the Fancy Dress Ball. Thanks to the efforts of the Dudgeon family I appeared as a creature which might, with imagination, be seen to resemble a Chinaman, but certainly nobody could have identified as F.O.G-W.

'The Dudgeons have given me some more introductions including one to Dutton, Chief Secretary at Lusaka, and another to Mrs. Bertie, the sister-in-law Lady Betty had never seen and wanted me to inspect in the Transvaal!! When showing me photos of Scotland, Jean Dudgeon showed me one of the house they always wanted to take - Lochdochart!! [This was the shoot that the G-W.s rented in 1936 and again in 1938].

'The voyage from a social point of view comes to an end at Mombasa, where all but 50 disembark. The games side of it is more and more like a private school - Frantic finals, prize-givings and hymn for end of term at Divine Service yesterday! My great relief is laughing at it with a very amusing man of about 30, Frank Howden a very good actor and just married to a most attractive girl called (till 6 months ago) Peggy Percival.'

On 28th October from Mombasa, Oliver recapped for his father details of some of the passengers, 'It was very pleasant to receive letters at a sad moment, when nearly all the friends I have spent the last month with, left by train for Nairobi last night. The boat seems deserted without them. Cross and Harper have now joined their wives, so that Hendry

42

and I are left in luxury. Major Dudgeon is aged 57, was at Winchester and Trinity Cambridge, and has a son, 16, at Winchester now. The 'Jolly party' referred to earlier, turned into a party of young men (about 5) running after the repulsive girl, 'L', the joke of all the other passengers. I escaped not without some ill feeling, and I foresee an awkward position tomorrow, when she is among the few passengers left and is robbed of adorers. I intend being very rude. She really is thoroughly mischievous and uninteresting.

'I had many tender farewells and was pressed to stay for any length of time in the future with the Dudgeons. Elizabeth Dudgeon will be Mrs. Grant after 19th November, as she is to marry a tea planter.'

3rd November, from Mozambique Channel, 'Zanzibar is about the most interesting town of the whole trip. It is really Eastern. A mixture of Arabs, Indians and Swahilis. We also saw the (U.M.C.A.) Cathedral on the position of the old slave market (recognised from the frontispiece of a book given me by Miss Backhouse!), the British Residency and the Palace of the Sultan, who celebrates his Jubilee this year. Zanzibar produces three quarters of the world's cloves, although only a very small island, smells accordingly.

'Dar-es-Salaam is the most beautiful and has beautiful avenues and a lovely lagoon harbour. The coast is low-lying with masses of green tropical growth and beautiful yellow sand. We hope to arrive at Beira tomorrow, Wednesday. The train leaves on Thursday at 6 p.m., arriving Lusaka on Sunday at 7.30 p.m.. I have avoided the vamping of 'L' so far, and made some new friends travelling from Kenya to Durban for the Exhibition.'

He also wrote to his brother on 3rd November to say that he will think of him at his confirmation at Eton on 5th December. He added, 'Imagine my thrill at Dar-es-Salaam, when I saw one of the 1st Class passengers disembarking had on a black, orange and magenta tie! [Sheepshanks' House tie]. He turned out to be called Logan and we had a good talk.'

43

OLIVER ON BOARD *S.S. LLANDAFF CASTLE*
AT TILBURY, LONDON.

OLIVER ARRIVES HOME AT SOUTHAMPTON

5th November, 'We arrived at Beira at sunset yesterday, stayed on board for the night and got through Customs early. The fare to Lusaka is £7, but excess luggage an extra £1. The train leaves at 6 p.m. on Thursday, arrives Salisbury Friday evening, Bulawayo Saturday morning, and Lusaka 7.50 p.m. Sunday (in darkness as the sun sets at 6 p.m. and there is no twilight whatever).'

7th November from Bulawayo, 'The arrival in Rhodesia was thrilling. The freshness of the mornings and evenings 5,000ft up after Beira is really wonderful. The country after crossing the border at Umtali is very good indeed. High hills with masses of rock, not unlike the west coast of Scotland without any rain. The trees, since it is just Spring, are a vivid green. As we got nearer Salisbury the hills turned into knolls, Kopjies I believe is the correct term, and eventually a broad plateau with distant views to the hills near Umtali and masses of cattle grazing. Quinn, one of my shipmates, who is manager of the Ford Depot showed me round Salisbury for the 2 hours we had. Very good of him. The City is very impressive. Streets broad enough for a span of 8 oxen to turn in them, good modern buildings and lovely Jacaranda trees, which are now a mass of lilac coloured flowers and Flamboyant trees with gold and red flowers.

'We arrived in Bulawayo at 7 a.m. and I have spent the time here eating, sleeping and washing in a hotel and making final purchases of quinine etc, and haircutting before the wilds, as Lusaka will be shut when I arrive.'

CHAPTER 5

MAKENI FARM, NORTHERN RHODESIA

9th November from Makeni, 'I arrived at 7.50 p.m. yesterday evening and after dining in the town, drove out here with Alan Hewitt and reached the house about 10 o'clock. The journey from Bulawayo was very comfortable as only one other youth going up to the Copper mines for the first time, in the compartment. The Victoria Falls Gorge was terribly impressive, but the Falls were drier than ever before since discovered, and from the railway bridge only the dry cliff, where the falls used to be, was visible.

'Hewitt is a very charming man, about 35, a good sense of humour and takes pains to put me at my ease. His wife will not be back from England till Christmas, so at the moment I am sleeping in the main house. Lovely to have a room and bed and bath again after 5 weeks. Gabb, another temporary assistant, is also nice and very friendly. Very dark, a good smile and a good bit older than me.

'The country here is pretty, but rather flat. Red soil, grass at the moment burnt, but in a week or so will be green, trees a vivid green as Spring. The house has a deep cool verandah. Outside are orange and lemon trees plus flowering bushes. It is hot, but there is a constant breeze, a wind which cools us.

'After breakfast, at 8 a.m. this morning, we first gave a bull a dose and then Gabb and I went off to superintend the reinforcing of a dam. Five teams of oxen dragging scoops, which were upset on the side of the earth wall, now dry through lack of rain. Tomorrow at 7 a.m. I go off with Hewitt by car 60 miles to the cattle ranch on the Kafue river banks, country with lovely hills. We are taking guns for duck, and valises to sleep out. There is a very nice bull-terrier here called Jane. The 'boys' are Billy, old and the cook, plus Josiah, young and looks after Hewitt and me. Must learn Kaffir.'

15th November, 'I do hope we can get Lochdochart for 1938, but I can easily return for 1937, if the family would rather go to Scotland then.

'The car expedition to the Kafue cattle ranch was very thrilling. Hewitt, Billy the cook and I set out in a hired Dodge as Hewitt's Morris 8 open car had broken a spring. The tracks for the car over the 60 miles were very rough. After 30 miles a puncture and found we had a jack with no handle and no pump. I lay under the car for ½ hour in terrific heat. Then after another 15 miles another puncture and had to go on to Kafue on a rim of front wheel. There we mended the tubes and found a pump. Kafue is open veldt land near the river of that name - terrible mosquitoes but lots of game and mirages. The rancher Lyon, a Boer enormous and extremely friendly, met us with the news that lions were troubling his cattle. He had shot one and wounded two. So at 6 a.m. next morning, while Hewitt went off to inspect the cattle, Lyon and I, plus boys with assegais, searched for his wounded namesakes in a reedy swamp, sometimes up to our waist in water. After 3 hours we had found the spoor and some blood, but had to abandon the hunt, as we had searched all the likely places.

'On the way back to breakfast, Lyon explained that at any rate lions were less dangerous than buffaloes. At 11 a.m., a herd of 80 buffaloes were reported by the native headman! Hewitt then returned with the car and we soon found the herd. For one awful, but thrilling moment the herd charged at us 200 yards away, but, thank God, they turned off and we were able to watch them charge away. A really wonderful sight. In spite of appearances, I don't suppose it was much more dangerous than driving on the Great West Road!

'We returned here on Friday. Work has continued on the dam, also mending a cattle dip. The rains started yesterday. If they stop we hope to play cricket in Lusaka this afternoon.

'I have discovered Hewitt was at Marlborough, is the

47

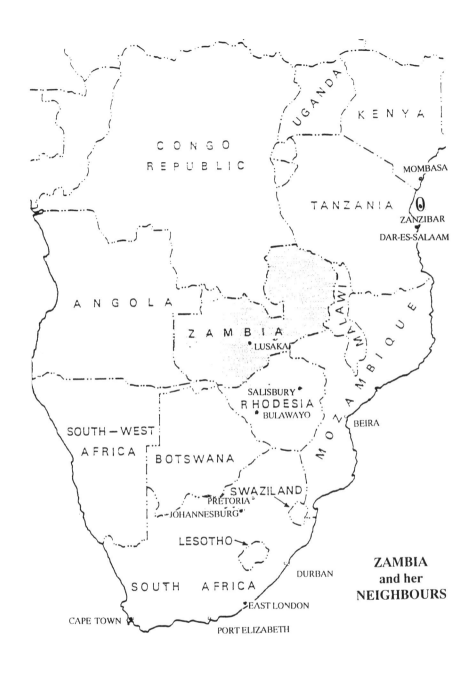

ZAMBIA
and her
NEIGHBOURS

MAP OF AFRICA

48

son of the rector of Stanford near Worcester, is a very keen cricketer and a good shot. He is a nephew of Lady Baker's 1st husband Boyd Cuninghame. I like Gabb very much. He is the son of a well to do farmer near Malvern. Hewitt knows Knighton and often stays with Arkwrights near Presteigne to fish.

'Have heard nothing of a church yet.'

22nd November, 'My bicycle arrived with 2 punctures in its front tyre. I have only had one fall so far. I think of Daddy as I pedal along [memories of his C.I.V. days in the Boer War].

'The first time that I was left alone in charge of work on the dam a snake was discovered. The head 'boy' present, after much fuss hit it with his long whip and then handed it to me in triumph. It was naturally still wriggling. I was in grave doubt how to make sure it was dead, and what to do with it!

'The 'boys' here are a splendid lot, as most of the head ones have been here ten or twenty years. Melik the head one is an ex-police 'boy'. Jim, who does the sowing, dressed in trousers ending just below the knee, is also a very old stager and incredibly fast walker. Billy the cook is splendid. Josiah is a bit crafty. This place is like a great industry, with masses of different things going on at the same time. I spend most of my time bicycling from one activity to another. I can now begin to make myself understood. At the moment we are mending the dam, ploughing with 18 oxen, planting maize with the tractor, building Kraals for the cattle, putting concrete floor on a sheep dip, apart from milking, gardening, shooting for the pot and doing a lot of reading and writing. The day begins at 6 a.m., bed at 9.30.

'I have just discovered Hewitt only met and married his wife on the voyage out to Cape Town this July!'

29th November, 'I have had a good week for letters ... Anne [Wigram] saying Major Dudgeon a great friend of Lady Wigram and Elizabeth (one of twins) her god-child ... Ted

49

Peel who loves schoolmastering at Rossall, and Seary who says the best moments of his life were at Bungay Station and in church with you [Lumley] and giving me most touching sympathy about home sickness!' Seary was a young man at the Magdalen Mission, in about 1905, at Somers Town near Euston Station, who told Lumley he was fed up and wanted to emigrate to Canada. Lumley was pleased to arrange this and eventually Seary went off with a barrow load of books to Canada and got a job as a night watchman, read the books and advanced himself. Lumley and Seary wrote to each other regularly all their lives and Seary made a visit to England, meeting the family on holiday at Bungay. His three sons made good and fought in the War. John is still in touch with Sidney and Pat Seary who came to England for a visit after the War.

Later he continued, 'The various parts of the ranch are Makeni, pronounced Mar-kay-nee, the headquarters, Manji-mushla, 4 miles away, where we are now planting maize, Casa Vera 2 miles from here, the centre for cattle ranching in the wet season. The house is on the edge of the escarpment looking over the Kafue valley to the most lovely hills. The blue lagoon where I camped soon after arrival, is the cattle centre for dry season. Real veld country. The rains have now started with terrific storms. Lovely and fresh between them and all now looks green. I have been having a lot to do with dairying lately. They milk about 30 cows here. There are 3,000 head of cattle in all, mostly for beef, oxen etc. I have also looked after building a new road to Casa Vera! Great fun except that I lost myself for half an hour in the jungle, and during that time 0.78 inches of water fell and one man was struck by lightning nearer Lusaka. A really terrifying experience. I shall be very careful in future. There is nothing to go by in this bush-jungle here. I *was* glad to find the open country.'

On 6th December, his letter gave a typical day's work, 'Called at 6 a.m. to watch the milking and butter making. Then shave before breakfast (perfectly delicious) at 8.30 a.m.,

10 a.m. to 12 noon supervise road construction. Lunch 12.30 and 2.30-5.30 driving the tractor with a harrow or mealie planter behind it. From then till 7 p.m. at dam to wait for teal or to the bush for pheasants. Bath and dinner at 8 and to bed at 9.30 p.m..' He was pleased to hear of Felicity's success at painting and had remembered John's Confirmation the day before. He ended, 'Everyone out here is staggered by the King's behaviour and terrified of its effect on the Empire, especially South Africa.'

11th December, 'We have just heard the sad news of the King's Abdication. It all seems a nightmare, but I suppose this is the best end to the crisis now.

'We have been doing a lot of cattle dealing lately. I have to entertain the prospective buyers while cattle are found. A good story of one buyer, Susmann, who said at a public meeting, when thanking for a presentation clock, "I t'ank you from de bottom of my heart, and my wife t'anks you from her bottom too." I have just heard from Hewitt that there are Anglican Services at Lusaka. He goes at 8 o'clock whenever he can, so I am hopeful about Christmas. A leopard appeared on the road the other day. Next day at the same spot I heard crashing in the bush. I stood clasping my knife in terror, to see 2 small buck even more terrified. The leopard has since been killed elsewhere.'

On 18th December, he wrote to his father, 'I am feeling fit again now (after a day with tummy trouble). The rains have set in fairly steadily now. I suppose in your bicycling in the more civilised parts of South Africa, you didn't have thorns. [i.e. in the Boer War]. Since every tree or bush here has them, cycling is very difficult. I feel so very sorry for the boy who has to mend my daily puncture and sorry for myself as I wheel the machine back to him. However, when there is air in the tyres, I think of you, as I bump over the veldt by sun or moonlight. Necessity has taught me how to mend the pump, which in my anger I pulled in two; as first mended, it sucked air out of the tyre!!' He then explains that he was unable to attend Holy Communion in Lusaka because the South African Railway Missioner was sick.

27th December 1936, 'Mrs Hewitt has arrived and I like her very much. The daughter of a distinguished medical professor. Her husband, though amusing and kind, is most off hand and silent at times. Gabb and I are now living at the White House, ¼ mile from the main house, where we have meals.'

10th January 1937, Oliver added, 'I paid my first visit to official Lusaka this week, when I took the nurse into the Hospital to have an anti-rabies injection. The capital is 3 miles from the Lusaka I know. It is on the top of a wind swept ridge with lovely views over the bush-veldt. Some really impressive buildings including the central offices... Lyon has now moved from the Blue Lagoon to Casa Vera and has brought back all the cattle with him. He is refreshingly unmechanical. We pushed his car a long way yesterday, before he remembered the petrol was turned off!!'

24th January, he said that Rosemary and Ian Henderson had been invited out to Makeni in April, by the Bakers, the owners, but would not come as the Coronation was due. Rosemary was greatly admired by Oliver, while Ian was at Sheep's House at Eton. He talked of visiting Bishop Paget in Rhodesia.

28th January, 'Hoeing mealies, road widening and mending on the way to Lusaka, and of course milking, have been the principal work of the week. One boy came to me with his toe nearly chopped off with a hoe, and another with a badly burnt wrist. He had gone to sleep and absent-mindedly left his arm in the fire. I am trying to teach Mrs Hewitt to ride on Lyon's Boer pony!'

5th February, to his father, 'I heard from Ted Peel, who writes from Bournemouth and reports having grown a moustache. The flats on our old vicarage site and garden are finished and he thought ugly.

'I have been an utter failure, as you foretold, as a fierce ruler of 'boys'. One of the foremen, Amos, said he understood I was going to buy a farm and all the boys would like to come and work for me!! Can you imagine me leaving Lusaka with 60 odd 'boys' plus women and children!!'

Oliver added a private note to his father, 'Thank you for praying for me at this time. At the moment, I feel fairly settled about ordination, but am horribly uncertain as to whether to follow my early hopes and be a thorough-going slum and mission priest, or to make what appears to me a compromise and continue to lead a modified social and sporting life. I feel I must have made up my mind when I return, because, though at the moment the position with 'X' is ideal and perfectly free, it would be a wretched thing to encourage her and then leave her in the lurch. However, for all I know, she may be married by the time I get back!'

Later he wrote another private note, 'Thank you and Mummy so *very* much for all your sympathy and advice. I entirely agree about the need for variety, in fact I love it myself; but you must surely agree that such things as Oxford Mission to Calcutta, Bush brothers in Australia and U.M.C.A., the fancies of my early days, would hardly be easy for a married man!

'As regards 'important positions in the church,' I have always felt that the great advantage of clergy over politicians is that the really important work in the former, is done by parish priests, and not those in exalted positions. Ambition is therefore unnecessary. 'Permanent' is the very last thing I should like. There are plenty always anxious for it, and well suited to it.

'I have always thought of starting work among miners, since I saw the film *Kameradschaft* at Oxford. They seem such a fine type of men and are in such terrible conditions at the moment.

'As regards 'X', I wish you knew her better, as I am certain you would like her the more, the better you know her ... The difficulties 'X' and I have had to face are something, compared to the complete ease I might have had, for instance, with 'Y'.'

12th February, 'Gabb and I lunched with the Bretts at Mayinda, 12 miles beyond here on a rocky hill looking straight

53

out over the Kafue valley to high hills by Mazabuka. A really wonderful view. They have an enormous chicken farm, getting 1,200 eggs every day.

'When working on Lusaka road the other day, a white man with a month's growth of beard, followed by a line of 'boys' carrying kit à la Dr. Livingstone on their heads, suddenly emerged from the bush and asked me where he was! He was on a 30 mile trek across the country surveying for the Anglo-American Mining Co. I have never seen anyone look half so disreputable, but he turned out to be a rather amusing cockney.'

Oliver wrote on 19th February, saying that Bishop Paget (from Salisbury) had written a most warm invitation for him to stay and that he would try to fix things so that Oliver could go on trek with him round his diocese, 'Sounds thrilling and just what I should like.'

26th February, 'Gabb went off to hospital on Monday with fever and a temperature of 104 degrees. I hear he is better now, but since he has got a job in the N. Rhodesian Police (more like soldiers here) he will not be here again for more than a day or two. I am very sorry and shall miss him very badly. On the other hand it may make my part in the farm work more interesting, if more difficult, for the last month.

'We have been busy building a kraal for the sheep, which have just arrived (62 of them) and digging a tennis court. The boys have dug so deep that I am terrified of its turning into a swimming pool and having to bathe in it!!

'I have discovered that the boys call me Longo Longo 'because I walk so fasty and so far.' A great relief that it is nothing worse!'

5th March, 'Mecky enjoys shooting birds with a catapult. The boys call him Funga Funga as his shorts are too big for him and look like falling off.'

Oliver then explained that he will not be able to stay with Mr. A. G. Hay, as Mr. Hay had been selected as one of the pioneers to represent S. Rhodesia at the Coronation. Brett asked Oliver to look after his farm for him, while on holiday late in April. 'I refused my first offer of a farmer's job!' He went on, 'My 60 cows were not producing enough milk so 15 were to be changed. The selected 'duds' had to be marked by cutting the hair off the end of their tails. You would have laughed to see me charge round the veldt hanging on to a cow's tail, waving the knife which you gave me.'

12th March, 'Mr. Hay has left for England but has given me 2 letters of introduction and a most pressing invitation from Mr. and Mrs. John Fletcher of Bulawayo to stay with them until June. He is a most distinguished engineer. I am writing to suggest myself from 3-15 April. On that day Bishop Paget has offered to pick me up and take me on tour to Francistown in Bechuanaland, and to Plumtree School, returning to Salisbury 22 April. The Bishop goes on to say it would be lovely if I could accompany him on a tour of the East of Rhodesia at the end of May. That is the country that I loved on the way out.

'Gabb left on Tuesday and we miss him very much. I shall hope to see him at Livingstone on my way south.

'Hewitt's car is now quite exciting to drive over these roads, as there is plenty of 'play' in the steering and only the gears for brakes!'

19th March, 'We are very short of rain here and have only 23 inches - 36 inches being the normal. The result is that very little wheat can be planted, which together with the loss of 3 imported pedigree bulls in the last few weeks, will be a serious financial loss to the Bakers.

'I have sent off some more photos - the chortles of delight from the boys were splendid. Mecky produced 10 more 'wives' to be photographed, but I was firm this time!!

'I don't think I have ever mentioned the weekly duty of dipping the trek-oxen in order to get rid of ticks. It is sometimes an exciting business getting them through, and always difficult to count about 160 through correctly. Lyon who dips the remaining 3,000 cows, bulls and steers, has to do it almost daily.

'Last Tuesday, St Patrick's Eve, we went to a dance in the Cinema at Lusaka. Of course no one had heard of 'Passion Week' out here! It was really great fun. My best partners were Mrs. Totman (detective's wife, I must be careful) and Priscilla Fergusson, a really very charming South African working for the British South African Co. here. Probably just as well I am leaving!!

'During my road work, now finished, Cholmondeley Dubuisson's rival for this seat in our parliament stopped and gave me 20 minutes of the best canvassing, in spite of my having no vote. In the end I discovered he had run out of cigarettes, but could not help him in that way either! He offered me land at 16/- an acre.'

26th March, 'I have had excellent letters from Kenneth Crawley with news of Oxford and the Verneys. Ted Peel [later to become Oliver's brother-in-law] is still full of enthusiasm for Rossall School and gives some very sensible views on schoolmastering.

'Today is Good Friday and the hour is 10.10 p.m.. At 11, I have to drive in to meet Hewitt's train. For the last 4 days I have been in sole charge of the farm! During my term of office: 1 bull (pedigree) has died, been dissected by Fern and myself, and its brain, spinal cord, liver (bright yellow) and nerves in its thighs sent to the research station; 1 sheep has died and been buried; 1 cow herd boy has come with a very deep cut into his ankle; we have run out of paraffin for the tractor and mealie meal for the boys; cut the poorest mealies and stored them in a pit for winter fodder for the cattle; dug an irrigation trench for the wheat land; taken Mrs. Hewitt in to the Bourlay-Green wedding and fetched her after cutting up the bull; *all the time* tried to prevent a marriage between Jane and the mongrel Burky, - what a Holy Week!! I have really enjoyed it all very much. Today there was time to keep quiet nearly all the Three Hours and I hope to get into Lusaka on Easter morning. I shall now feel I really took a part in farming at Makeni.'

CHAPTER 6

VISIT TO SOUTHERN RHODESIA
AND SOUTH AFRICA

5th April, he wrote from Mr. and Mrs. Fletcher, Bulawayo, Southern Rhodesia, 'Easter day at Lusaka was very nice. Hewitt drove me in to Lusaka and the church was packed. I was able to say goodbye to many friends. My last days at Makeni were enlivened by the arrival of the Bloomfields' two polo ponies, which had to be exercised. I thoroughly enjoyed the early morning rides and was able to give Mrs. H. 3 lessons!!

'I had many sad farewells at Makeni, especially to Lyon and to Mecky and Melik. The latter made a short speech with tears in his eyes, repeating the offer of all the native labour! Though sad to leave, I felt I had been there long enough.

'I met interesting people on the train: copper miners, Border policemen, a Rodent (anti-plague) officer and a most charming U.M.C.A. [University Mission to Central Africa] padre, travelling 'Lay' - Fiennes by name. He had been at Winchester, Trinity College, Oxford and Cuddesdon [theological college] then St. Albans. Such a nice man of about 30 and most interesting about his work at Choma [we hear more of him when Oliver was Bishop].

'The Falls are quite as thrilling as they are made out to be - this time there was such a flood that some views were spoilt by too much spray!

'The journey from the Falls was made interesting by King Yeta of Barotseland being on the train. At every station there were vast orderly crowds kneeling to await him and hear a speech from him.

'As I approached Bulawayo, I must confess to awful apprehension as to what the Fletchers would be like. This was more than dispelled the moment I saw them. They really are as charming a couple as you could imagine. By 12 o'clock we were using Christian names, after 5 months of surnames with the Hewitts!

57

'John is full of life, keen on tennis, squash and riding, and a member of the family Engineering and Timber works. Maureen is something like Priscilla Bacon and certainly as good-looking and charming. I have been *very* lucky.

'Since arriving we have played much tennis and been on a moonlight picnic to the Matopos hills, where Rhodes is buried - a most thrilling spot.'

13th April, Bulawayo, 'I heard this week from Alan Wigan with news of his attachment to the Rifle Brigade and a splendid letter from Mark Meynell, who is doing an Art Course in London. I don't know which of the Fletchers I like best. Both are Rhodesian born and a good type of Roman Catholic. This is a beautiful house and though they have been married two years, they have only been in it one year, as it had to be built. I am their first guest!

'John and I have been again to the Matopos to Rhodes' grave. The country is very odd, rocky crags with boulders at odd angles plus red and green lichen on them. We went to a very good dance at the Grand Hotel. Maureen is a really good waltzer!! On Sunday John dropped me at our church on his way to 7 a.m. Mass, and I found a crowded church (about 120) - a very nice service.'

21st April, Salisbury, 'I am so glad Daddy's heart is not seriously bad and do hope the pains have gone. They were probably just like mine [presumably referring to when he strained his heart rowing at Oxford]. So glad you have Coronation seats. John and Maureen really were the most perfect hosts and I was really sad to leave. My sadness at leaving was considerably relieved by meeting the Bishop. He really is the greatest fun and also a very inspiring man. Last Friday we went down in the Headmaster, Mr. Mikie's car to Plumtree School. We spent the night there. I saw all round the school, which is run just like a Public School and has some fine buildings. On Saturday we went on to Francistown, the principal town of Bechuanaland and a gold mining centre. The Bishop consecrated a new church. I went over 2 gold mines - thrilling to see the yellow dust.

'We left by train (lunching with the Fletchers at Bulawayo on the way) and I travelled in new luxury as the Bishop's friend, having a coupé to myself; very different from sharing the compartment (and incessant drinks) with miners, as I have always done before!

'I went to a native church at Francistown - the first I had visited. The singing is most impressive and I thought the Bishop spoke very well.

'The Bishop asked me to join them on a tour of Portuguese East Africa, Nyasaland, Lusaka and Victoria Falls in June, but I think I should go down to the Union then. We hope to be here about a fortnight and then go on trek including Marandellas, where the Nashes live, return here for the Coronation, and back to Umtali and the Eastern Border.'

1st May, from Salisbury, ' ... could you make some enquiries about Westcott House [theological college] for next year?

'I have been much enjoying my time here. The Bishop really is a most amusing man and also a tremendous fighter for the Church out here and for the rights of natives. Mrs. Paget is quite young and attractive and a really good horsewoman (including show riding). They have been most kind in taking me to beauty spots like the Prince Edward Dam and the Dombashawa Rock, a great granite hill from which you get a view of the distant Mashonaland hills - far grander and more extensive than the celebrated 'World's View' near Bulawayo (Rhodes' grave in Matopos).

'I am glad to say they also make full use of me, correcting letters, supervising the garden boys, mending blinds and bell, plus driving the car.

'The Bishop, Mrs Paget and I went to lunch at Government House yesterday. Sir Herbert is a dear old boy and a fanatical Old Etonian. He at once said I must dine with him on 4th June and would accept no refusal - an extravagance, since I shall then be in Bulawayo - but a pleasant one. We have just had our invitations to Government House Garden

Party on May 13th (Coronation Day). I shall think of you in Westminster Abbey.' His father was attending as one of three chaplains to Archbishop Lang.

On 7th May, his birthday, Oliver wrote from the Pagets, ' ... I shall not tell the Pagets till too late for a present, but we go to the Rhodesian Regiment Coronation Ball tonight. I shall think of you entertaining 'Colonials'.' Lumley arranged for a visit of 'Dominion Guests' to Lovel Hill in Windsor Forest, and wrote a letter to *The Times* on 18th May. It had been suggested in *The Times* that visitors from the Dominions would like to visit ordinary English country homes. 'My family begged me to invite a party of six to Sunday luncheon and tea. The Coronation Hospitality Committee put me in touch with the Victoria League, who informed me that four visitors from New Zealand, one from Southern Rhodesia and one from Australia would arrive at Windsor Station on Sunday morning. We drove home to be welcomed by my wife and four daughters, complete with governess - a 'Victorian' touch much appreciated.

'After a typical Sunday beef and exploration of the house - parts dating from 1578 - two car loads left for Eton, where our younger son was 'discovered' pen in hand, writing his Sunday letter home.

'Our return was via Runnymede, Magna Carta, Fort Belvedere and Ascot Racecourse - to combine old and new interests - for tea, with some time in the garden, before the train back to London.

'I hope, Sir, that this was the kind of entertainment suggested in *The Times*. I can only say that we enjoyed every minute of it, and delighted letters from our guests lead us to believe the pleasure was mutual. I venture to write of our experience to encourage others. Signed, Pater Familias.'

The signature did not fool Reggie Boyle, who guessed who the author was and wrote a bogus reply to *The Times* a few days later, purporting to come from one of the visitors. It was on the lines that on their return from Windsor, the visitors found that they were missing a whole list of articles! Reggie was a great practical joker and cartoonist for Punch magazine. He sent Lumley, on another occasion, a limerick, beneath a sketch of a headless man holding an axe:

A certain young fellow of Datchet
was shaving himself (with a hatchet)
He exclaimed, "Here's a go
At the very first blow
I have cut off my head -
Can you match it?"

This was hung by Lumley in the gentleman's loo by the front door, which prompted a second sketch, with the poem:

Then up spoke a fellow from Windsor
"I think it a terrible sin Sir
To show me a story
So gruesome and gory
The moment that I have
Come in Sir."

A CERTAIN YOUNG FELLOW   A FELLOW FROM WINDSOR
FROM DATCHET

61

Returning to Oliver's letter, he said that he would be staying at Bishop's Mount until 26th May, when he would be going to the Fletchers for a few days. 'Tomorrow we go to Glendale, north of Salisbury in Mazoe hills for the day. Next Friday to the Marandellas for some days. I am camping at the Mission. 20th-25th May, the Bishop and I go to Umtali to the Mirfield Fathers in the mountains near there.

'The visit to Gatooma (100 miles south west of Salisbury) last weekend was most interesting. I stayed with the rector Pughe-Morgan, grandson of the rector of Beguildy. A nice man and knew Radnor well. We went to a native confirmation at the huge Eiffel Flats Goldmine and I was photographed with the choir! Also out to a farm called Handley Cross, which has a most charming private chapel. A lovely service with sheep bleating all round us. The Bishop has a lovely chapel in which he has daily services. It is open to the garden on one side. The nave of the Cathedral is being built. A fine granite building. Chancel finished some years ago.'

20th May, from Bishop's Mount, 'The Bishop is still down with fever and though better, they fear it may be mild typhoid. Marandellas visit was cancelled entirely. Tonight I leave alone for Umtali, where I go out 15 miles to Mirfield Fathers at Penhalonga.

'Apparently, at native sports for the Coronation, a pipe band of Highlanders (coloured) appeared, and dances were in full swing till the clan had to rush to the rescue of one dancer whose knowledge did not extend to keeping the kilt up!

'A good story from Mike Furse [formerly Bishop of Pretoria] when showing petunia flowers to a guest, who said 'Oh, Bishop, how I love your spitoonias,' to which he replied, 'Yes madam, but what about my salivas!'

27th May from Strathearn, Maryland, Salisbury, 'The night journey to Umtali was slow but comfortable, as I was the only passenger in coach attached to goods train. Arrived at Umtali at 5 a.m. and found a car to meet me in the dark.

The 12 mile drive to St. Augustine's mission over the Christmas pass was thrilling as in first light of dawn. The country is as beautiful as I have seen *anywhere*. Masses of great rocky hills with most beautiful valleys and brilliant sun, but quite fresh and cold at night.

'The mission is set on a Kopje and has many fine buildings, all designed and made locally. I was met by Father Buck who knew D. (Lumley) when he was up at Trinity. The other 5 Fathers included one Hewitt, who had for ten years been in the Carl Rosa Opera company and B.B.C.. Another, Richard Barnes, on holiday from England, whom I particularly liked. I did a lot of walking over the hills and visited the most impressive bushman paintings on rock, of men and buck, about 1,000 years old. We visited industrial schools, where locals were taught to cobble, tan, carpenter and tailor. They run a debating society and all spoke well, except one who started by saying, "We must speak before we think," and proceeded to do so!!

'I left Umtali and spent a night on a mission station at Rusapi. The Blue Gums (Eucalyptus trees) there, were magnificent. Then I spent a night at Ruzawi Preparatory School, at Marandellas. It is new with buildings worthy of Eton's best - thanks to the Beit Trust. The headmaster, Grinham, is a great friend of Adam Fox at Magdalen.

'I returned to Bishop's Mount in Grinham's car and found the Bishop up and convalescent. After repacking, I met MacEwans in Salisbury and motored 60 miles out here.'

3rd June, 'I enjoyed my visit to the MacEwans. He was a most interesting man. Had been navigating officer on the flagship during the battle of Falkland Islands, Commander of an Airship, a cow-boy in Texas and a gold miner. They took me to see Turkish tobacco grown, picked and graded. I also visited the chrome mines, now working to capacity for armaments.

'I motored to Salisbury with the MacEwans on Saturday. After writing my name for the last time in Government House book, I spent my first night in an African Hotel! Went to the Cathedral on Sunday morning and said goodbye to various friends.

'Sunday night, I spent in train to Bulawayo in great comfort with only one companion. I wish he hadn't begun drinking brandy and water and smoking boer tobacco at 6 a.m.! No time to see Fletchers at Bulawayo.

'Horror at finding we were 6 in compartment after Bulawayo, but we managed to reduce numbers to 4. They were 2 Boer youths being deported from Southern Rhodesia. Quite friendly, but kept saying they looked forward to Boer conquest of Southern Rhodesia. The third was a dear old Scot from Durban named Adam Smith, with whom I had all my meals.

'Monday night we went through Kalahari desert, a desolate country of sand and thorn bush, rightly called by the Boers, 'Wait a minute thorns'! Tuesday morning we reached Mafeking, a dull railway centre, in spite of historic interest and the thrill of being the first place I had set foot in, in South Africa. The last hour from Krugersdorp to Jo'burg was all through great dumps of the gold reef mines. Later I could see the sky-scrapers of Jo'burg and felt uncanny on the local suburban train out to Pretoria. I had forgotten the feel of a great city.

'The Bishop [Parker] met me at Pretoria and drove me

to this beautiful house, built by Neville Talbot. It is on one of the high kopjes which surround Pretoria and looks straight across at the fine Union Government Buildings.

'The Bishop is the first person I have met since saying goodbye (in London) that I have ever seen before! I like him *very* much. Quieter than Bishop Paget, but with a great sense of humour. Mrs. Parker is a most interesting person. Her brother, Sir George Albu, is the young Christian Jew owner of the biggest gold syndicate in Jo'burg. Whether I shall be able to visit him or not depends on the date of arrival of what he hopes will be his son and heir!' Mrs. Parker took him to a cocktail party where every country under the sun was represented, 'Oh, the daughter of the Swedish Consul!!! I really must visit Scandinavia one day!

'Last night Bishop and I went to hear a Zulu poet speak on race relations and heard some Zulu singing, which was something quite new and very beautiful. A strange mixture of humming plus the most lovely voices. I feel that I have reached the important part of my tour, now that I am in South Africa.'

ON TOUR WITH THE BISHOP

9th June, Barberton, Transvaal, 'Barberton is a most lovely place in the Drakensberg mountains. The country is just about as beautiful as the North of Italy. The mountains and climate are very similar, and the lack of lakes here is made up for by much grander distant views than I ever saw in Italy.

'The Bishop and I left Pretoria last Friday and took it in turns to drive his powerful Plymouth car over the 240 miles to Barberton. The first half was over High Veldt, open down country; the last part Low Veldt, mountainous country with almost tropical valleys. We are sleeping at the hotel here and having our meals at the Rectory. Mr Carlisle is about 35; was at Radley, Cambridge and Cuddesdon [theological college]; has a brother as partner to Hugh Parker [the family solicitor].

65

His wife, a South African is most attractive. They have 2 small children.

'Since being here we have done a lot of walking in the mountains and seen Swazi warriors. They have very little clothing, wear masses of beads, paint their hair yellow and carry a spear, a club and a hand-mirror!!

'We have been to many functions connected with the Church Jubilee. The church itself is a beautiful one, most suitably Italian in design, and it is one of the very few in South Africa, where Europeans, Indians and coloured worship together.

'We have been meeting, here, Dr. Rheinalt Jones the greatest authority on race relations, now standing for senate. He came from Caernarvon and knew Granpapa. [Sir Francis Edwards].

13th June, to his Uncle Louis, from Redhouse, Plaston, Eastern Transvaal. 'Northern Rhodesia was just what I wanted: exciting, wild, full of the sort of people I should never have come across elsewhere, and not altogether easy to get on with. Southern Rhodesia was pleasant, but I got rather bored with its super-British sentiment at times. This country is far more interesting and this part of it the most beautiful mountain scenery (the Drakensberg range) that I have ever seen since we parted at Tilbury. Really grand mountains with valleys wide enough to show them off well.

'At the moment, I am staying on an orange plantation which is very busy as they are now starting to pick and pack for the British market. My host, Major Graham, was in the Egyptian army, but after the Boer War, so you couldn't have known him. He also grows on his farm a delicious fruit called Avocada (!) Pear. Did you come across it in British Columbia? If not I must introduce you to it. ... on 16th August I hope to land at Southampton. It will be delightful to see you again and introduce you to my most attractive little wife.' Uncle Louis was always pulling his leg about marriage, so this was a return leg pull!

17th June, from Waterval Boden, Eastern Transvaal, 'We left Barberton on Thursday and spent two days in Game Reserve, where we had amazing luck. ... Friday to Sunday at White River; we stayed on Major Graham's farm. White River was charming and orange picking and grading most interesting. We lunched with Statens. [Oliver's correspondent, Oscar Staten, had invited Oliver to farm with him]. A lovely house with mountain views, but it would have been too pleasant, compared with Makeni and far less wild.

'Monday night, we went to a farm on which coloured farmers do mission work. A thrilling spot under a mountain range on Swazi border. Very African and after confirmation we watched dancing and singing round camp fire by moonlight. I was a trifle surprised to find my bedroom festooned with orange blossom, but apparently there had been a wedding and it was left up for me to see whom I dreamt of!! Needless to say, I didn't dream at all!!!

'We then left Carlisle's parish and went down to the Portuguese Border at Komatipoort, a very hot spot, where we met Raymond White, the Railway Missioner. Young, cheery and very good type of businessman turned parson. Wednesday we drove up the Crocodile valley, with splendid mountain views and passes to Elands Hoek where we slept in a most primitive hut on a huge orange farm. Confirmation on arrival and Communion at 6.15 next morning.

'The Bishop is a most perfect companion and I have enjoyed it all tremendously.

'The Dutch now refuse to use any English word, and therefore call the fox-trot, the jackal stroll and spell the green things you eat, wechitippels! But I like some Boers very much and they look most picturesque with beards and donkey carts.'

25th June, Bishop's House, Pretoria, 'The weather is now quite perfect - cool at nights, but always warm and sunny in day. No rain since March! The trek ended well. The night at Waterval Boven on the stoep with one blanket and frost toughened me up! Next day we went over top of mountains to a fairly large gold mine called Slyhoek, interesting and a model village for white and black workers. Saturday we returned here over the High Veldt and past Diamond Hill. We had a terrible moment when Bishop was driving. A car came round a bend at about 65 mph on wrong side of the road, tried to get over and came broadside at us. The Bishop drove straight off into the veldt and we only struck one large stone. The other car didn't stop!

'On Tuesday, Mrs Parker took me to Johannesburg. A great thrill to see the city with all its bustle and sky-scrapers. We lunched with her mother, Lady Albu and had tea with her brother, Sir George Albu and his perfectly delightful wife.

'On Wednesday Rosita Forbes, the novelist and traveller came to stay and we went to her lecture on travel in Afghanistan and Siberia. She was great fun. She horrified us with her stories of loose living in Kenya. At the first hotel she and her husband stayed at in Uganda, the hotel keeper asked, "Are you married, or do you live in Kenya?" Thank goodness I did not go to stay there!!

'On Thursday, we went to visit a chieftainess, about 40 miles north of Pretoria, and had a good African day pushing the car through sand.'

JOHANNESBURG

30th June, staying with Dowager Lady Albu, Northwards Johannesburg. 'I loved the Carl Rosa Opera Company's performance of *La Traviata*, especially the first two acts. The most amusing part was the audience, which varied between apparently Spanish ladies in mantillas and Boer gents puffing foul tobacco from their pipes.

'Sir George Albu had arranged for me to go over a gold mine on Tuesday morning. I met a party of 15 females, American Tourists, all repulsively ugly. We went down in a cage. All repulsive females who could, held on to my arms, as we descended in the dark!!! Back with Sir George to his house, where I had long talk with him about goldmining, accidents, workers etc. He is one of six group managers of the whole Rand.'

DURBAN

6th July, Woodley, Durban, 'I have really been most terribly lucky in coming here at the height of the season to stay with Mr Mackeurtan, a most delightful, wealthy bachelor of 48, whose house is constantly full of the youth and beauty of South Africa! He really is a most charming man. He has a beautiful Dutch house full of works of art, with a most lovely garden looking out to sea. It is on the Berea, the hill behind Durban. He is a solicitor by profession and South African born.

'Malise Mackeurtan, his nephew, was once 'fagged' to me at Eton by Charles Maclaren, in 1931, and is now about the gayest young man in Durban. The delightful result is that we go to cocktail parties every evening and dance most evenings. It is a definite change from Lusaka!

'On Thursday, I hope to set sail in the *Winchester Castle* for Capetown.' Later he describes going to the Durban beach to feed the monkeys with Bobby Burnett, a young actor, now writing the life of Empress Josephine, and then visiting the valley of the Thousand Hills, the show place behind Durban, which he thought was not so good as the Eastern Transvaal.

SEA PASSAGE

11th July, *Winchester Castle*, 'On the gangway I spotted what I thought was a particularly attractive girl. Later I found myself dancing with her immediately after dinner, when I discovered that: 1. she was married, 2. she knew Philip Stent well and was married to his brother, 3. she was disembarking at East London next morning. I hope to go to a dance with the Stents (in Cape Town) the night before I sail (home) on the *Llandaff Castle*, as she arrives from East London on the *Llandaff Castle*.

'At East London, it was too rough to go ashore. Passengers were slung overboard on to the tug in baskets! I have done little but sleep and read, to recover from my week in Durban. Today we were in Port Elizabeth. Being Sunday I went to an extremely nice Sung Eucharist at the Collegiate (why?) Church of St. Mary. I also went to the most celebrated snake park, where anti-snake bite virus is made. Port Elizabeth was on the whole attractive, founded in 1820 by English settlers.

CAPETOWN

16th July, The Sanctuary, Milnerton, Cape, 'The night before we arrived was *very* rough indeed, but thanks to my bunk I never felt unwell. Snow had fallen on Table Mountain. We arrived just before dawn and Table Bay and the Mountain were a very thrilling sight, the same as Daddy saw it from the Ariosto [the dreadful troop ship that his father sailed in as a private with the C.I.V. for the Boer War in 1900].

'I arrived here to stay with Bishop Parker's commissary in Cape Town, expecting a retired parson. I found a most aristocratic country gent - with a large hunting and polo establishment! Mr. Hankey is very nice and Mrs. Hankey is a very friendly person. I found that their son is married to John Medlicott's sister, and Jim Lewis came here often to ride! [both friends of Oliver].

'The house is close to the sea with a glorious view across Table Bay to Cape Town and the mountain. Mr. Hankey has really good horses and I have had an excellent ride on Champagne, every day. I have prevailed on Mr. Hankey to teach me some of the finer points of riding and jumping. I have been up to the top of Table Mountain. It was a perfect sunny day with snow on the mountains, which was incredibly beautiful.

'Last night we went to hear the Carl Rosa Company's *Rigoletto*, which I loved. Great was my surprise to hear our old record '*La Donna e Mobile*'!'

23rd July, de Grendel, Cape, 'Lady Graaff is *most* amusing, interesting and attractive person, though at times alarming and very outspoken. Old Sir David was Botha's great friend and was acting Premier and South African representative at Imperial and Peace Conferences. Lady Graaff is most ambitious for her sons, David at Magdalen Oxford is retiring but nice, and Janny aged 9 is great fun. De Villiers is a perfect host on the farm, but has to go into Cape Town to work most days.

'We ride a lot, often before breakfast. I ride Lady Graaff's horse, Mystery, which de Villiers told me badly needed a man to ride it, to get it out of bad habits! Riding is absolutely ideal here. Tiggerburg rises up behind the house and the view over Table Mountain is glorious. Masses of wild arum lilies everywhere.

'We went to the opera *Faust* on Monday. Tuesday, Yvonne de Villiers, whom I met at Durban, came up to ride with me here and today I hope to go over to their lovely old Dutch farm at Rustenburg.

'We have been over to Somerset West to the wonderful old Dutch house, owned by Lady (Lionel) Philips. She was most alarming lady, but very amusing. Her grandson was with 'Dodo'.' [Oliver's Aunt Constance had many graduate lodgers, while they were working in the City of London].

26th July, de Grendel, 'Since I last wrote we have had a good deal of rain, but it is now fine and lovely. I have enjoyed lunch with Sir Alfred Hennessy whom I met in England, and my visit to 'Bishops,' the Public School, at which Adam Fox [tutor at Magdalen] taught de Villiers. On Saturday night de Villiers and I took Yvonne and General Botha's grand daughter to dance at the country club.'

30th July, de Grendel, 'I have continued to enjoy life

71

here immensely. Riding over the veldt is quite splendid. I have ridden an Arab and a Basuto pony the last two days, the latter very comfortable. David is really the greatest fun and makes me laugh a lot. He is a real backveldter, but is surprisingly keen about Magdalen. A woman hater. The latest amusements are putting the 16 lb shot and kicking a rugby football, at neither of which do I excel, but they give a lot of laughs.

'Well, it is simply thrilling to think of seeing you all again. I shall of course, not expect you at Southampton.'

He sailed home on 31st July on the *Llandaff Castle*, arriving at Southampton on 20th August, where he was met by his father, who brought him down to the family in Devon. They had taken Bradiford House, near Barnstaple, for the month of August. A very happy holiday was spent surfing at Hope Cove and a drive to Lands End via Tintagel and Clovelly. On the way back they called in at St Michael's Mount, which was all rather tame for Oliver, after his great travels in Africa.

Previously on 22nd June Edward Paget, the Bishop of Southern Rhodesia, had written to Lumley, 'I wanted to start Dear 'Grugger' for though a junior, that is the name by which in olden days I often heard you mentioned [his nickname at university].

'It was quite delightful having Oliver with us - an ideal guest - and we enjoyed his time with us enormously.

'I may as well tell you straight away that I have solemnly pledged Oliver to return to this Diocese some day as a priest, and I hope that no parental influence will obstruct this arrangement! (and I have warned Wilfred Parker off!) As far as I could gather he is quite clear now in his mind as to Ordination and he hopes to be ordained. He talked much with me about Cuddesdon [Lumley's theological college] and Westcott House. Of course Cuddesdon means very much to me. I put Westcott House fairly strongly before him, partly from what I have heard of Westcott House under B.K. Cunningham, but mainly because of what I know of B.K., whom I love. It would be a great privilege to live under the daily influence of B.K. for any man moving towards the Ministry.'

Then on 30th June, the Bishop of Pretoria, Wilfred Parker, reported, 'I must write to tell you how very much we enjoyed having Oliver with us. He really is a most delightful person and having been with me constantly for nearly a month I have failed to discover any faults in him at all!! He is cheerful and unselfish and very much on the spot. One day he will make a splendid priest. I only hope that when he has done 2 or 3 years in England he will turn his thoughts to working in this diocese, and that you will spare him to us.'

In fact Lumley was to die a few weeks before Oliver sailed for Pretoria, as a priest in 1949. Pretoria had won against Salisbury.

CHAPTER 7

PREPARATION FOR ORDINATION 1938

During the autumn he visited friends in Scotland and had a few days stalking with Victor Balfour-Brown at Ardkinglas by Loch Etive.

On 10th October 1937, Lumley wrote to Felicity, who was at a small finishing school in Paris. 'Oliver will be going to Cambridge to see Canon Cunningham the Principal of Westcott House some time this week I expect. He has shot at least 7 stags and the last was 16 stone 10 lbs, the heaviest and best at B.B.'s this year.'

Then Oliver wrote to Felicity on 22nd October, 'Your letters are always splendid and full of interest. I expect you have heard all about my time in Scotland - what fun it was, until I strained my wretched heart. However, it is already far better and I hope it will be quite right again in another fortnight.

'On Tuesday I went down to Cambridge for the first time to see Westcott House. I was very surprised to find how much I liked it at first sight. Quite a cheerful looking place, with a very charming man as Principal. I was delighted to find that Ronald (Loopy) Lunt was there and gave me a lot of useful information.'

Lumley reports to Felicity on 15th November, 'Dr. Halley came to see Oliver this a.m. after his month's rest, and said he was quite fit again and can ride, but not to hunt or play hard games till January.'

As he had been unable to get a place at Cuddesdon Theological College, where his father had trained, he now started training for the priesthood at Westcott House, Cambridge, on 13th January 1938.

Towards the end of his theological training, he met up with several Oxford friends in April 1939, when a party of

74

them went on a cycling holiday in Holland. Mark Meynell, later to be ordained and become a Canon, reports that the party consisted of: Diana Ponsonby, who became his wife, plus Lavinia Ponsonby, later to marry Sir Michael Hamilton, son of the Dean of Windsor, Judy Leslie Melville, David Coke, Innis Dorrien-Smith, Jean Riddell and, of course, Oliver. Mark remembers the occasion when it was Oliver's turn to go to the nearest farm for milk, 'The rest of us were lying at ease on the little clumps of hay (rather than hay stacks). When he appeared he had put two large long necked bottles in his breast pockets - no doubt to free his hands for the handle bars. And of course we all laughed at the quickness of his sex change, but equally, of course, he had done it on purpose. We all enjoyed that!'

During the summer he completed his theological training and was due to be ordained and work in a parish in Wigan. He felt that he might look like a draft dodger to escape the army, to the tough Wigan men. It was not possible to become an Army Chaplain until he had several years of experience, so he decided to postpone his ordination until after the war.

He volunteered to join the Green Jackets, his uncle's regiment, and his father had been chaplain to them in the First War. As his brother John was planning to be a regular soldier, he agreed to let him join the Rifle Brigade, to please Uncle Louis, while he chose the King's Royal Rifle Corps, the 60th Rifles. This would avoid any awkward situation, if one brother had to order another to carry out a dangerous task.

During that summer Lumley was shattered to hear that John had not been accepted by Magdalen, Oxford. Oliver was still at Westcott House and had the bright idea of visiting the Ram (Ramsey), Master of Magdalene College at Cambridge, who readily accepted John on the strength of Oliver's personality without even interviewing John! Another example of Oliver's concern for the family.

While Oliver was waiting to be called up, he took a job as a butcher's boy. There was a well known butcher, Mr Smith, at Cranbourne in Windsor Forest, who provided meat for many houses in the Ascot area. He was a great character and much loved. He was looking for someone to deliver meat to the large houses, as his butcher's boy had been called up. So Oliver volunteered and had a lovely time chatting up the various cooks, coming home with some most amusing stories.

On 15 November 1939, Oliver joined the Oxfordshire and Buckinghamshire Light Infantry as a private. Lumley notes that on that very day his father, who had been Colonel of the Regiment, would have been 114 years old!

SMITH'S BUTCHER'S VAN OUTSIDE THE BACK DOOR
OF LOVEL HILL WITH BUTCHER'S BOY AT WORK!

CHAPTER 8

THE ARMY - TRAINING IN ENGLAND 1939

Lumley kept all the letters Oliver wrote during the war and when he was in Germany, until he was demobilised. We are able to build up a picture of his activities from these letters They are all to various members of the family, except where stated.

Although Oliver was attested to the Oxfordshire and Buckinghamshire Light Infantry, he was posted to the Warwickshire Regiment as a private, designated a Potential Officer. He was then sent to an Officer Cadet Training Unit (O.C.T.U.) from March to May 1940, and arrived at the 60th Rifles Depot at Chisledon on 7th June.

It is interesting to note from his father's Anniversary Book that Oliver conducted a Lenten Service at St. Peter's, Cranbourne, on 1st March as the vicar was ill. Although he was not yet ordained, he was making use of his training.

By the 20th July, he was posted to the 2nd Battalion 60th which was reforming at Tidworth, after their gallant defence of Calais the previous month.

Nothing is known about the rest of the year, except for a letter to Prudence on 15th December saying what a blow it had been that he had to cancel an invitation to a dance, due to the absence of so many officers on a course, which left him on duty. He added, 'I had rather set my heart upon going to the dance and introducing you to some of my brother officers. My depression has been slightly cheered by the arrival of Jasper Ridley to join the Battalion. You remember he is the third of the trio, with Con O'Neill and Jo Grimond. He is married to Jo's sister in law, a Bonham-Carter.'

8th June 1941, from Trowbridge, Wilts. He was by now Technical Adjutant of the Battalion and had to look after all the mechanised and motorised transport. Being painstaking and methodical was a help, but he was no engineer, so the work was very difficult for him. He wrote to his parents, 'I changed my billet, so as to be nearer the mess for Battalion H.Q. and D. Company. I am therefore in a beautiful little house a mile outside Trowbridge, in a village called Hilperton and the house is called Palmers Close.

'The mess is far better now that D. Company have joined us, as it is less dominated by the Colonel and can get away from him. Richard Tindall and Richard Wood are among the D. Company officers ... Trowbridge church is a very beautiful one with good services.

'I heard from Lavinia Ponsonby that you were at the Fourth [at Eton] and it was a good day. Mindy and Priscilla [Bacon] are now at Oxford.' He was reporting on Lavinia's sister, whom the Green-Wilkinsons used to meet at the Tabley theatricals with the Leicester-Warrens.

3rd August, from Tidworth Park Camp, 'Splendid news about John Leicester-Warren [reported missing at Dunkirk, but now a Prisoner of War]. I saw John [his brother] in Salisbury yesterday. I had gone in with Jasper Ridley and spent a glorious summer evening wandering round the town with him. Being a publisher and an ordinand, we spent most of it in the Cathedral Close. Dinner at the White Hart was excellent and it was there that John turned up with a large party of braves from the 95th!' i.e. Rifle Brigade.

19th August, 'There is no doubt that we are planning to go. Apart from the wrench of leaving the family, I am simply delighted. John came and told me the news that they were off too, with the greatest pleasure.' Oliver was in the 2nd 60th which was Motor Battalion to the 22nd Armoured Brigade, while John was in the 1st Battalion Rifle Brigade, who were supporting infantry for the 2nd Armoured Brigade. Both these Brigades were in the 1st Armoured Division, due to sail to Egypt. The 22nd Armoured Brigade Tank Regiments had already sailed for Egypt. Oliver continued, 'I have seen quite a lot of John this week. He asked me to dine in his mess [in Swindon]. That was the greatest fun, except for the terrible blow that a Major [probably Vic Turner] asked me if I was John's twin!! [There was 8 years between them]. I gather from John's brother officers that he is considered efficient, but often late!'

23rd September, from Tidworth, 'Daddy's visit made a great impression ... I never got to bed on Thursday night after he left. It was hard work, but I was amply rewarded by the pleasure of seeing train loads of carriers slide out of the station at the correct time in the middle of the night, and standing by the Colonel at 7.30 next morning, as the wheeled vehicles drove past for some three quarters of an hour. David Graham-Campbell kindly gave me a day off on Sunday, so I had a very happy day with the Ryders. [Hilaré, his sister, had just married Bob Ryder, a Naval Officer, and they were living at Wilton, nearby].

'I enjoy working with David Graham-Campbell very much. He is much easier to work with than expected. His coldness is only superficial. [An Eton master; there were five of them in the Battalion, David, plus Alan Holmes, Alan Wormald, Richard Tindall and Peter Blundell].

'It is thrilling to be able to realise what an adventurous prospect lies before us. How lucky I am to be setting out among so many friends for overseas service. I have always longed for this, since soldiering was first suggested for me, when we were at Argentière' in 1927.'

Richard Wood (now Lord Holderness) writes that he joined Oliver's Battalion in February of that year, and because of the dispersion of the Companies, he seldom met Oliver and little knew him until, 'he hailed me one splendid summer evening, when we were all at Tidworth Park and Oliver's father and mother plus brother John were visiting him. John I had not seen since we served together in the same platoon of the Eton O.T.C..' Hill's and Sheepshanks' Houses shared a platoon. Richard was the platoon officer and John was his platoon sergeant. Richard continues, 'When the battalion embarked on the S.S. *Franconia*, having proved my lack of business acumen as messing officer of D. Company, I was none the less appointed Assistant Technical Adjutant to Oliver. His duties were to establish records of the Battalion's vehicles. Alas for Oliver, his impeccable records were all blown away in a fierce storm a few days after our arrival in Egypt. One immediate result was the reduction of any effectiveness the Assistant Technical Adjutant may have ever possessed. He was quickly returned to where he properly belonged, the command of a platoon in the company then commanded by the taciturn Peter Chapman. My only regret at the justified dismissal was that I saw little of Oliver for the rest of my time in the desert.'

CHAPTER 9

THE VOYAGE TO EGYPT, 1941

Oliver's first letter from the troop ship was written on 26th September and said, 'Here we are on board a luxury liner. The men are horribly overcrowded. Your descriptions of the Ariosto [his father's troopship to the Boer War] are painfully true. The food is excellent for all. I am sharing a cabin with Jasper Ridley, John Bunbury and Edward Voules. John B. was a farmer in Southern Rhodesia. Edward V's brother-in-law lived at Lovel Hill. He is messing officer and used to work at Gunters. [Tea Shop].

'At the moment I am having a wonderful holiday after some very busy times lately ... I wish I could visit Uncle Cuthbert [Leicester-Warren, an honorary uncle, and was inserted to indicate that they were near Knutsford, and therefore at Liverpool docks]. John is not here.' He was, in fact, embarking on the S.S. *Strathaird* at Glasgow, and they would all join up later in one convoy in the Atlantic.

8th October, posted from Freetown, 'We have, on the whole, had a very good voyage so far. I must admit to having been sick for the first time. We have only seen one German plane so far, and from the consequences of that we were most providentially delivered. [No doubt due to the storm]. I see most of Jasper Ridley and Alan Holmes, both are great fun. Alan is Transport Officer. He was in College at Eton and Captain of the School and XI. We have a padre on board, I am glad to say. The congregation on Sundays at 8 o'clock consists of large numbers of 60th officers. A very pleasant surprise.

'I forgot to tell you, Rifleman Byrne was tried by Court Martial for absence without leave. His explanation was simple. He had gone on leave to Eire, and had been given two months imprisonment for absence without leave from the Eire Army. I see no reason why he should not spend the rest of his life in the military prisons of the two countries!'

25th October, written between Freetown and Durban, 'I haven't seen John, but Michael Edwards [John's Company Commander] did manage to get over to this ship [when they were stuck outside Freetown in sweltering heat]. He reported, to my immense relief, that John too had been sick. [Actually untrue - he had only been confined to his bunk!]

'We had a great ceremony at the crossing of the line. Great excitement when the Brigadier and the Nurses were shaved and ducked.

'The Colonel is an enormous success. I like him very much. Jasper Ridley, Alan Holmes, Richard Wood and Alan Wormald I see most often.

'It is a long time since we heard depth charges and we are looking forward to going ashore at our next port. Love to Mr. Mackeurtan.' This was a code to indicate Durban, as the family knew where Mackeurtan lived.

VISIT TO DURBAN

16th November, written between Durban and Aden, 'Our days ashore were an unparalleled success, except for the great blow that John wasn't there, as his ship had put into a different port. [Cape Town]. I had looked forward so much to seeing him, and introducing him to my friends.

'As soon as I landed, I walked off to Douglas Mackeurtan's house. I was surprised to find myself simply overwhelmed with pleasure at returning to sights and sounds and smells which I hadn't experienced for four years. I had forgotten how very happy I had been in that country. Luckily he remembered me all right. He had a guest staying, who

82

turned out to be Simon Elwes, whom Felicity may have heard of as a rival portrait painter. He is now a soldier and was waiting to join a convoy. Very amusing and a good story teller. He was painting two girls. Douglas was a most perfect host. For four days he invited me and my friends to luncheon, sherry party, and dinner; and his food is such as you can never have tasted. Every afternoon he sent us out into the country in his car. I brought Alan Holmes, Peter Blundell, Geoffrey Jameson and Richard Wood up to him, as they all knew his nephew at Eton, the first two as beaks and the latter two as fellow members of the Cricket XI. Every evening we returned to my old haunt, the night club, before hurrying up the gangway sharp at 2 a.m. Each morning we went for a route march, very welcome exercise.

'The people of the country have simply surpassed their own record of hospitality. General Smuts seems to be doing wonders, in a very difficult situation and has sent a large and efficient expeditionary force 'up north.' I set sail again much refreshed by the best holiday since my bicycling tour in Holland.'

Richard Wood adds, 'Aboard the *Franconia*, I had quickly come to realise what a delightful companion Oliver was. During our four days' pause in Durban, I spent many hours in his company, entertained and driven over much of the surrounding country. I happily listened to his stories of fox-hunting on Exmoor with the then Master, my brother Peter, then just over twenty, but still much nearer Oliver in age than I was. On one memorable occasion he had been summoned to Somerset and told to make sure to bring his red coat and top hat. The Master's friend must be properly dressed. Peter and Oliver duly appeared at the meet, but one horse only was led there by the groom. "Where is my friend's horse?" thundered the Master as he mounted the only available animal, at the same time bidding the groom to collect a small shaggy pony from a nearby farm. Oliver climbed on to its diminutive saddle, but, however shortened the stirrups, he had the greatest difficulty keeping his feet clear of the large stone boulders that abound in that part of the country.'

29th November, between Aden and Egypt, 'Since I last wrote we paid a long visit to a port which I had visited before, but had not been ashore. [i.e. Aden]. I didn't get ashore this time either, as I was 'Officer on Guard' the only day we were allowed ashore. This disappointment was more than made up for by the kindness of the Colonel, who arranged for me to go with him on a visit to John's ship. I had about an hour and a half with John. He was in great spirits and seemed very happy. I laughed a lot when he told me he had been ashore and on his first visit to the mysterious East, had gone at once to the Cinema. East and West may appear to be different to Rudyard Kipling, but not to the imperturbable John G-W. However, the 'Flick' seems to have been not altogether lacking in mystery, as John assures me it had no roof. [Also it was in a native language, so he did not understand a word of the story!] It is very thrilling that at last we are coming into the fighting zone. I wouldn't wish to be anywhere else at the moment, except for a sneaking wish that I was back with old friends and the 'Carriers' in Number One Platoon.'

ARRIVAL IN EGYPT

8th December, 'Here we are where Uncle Louis had the worst day of his life, a day I can fully understand now. Sand in the food, in the hair, in the eyes; and yet it is good to have ended the journey at last, and I am delighted to be able to stretch my legs and recover my 'rowing man's appetite!''

Christmas Day at Amyria near Alexandria, 'Our plum pudding was excellent and I then went on and had another one in the A. company mess. It is sad that John and I could not be together today.' He had seen John several times, but his Battalion had gone up to the desert a few days earlier.

'I have been most desperately busy lately; but I am beginning to get my 'second wind' now and shall be glad to move. David Graham-Campbell and I have shared a tent, except for one night, when it ceased to be there to be shared.' He does not add that this was the occasion when all his careful records were blown away.

The amount of work that Oliver had to perform can be judged from the War Diary of Geoffrey Jameson, who says, 'Needless to say there was a shocking G.H.Q. muddle over vehicles. Half of them we never saw again. As it was, the Battalion was not fully equipped until two days before we left for the desert. All the carriers we brought out from England were sent elsewhere and we were given mediocre carriers in their place. All vehicles had to be taken into the workshops in Alex. to be desertised!'

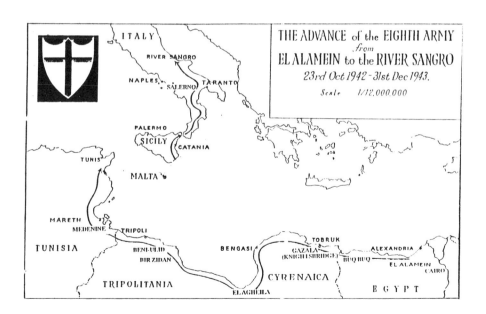

THE ADVANCE of the EIGHTH ARMY *from* EL ALAMEIN to the RIVER SANGRO 23rd Oct 1942 - 31st Dec 1943. Scale 1/12,000,000

CHAPTER 10

EGYPT TO TUNISIA. 1942

Oliver wrote to Felicity for her birthday early in January 1942, 'on a pitch dark night the Staff Captain and I were returning to camp and strayed out of our way into another camp. Imagine my surprise when the head that emerged out of the first tent was John's. I didn't know he was within 200 miles at that time.' Both Battalions 2nd 60th and 1st R.B. were at that time following the advancing 8th Army to the border of Cyrenaica at El Agheila.

El Agheila and Retreat

The day that the 1st Armoured Division took over from the 7th Armoured at El Agheila, 21st January, Rommel started his advance East. John's group were attacked from the air in the Wadi Faregh soft sand, and many 15 cwt. trucks were destroyed, including his. They were all withdrawing in difficult conditions. Oliver writes about this withdrawal on 6th February, 'Here it has been rather a case of 'Hooge' again, [his father's battle in the First War] but mercifully without the cost in men. I expect you have seen Richard Tindall's death in the papers. That is a great blow, as I used to see such a lot of him as M.T.Officer. I had been with him an hour before.

'There was a great evening, when I was issuing out petrol in a Laager, entirely surrounded by the enemy. It was reported that an officer had come in on his own and needed petrol. Up came John! We had a great supper together of bully beef and cheese and jam, and then we drove through the night and managed to escape. He was very well and in splendid spirits. I was able to give him a few things to make up the kit he had lost.' John had been sent back with petrol for George Miller's

86

carrier platoon, in a dingo scout car, as his truck and all his belongings had been lost. The petrol was handed over, but George Miller then got lost and was eventually captured, as described in his book, *Horned Pigeon*. John returned to his column, only to find that it had moved and in fact on a different bearing. He continued on the old bearing and just as dusk fell, over the last brow of the last hill, he saw a column in Laager. Luckily it was not German, so he was able to ask for petrol, only to be told that the Technical Adjutant had said that no more petrol could be given out. To his joy he found that it was Oliver's order, so petrol was found. Oliver ended his letter, 'on the whole I am very happy and enjoying life. The cold and the wind are really the worst part, except for certain rather unpleasant visitors overhead.'

REFIT IN CAIRO

21st February, Cairo. He just refers to a long journey and wallowing in wonderful baths and eating delicious food. He could not say where he was because of censorship. He was sight seeing with David Graham-Campbell and dining with Ian Whigham, a Cranbourne neighbour, 'Tony Mellor is now my immediate superior. John Robinson has taken over H.Q. Company from Lionel Morris to my delight ... When removing my beard, I left my upper lip unscathed. The growth is positively alarming to me, if not the enemy. It is a positive Walrus already and absolutely defies nose blowing ... I do feel sorry to be completely parted from John. Perhaps it will be a good thing for him to be quite clear of his elder brother.' John's Battalion had been left behind south of Tobruk, where they stayed until the Knightsbridge battle in May, while Oliver's Battalion was refitting in the Delta.

3rd March, on leave in Cairo, 'When I left camp, I feared

that it would be rather lonely. Unlike boarding the train at Warwick, Ashvale or Tidworth or throwing my leg across the 'Tempest' [his motor bike] at Whitley with the prospect of arriving for tea at Lovel Hill; but short of that I couldn't have been less lonely or more happy. I have met a wonderful selection of friends. Michael Wills is an instructor at the O.C.T.U., who took me round to his flat on the banks of a big river [Nile] and there I found John Loyd, who lives at Lockinge near Wantage and is a son of Daddy's friend, and John Harley recovering from being blown up by a land mine. [His parents lived at Brampton Bryan not far from Knighton, so the families knew each other, and Jane Harley, his sister, was probably the girl photographed by the Tatler at the meet]. Michael seems to have quite recovered from his wound and has an M.C.

'My first night at the Hotel I spotted an amusing and interesting little padre, a Lt. Col. in the S. African army with D.S.O. and M.C. and bar. He turned out to be Father Runge, whom I had met with the Mirfield Fathers in Johannesburg [after farming in Northern Rhodesia]. He is a most splendid man, full of original ideas about everything. He is a great friend of Adam Fox [Magdalen].

'On Sunday, I went to the Cathedral. It is packed in the evenings and well attended in the mornings. Imagine my surprise in finding Wilfred Parker [Bishop of Pretoria whom Oliver stayed with in 1937] was celebrating at 8 o'clock. We had a great reunion and are going sight seeing tomorrow with his brother, who was at Radley with Daddy and met us all at Glion' [on Lake Geneva in 1927 during the Tour of Europe].

A REST IN CAIRO

After his leave, on 5th March, he went back to the Battalion to complete the re-equipping before returning to the

88

desert and on 29th March, 'I am writing from a very comfortable and well run hospital, in which I am an entirely bogus patient. I can't explain everything, but there was a sudden terrific pressure of work and most of the other men to help me were either away or not yet posted. For the moment it rather cracked me up, and when the job was finished I was left behind in hospital, really only for a rest. The doctor, a Major Kennedy, is a most skilled specialist and has made me feel 75% better in two days. In a few more I hope to be on my way back to the Battalion. Whether I shall be given a change of job or not I don't know. A year as Technical Adjutant is a long time.

'John Harley is a fellow patient in this ward. I enjoy seeing him very much. He is now a very keen soldier and very full of interest ... My 'sister' is friendly but not dangerous. The Night Nurse is friendly and dangerous!!'

1st April, from hospital, 'You can imagine how thrilled I was when John Harley's wireless suddenly announced news that Bob [Ryder] had been in command at St Nazaire. John very cleverly spotted it as soon as I did.' He also wrote to Bob, 'It is difficult to convey to you adequately the congratulations which are due to you, or to explain what an inspiration it is to have a brother-in-law capable of such thrilling and outstanding actions.'

10th April, from the Base Depot, waiting for a posting. He wrote to his father and had just heard of Cosmo Cantuar's retirement, 'It will be the end of thirteen years of wonderful service to C.C. and I do hope that he will be properly appreciative.' On his own health he added, 'The week here has allowed me to recover a good deal more from when I left the hospital. My heart is quite all right - I have been doing a hardening course running up and down the very steep hills here without any bad effects. It was merely a case of working myself to a stand still and getting mentally addled with technical matters. David Graham-Campbell is as unmechanically minded as I am and couldn't appreciate the difficulty of doing my job, when there was no R.A.O.C. officer to help me. For the past year it has been one long struggle to keep an uncongenial and difficult job under control.

'By wonderful good fortune I was able to spend the three hours [on Good Friday] at the Cathedral under my friend, Father Runge of Mirfield.'

A Platoon Commander of D Company
in 2nd Battalion 60th, near Tobruk

21st April, 'Here I am back among my old friends and once more a platoon commander, owing to doctor's orders not to meddle with motor cars for a bit. I am delighted to be back with the men again, but of course there is a terrible amount of lee way to be made up after a year. It is grand to be under Peter Chapman once more and to have Alan Holmes as 2nd in command of the Company. ... I saw Bobbie [Erskine] yesterday and he asked much after Bernard and Blanche [Branston]. The flies here are a perfect plague.' They were somewhere behind the Gazala defence line.

30th April, 'A few days ago a car drew up outside my dug out and from it emerged Ronald Lunt. He is now a padre with the Guards and seemed extremely happy. Very clever of him to have found me. We had a great lunch together.

'We have been bathing lately. Even I am enthusiastic for bathing at the moment.'

7th May, 'I can say that I am having a heavenly time, away from the Battalion giving my platoon a swim in the sea. There is a cove worthy of Lulworth. The men are all in and happy. I am out and happy and to crown all, Bill Heathcoat-Amory from H.Q. Company has turned up. I am absolutely devoted to him, a very enterprising and amusing Major. My bathe was short but very good.

'Alan Holmes is a great help and friend in D. Company. Peter Chapman I would do anything for.' [The Company Commander].

17th May, to Prudence, 'It is Sunday afternoon, so like a good boy I sit down in the desert to write home and tell you the results of the school sports, but I cannot, unfortunately, add that we are just going into chapel. It is well over a month since I have 'been to church'. We are unfortunate in our lack of padres.

'A few nights ago you must have heard an anonymous reference to my platoon's behaviour in a phrase from Cairo. We had an exciting night and all returned very well.

'My company commander, Peter Chapman is a most inspiring man. Rather old for 34, because he is a bit bald. He is very quiet, with a great sense of humour and the most tremendous power behind him. His family lives in North Wales near Carnarvon.'

MACHINE GUN COURSE IN PALESTINE

24th May, 'I have no letter to answer, but better than any letter is the wonderful, thrilling news that Bob has been awarded the V.C. I saw it in the very first newspaper I picked up on my return from the desert. It is a perfect end to his daring and successful action.

'Nearly a week ago I left the Battalion, at very short notice, to go on a Machine Gun Course. Something quite new to me and I am delighted to have been chosen for it, doubtless due to the kindness and thoughtfulness of David Graham-Campbell. It is good to have a chance of becoming a specialist again, after my short and happy time as an ordinary

Platoon Commander; and this time it is a real soldier's job. I shall for the next month be a Philistine. How very greatly I hope that I may be able to have a few days off to visit the place we have read about so often. [Jerusalem].

'There is a fly in the ointment. On the very first road I reached, near [Tobruk crossed out!] a truck swerved into me, ran over my foot and drove on. The desert is in many ways a safer place for motoring! Luckily my ammunition boot took the weight. My heel is badly bruised and cut. The nice surgeon at the hospital sympathised with my desire to go on the course, and put my whole leg in Plaster of Paris.

'I hope to hear Bishop Gwynne preach this evening, Whit Sunday [in Cairo] and continue my journey tomorrow morning.'

3rd June, Australian I.F. Reinforcement Camp, 'This new work is full of interest. It is difficult, but infinitely better than my last job. It is a most terrible blow to be away from the Battalion just at this moment. [Battle at Knightsbridge near Tobruk was in progress]. It is horrible to be away from all my friends and my men, when they are in action. I should like to be sharing dangers with John.

'I have had the plaster off my foot and the cut is healing well. So sorry to read of the raid on Canterbury. I do hope the Cathedral has not been ruined.'

25th June, from hospital in Cairo, 'I have had a short leave in Jerusalem, have finished my course and am waiting for orders to rejoin the Battalion. I am spending the time in the same hospital as before, having a wisdom tooth cut out. Roly Gibbs' brother is a fellow patient. Visitors include Alan Wormald [Eton master] and Guy Haslewood, villain of Magdalen plays. No news of John so far.' His Battalion had been driven out of the Knightsbridge area on 13th June, and on 25th were bathing and refitting at Buqbuq.

25th June, Oliver wrote a long letter with a full description of his visit to Jerusalem. 'The great event of my life,' during his recent leave. His arrival by road from Jaffa, 'along the road where Christ and his disciples walked on the first Easter day, was made more thrilling than ever by a perfect sunset. These were the first hills we had seen for months. Their beauty in the setting rays combined with all their association made a deep impression.' The next day after he had visited the Anglican Cathedral, 'painfully English and cold and unsuitable,' he joined his companions and an Arab Christian guide to enter the old city by St. Stephen's Gate, 'then the excitement and wonder at being on sacred ground returned.' After visiting the Temple area, wailing wall and the vast Solomon's stables, they saw the 'reverent and beautiful' Garden of Gethsemane. He found it rather incongruous that the Mount of Olives, from which Jesus mourned over Jerusalem and the alleged scene of the Ascension should have mosques built on them. But his visit to the Church of the Holy Sepulchre abated his anger at the Moslems. They had left those two spots unspoilt, while the Christians had shown 'the most abominable taste imaginable. The church itself is robust and fine; but the scene of the crucifixion and the tomb (for some reason now within a few yards of each other) are revolting in their ornate gaudiness. I wish I had never been there.'

They drove to Bethlehem after lunch and found it 'really beautiful set on a hill ... It was interesting to see other ancient houses in which the stables were immediately below the living room, half below the ground. Last winter there were several feet of snow at Bethlehem at Christmas time, so the clever ones, who try to laugh at the references to snow in carols, are quite wrong.'

On the last day of the course, 'before the final orgy of Australian hospitality, my left jaw began to swell out like a balloon.' So, in great pain, his dentist sent him to hospital in

Cairo, as previously mentioned.

1st July, 'I have been released from hospital, but still this wretched wisdom tooth, or rather what was the wisdom tooth is causing trouble. It is exasperating to be kept away from the Battalion, but I hope to set off in a couple of days. My enforced stay here has been cheered by seeing Father Runge, full of good spirits and optimism, Peter Wood now a Major, and Alan Wormald.'

BACK TO 2ND BATTALION 60TH,
2ND I/C OF COMPANY

10th July, 'I have had a very successful and happy return. On the way, I spent the night with Bobby Erskine. John Brewis' death is a terrible blow. He shared digs at Haslemere with me, and tent at Cairo. Am now 2nd in Command to Peter Chapman. No better job in the Army. No Captaincy, as I am not sufficiently senior. At the moment I am enjoying good company and food with friends of Triggs.' The Triggs, New Zealanders, came to Lovel Hill in 1935 as friends from the Commonwealth. He mentioned them to indicate that he was with the New Zealand Division, who were just north of 4th Motor Brigade. He was for a short time liaising with them. His Battalion and Brigade were by then operating at the extreme southerly end of the El Alamein defensive line.

The next letter was written on Gaudy Day. Magdalen men will know the date, 22nd July, 'Yesterday was a great day as John visited me; he looks robust and well, but his face is in a very painful state from the sun. He said he had cream for it. It was our first meeting since January and only lasted an hour, luckily a quiet one. I am still with Bishop Crossley's [N.Z.] friends and having great excitement.' John eventually had to spend a few days in an Advance Dressing Station, being given M & B, the new wonder drug. After that he wore a peaked cap to shade his nose, as tin hats were rather scorned.

26th July, 'I am now back with the Battalion after a very happy, exciting fortnight on liaison duties. Now back with Battalion H.Q. as Intelligence Officer. About the only subaltern's post I have not yet held!' He also wrote to his father on the same day, 'I am also doing David Graham-Campbell's job for a day or two,' as Adjutant.

12th August, to his father, 'This morning a padre turned up and we have had a Communion service. Very impressive in the lovely cool of the morning. Richard Wood, several other officers and more men than usual were present. I am trying to persuade the padre to come weekly for a night, Evening Service and Communion the next morning.

'Roly Gibbs has returned from a course in great spirits and is now a Captain. [To become a Field Marshal later].

'David is now evacuated sick and once more I am doing Adjutant. Colonel tried to make me a Captain, but can't be done until David has been away longer, which I sincerely hope he won't be!

'Your letter about all your anxiety during the battle touched me very much. I wish I could explain to you how tremendously happy I am in the desert with these men and, at the moment, with a job as good as President of J.C.R.! [Junior Common Room at Oxford]. There are bad times, but many more good ones. I should be very happy to think that, if I were to be killed in action, you realised what a happy thing it would be and any memorial service must have cheerful hymns. Personally I anticipate a big job of work to be done among these men after the war.'

19th August, 'I do wish I had seen Bob get his V.C.. Robin Eden and John Earle, John's friend at Sandhurst, both presented me with *Country Lives*. [Picturing the presentation].

'I am now Acting Adjutant and I have secured a tin of Golden Syrup, so life couldn't look better (until the next sandstorm). I went out to dinner last night to visit Martin Charteris, a Major now. [After the war he became H.M's Private Secretary and is now Lord Charteris of Amisfield]. He was in good form as ever, and full of enquiries about Daddy. Roly asked about Uncle Louis and the Admiralty Arch.' Louis, a Brigadier General was acting as a private in the Home Guard, with duties to defend Admiralty Arch.

22nd August, 'Am having a great deal to do in David's continued absence, but I enjoy it so much, that I don't find it tiring. Also it is much cooler now ... I had a prompt reply from D.C.G. [Deputy Chaplain General] enclosing pocket New Testament and other books asked for. Also bundles of papers from my faithful friend in Durban, Mackeurtan.'

31st August, the first day of the battle of Alam Halfa, when Rommel aimed to reach the Delta, 'An exciting day has a lull in it, so there is just time to write an airgraph. David is still away. This job is made far pleasanter by the fact that my chief is now Bill Heathcoat-Amory, to whom I am devoted. It was good to be able to go to communion together yesterday morning.'

PROMOTED CAPTAIN AS ADJUTANT
2ND BATTALION 60TH

3rd September, 'David Graham-Campbell has not returned and I have taken over his work [adjutant] on a permanent footing (i.e. a very large increase of pay). I am certainly thrilled at the prospect, in spite of many difficulties. No use discussing the battle, as it will soon be out of date.' On this day Rommel started his withdrawal, which continued to the end of the war.

17th September, 'We are much enjoying bathes and imagine my delight at being camped in a ripe figgery. A couple of days ago I had the pleasure of being smartly saluted, as I sat at work in my office truck, by a subaltern in the R.B.s -

John looked exceedingly well after an illness, which has done him a world of good by resting him. He may not be so well now, because we ate many a fig together in memory of Lovel Hill. Luckily the men are suspicious of figs. 'Like eating an abscess' almost put me off my tenth fig the other day. [There were two fig trees at Lovel Hill, which produced between them about 25 figs a day in September].

'David Graham-Campbell should be back any day now, and my old D Company is impatiently waiting for him now that Peter Chapman has become 2nd in command of the Battalion. I hear that Oliver Leese is now out here. Unfortunately we aren't likely to meet.' Oliver was in 13 Corps in the south, while Oliver Leese had taken over command of 30 Corps in the north.

25th September, 'I have been very busy lately and am just beginning to 'come to' again [training for the battle of Alamein was going on at this time]. Had a very good dinner with Peter Wood in our mess last night and talked much about our badger digging. Peter found our Colonel a good audience. The Colonel is the most charming man you could imagine. A wonderful sense of humour, keen church man, master of foxhounds and air pilot among other things.

'We were thrilled to hear of Bob's successful return from Dieppe. Tell Felicity my moustache is based on Sir Ralph Verney's, but not yet quite so bristly!

'P.S. I now have Luke Asquith as Assistant Adjutant, a great help. My orderly Room Sergeant, Rainbow, is the most delightful and amusing old Rifle man.'

14th October, ' My name has been put in for the Staff College here, but there is no chance of getting there for very many months or even years. Not that I should want to leave the Battalion while I am in my present work.'

19th October, 'I am at the moment back on a busman's holiday, picking officers and men. [From the Depot at Geneifa]. A great opportunity for washing and cleaning up. Yesterday I went to the Cathedral. The dear old Bishop was due to preach, but he had fallen down and broken his arm, while playing golf!

'Peter Chapman has been taken away for important work. [To command the Yorkshire Dragoons, who had been made a Motor Battalion, to work with the 2nd Armoured Brigade]. A great blow to me, as I was so very devoted to him. I now have a very able right hand man in Luke Asquith, grandson of the P.M. I have always liked him very much since he was a brother officer in A. Company long ago.' He ends by saying, 'The barber evidently never met Sir Ralph Verney and has cut the moustache down rather a lot!'

El Alamein

30th October, written during the battle of Alamein, 'A great excitement in the battle was to discover John attached to us for a day, as a Captain. His new job must be a very interesting one and I hope it will lead on to others. [He had been appointed G3 Liaison to T.A.C. H.Q. 30 Corps working under Oliver Leese]. John was very well and we had an excellent opportunity to talk to each other all night. We have been extremely busy. The deaths of Peter Wood and Berkeley Paget, my twin in the regiment, arriving at Chisledon the same day, are great blows.' 'Extremely busy' refers to the great battle which took place on 25th October on the Kidney Ridge, when Vic Turner commanding the 2nd Bn Rifle Brigade, won a V.C. and 2nd Bn 60th on their right held the German counter attack and destroyed many tanks. Luke Asquith gave a lovely description of Oliver, with his head out of the 'Gin Palace' control vehicle, while shells landed all around. Then Martin Charteris writes, 'If I close my eyes and think of Oliver, I see a picture of a man - not only standing up when the shells were flying - but standing on tip-toe and by doing so proclaiming that it was wrong to be afraid of shells.'

Oliver's movement order No. 2, dated 23rd October

1942, for the start of the battle is shown in Appendix A.

7th November, 'It has been a terrific battle and thank God it appears to have been successful. How far we shall be able to drive the enemy right out of Africa remains to be seen.

'The Battalion has done brilliantly well, but there has been a painful price to pay. David Colman, after his gallant action in leading his carriers out to test the strength of the enemy strongpoint for us, was sent back to H.Q. in his own carrier by the M.O. When he reached me he was sitting in his carrier commander's seat, dead from loss of blood from the wound in his head. We buried his poor body wrapped in his blanket and the excellent R.C. padre said the burial service. Michael Moseley's death is a great sorrow to me. Although I have never been an intimate friend, we had so much in common - rowing, Oxford, theology and Green Jacket life - and I was longing for the days at Jerusalem after the war, when we should be fellow theological students together. God had other plans for Michael, but it leaves me feeling strangely alone. [Oliver had heard of a training school at Jerusalem, which he hoped he could attend, while awaiting demobilisation]. David Graham-Campbell has been an enormous help to me during the battle. Alan Holmes was not with us and Peter Blundell is wounded, but Roly Gibbs has returned, I am delighted to say.'

11th November, 'Armistice Day - it has a new meaning now with many of my friends among the killed - what a magnificent end most of them had. They must be rejoicing in our victory, as I hope you are. It has put new heart in us all to hear that the bells are being rung in England for the 8th Army. I wish I were in Oxford to hear them.

'At last a Magdalen man has appeared - George Palmer the new Signals Officer was at Magdalen immediately before the war and it is very pleasant to be able to gossip about the past. The Colonel goes from good to better and it is an inspiration to be with him. Alan Holmes has rejoined us. He really is much my greatest friend among the Green Jackets, with Roly as a good second, though much younger of course.'

30th November, 'Dodo [his Roman Catholic aunt] complained much at my having a moustache, but didn't explain whether she disliked it on aesthetic or religious grounds ... Very glad to say Robert Cecil and Tom Miller have rejoined my staff. Both great friends and very efficient.

'Hetty looks well, but won't lay. Great discussion as to whether a cock is needed. I say no, especially in view of the exorbitant stud prices demanded by the Quartermaster. As a scientific poultry breeder [Lumley], you must surely support me. I attribute the failure entirely to over feeding on Bully.'

4th December, 'Thrilled to hear you had Lady Margaret Alexander to dine. Her husband must be a really great man. [The Alexanders had moved to a house in Cranbourne]. Pat Sykes has come to join us as a Major. [2nd I/C of Battalion]. He has a house near Bishop's Castle and knows Harleys, Ripleys and Green Prices. A padre major came to take services last Sunday. Very good services and attendance. The Colonel and Pat Sykes present at H.C. as usual. I am incredibly lucky to have those two to work with.'

10th December, 'We have just had John Robinson over to dinner and had a most hilarious evening. We had great competitions.' One was on the number of countries they had been in; Oliver beat Pat Sykes by producing Vatican City. Hunts they had been with was won by the Colonel. Cathedrals visited was an easy win for Robert Cecil. Voyages they had been ill on, a walk away victory for the Colonel.

THE ADVANCE WEST

Christmas Eve, 'A beautiful cold night with a full moon and my thoughts naturally turn to you, engaged in decorating the house.

'Two days ago, while leading the Battalion, I saw John standing by the side of the road; great luck, as a complete chance. I managed to have a few words with him, but had to rush on to regain my place. I hope now we may see Oliver.' His Battalion was now fighting in 30 Corps under Oliver Leese. John had contracted jaundice on the last day of the Alamein battle, but had just rejoined Tactical Head Quarters 30 Corps, which was then in the area of El Agheila. As liaison officer, his task was to guide Oliver Leese round the desert.

1943

New Year's Day, 1943, 'We found a padre, Wingfield-Digby, an excellent chap, who gave us a short Carol Service and address in the afternoon. The next day we were able to make our Christmas Communion in the evening, a thrilling service in the darkness.

'The news of Richard Wood's wounds [on 30th December at Bir Zidan] has shocked everyone. Both legs - but if anyone can get over it, he will.' Prophetic words.

31st January, 'Oliver Leese came to visit us a few days ago. He was most impressive and we thought him at once friendly and inspiring. He has changed a great deal since I last saw him [at Tabley theatricals]. He invited me to stay with him and John near the town [Tripoli]. I saw John just before the battle. He was so covered in sand that day that it was hard to say whether he looked well or not. He seems to enjoy his work and was in great spirits.

'John Robinson's death, on 17th January at Beni-Ulid, has been a terrible blow to all of us. I was so very fond of him and he was one of the few links with home left. He had been in such extra good spirits since he took over the Company and I enjoyed working with him enormously. He stepped on a mine and never recovered consciousness. I am glad to say Roly has taken over from him.' This letter was written on the day of the Victory Service and Parade in Tripoli attended by Churchill.

A SHERMAN TANK APPROACHES TRIPOLI

GODFREY TALBOT REPORTING TO THE BBC
ON THE OUTSKIRTS OF TRIPOLI

102

IN A 'JEEP' (NOTE THE SHRAPNEL HOLES)
L. TO R. - LIEUT. P.D.B. COCHRANE, CAPT. D.A.V. ANSON, LIEUT.
J.H. POWE, CAPT. F.O. GREEN-WILKINSON

C COMPANY ORDER GROUP
L. TO R. - LIEUT. G.S. PALMER, CAPT. F.O. GREEN-WILKINSON,
CAPT. R.C. GIBBS, M.C.

103

4th February, 'Bobbie Erskine came to visit us last week. He is very impressive in his new job [Divisional Commander] but still as friendly as ever. Robert Cecil, who was my Intelligence Officer, has gone to him as A.D.C. and should do very well. I am sorry to lose Robert, but luckily Luke Asquith is available to take his place, with whom I share a truck at present, as mine was blown up (I wasn't on it at the time and Wells was quite unhurt). We have a nice little mess of two. When it used to be Robert, our conversation was gossip, religion and scandal. With Luke it is scandal, politics and gossip. Luke's stories are endless and improbable, but always amusing.'

4th February, to his Uncle Louis, 'I am trying hard to get hold of some whisky and camel milk [his uncle was in the Camel Corps in the Sudan at the battle of Omdurman, and was always full of strange ideas]. It sounds just the thing for breakfast, but the former is hard to obtain and I couldn't face the latter 'unlaced'.

'I often think of our walks at Argentière and Cadenabbia, when you instilled into me the ways of the Green Jackets and the love of soldiering.'

22nd February, 'Pat Sykes and Roly Gibbs have been wounded. Neither very dangerously when they left here, but I shall miss Roly very much.

'I have had a wonderful letter from Richard Wood. He has taken the loss of both his legs in the most inspiring way.'

At some stage Oliver and Colonel Heathcoat-Amory visited Richard in a Cairo hospital. Oliver reported a splendid conversation he had earlier with Richard's brother Charles, who was G3 at Brigade Headquarters. Oliver had applied to Brigade for a padre to replace one who had recently left. As Richard says, 'My brother, always a little vague, had been unable to remember the details of the conversation and had to telephone Oliver again to ask, "Did you want - or particularly NOT want - a new padre for the Battalion?" '

2nd March, 'I haven't seen John for a long time, but I often hear of him from his fellow staff officers, 'while John wrote home at the same time, 'I frequently hear reports on how Oliver is from Bobbie Erskine. It doesn't look as if Oliver will be able to stay just yet. It is time I paid him a visit.'

8th March, 'A very great day today - John came here on his birthday with his Military Cross. It was the first I had heard of it ... he described to us all the details of what had happened in the battle just over. [the Battle of Medenine] Our padre Gregory is a really excellent man in every way. I am afraid he has a difficult job. It is uphill work after years without a padre.'

16th March, 'David Graham-Campbell is off to the Staff College. [Haifa. John met him there in the Autumn, by which time he was an instructor]. He badly needs a rest and change. We shall miss him, but his health has been very trying for a long time.'

22nd March, 'Tom Miller was killed on a mine. His death has upset me a lot. The number of my friends who have been killed is growing enormous. It is hard to adjust one's mind to what the losses really mean. Poor Tom died very gallantly leading his platoon and we were able to get the padre to bury him. His grave lies in the most beautiful country covered with spring flowers.' The battle for the Mareth Line started on 20th March. The Battalion was then towards the south of the line, before it made a dash to join the 'left hook' by the New Zealand Corps, which finally dislodged the Germans on 31st March.

30th March, 'Since I last wrote poor Alan Holmes has been wounded in the leg. Not bad, we believe. It should give him a good rest, which he deserves. Yet another friend gone, and one of my very closest. Toby Low [now Lord Aldington] an old friend from New College, has joined us and taken over Alan's Company.

'Just over a year now since the nightmare of my breakdown at Cairo last March. What a lot I have to be thankful for since then.'

30th April, 'Alan Holmes has written from hospital. He seems to be recovering well. Thank goodness Roly is still here.'

WOUNDED

25th April, Easter Day, 'At last they have hit me, yesterday, but only after a good run for my money. I was standing with the C.O. and an officer from Division H.Q. discussing plans, when a shell fragment went clean through my left thigh, fairly high up. Very little pain and I should be back in a month or 6 weeks.

'I was able to hand over the Adjutancy to Jim Harries before I left. My disappointment at not finishing the campaign off is offset by enjoying my first rest since last April.

'It must be some time since a G-W bled on the battlefield. I can't say it was very dignified as Humphrey Woods had to 'debag' me in front of all H.Q. and I was painfully aware that I hadn't had a change of pants for two months.'

Richard Wood reminds us that Oliver embellished this incident, when recounting it later on. The Colonel, Humphrey Woods was stone deaf, so he never heard the shell burst behind him. On turning round, he saw Oliver apparently 'taking cover' and rebuked him saying, 'Stand up Oliver - not in front of the men.'

The idea of Oliver being a coward is amusing to those who knew him well. You have Martin Charteris saying that Oliver 'stood on tiptoe, when shells were flying.' Then, Luke Asquith has written, 'In Tunisia when mines were the worst

106

weapon of the bosch, Oliver reconnoitred a Laager, halted us all, and then travelled himself in a jeep over the whole area in ever decreasing circles, before allowing us to settle down.' Such was his fearlessness, since the jeep could have driven over a mine at any moment.

6th May, 'I am still in hospital near Tripoli and have healed up so quickly that I am now allowed up and out. Yesterday, for the first time I went into Tripoli. After all the hopes we had of being the first troops to enter the city, it was strange to be entering it for the first time three months later, with a wounded leg, four hundred odd miles from the front.

'It is hard to believe that tomorrow I shall be thirty ... I wish I could expect to be ordained this year. Thirty seems to me a good age at which to take that step.'

13th May, 'My leg is far better and I can now walk about almost normally; but still the 'entrance' wound won't quite heal up, unlike the 'exit' which is almost healed now.

'That the war in North Africa is over is good, but the size of the haul of prisoners is thrilling and should be sufficient to affect seriously Hitler's plans for the defence of Europe. These were mostly picked troops. The other really promising feature seems to be how well co-operation between Americans, French and British seems to have worked in this battle. How is the tricycle?' Myfanwy was unable to ride a bicycle, so at the start of the war, when she was billeting officer for the London evacuees, she bought a tricycle to get around Cranbourne. It was a 'special' made for her with two wheels in front, which was considered less dangerous. It was based on the old 'Stop me and buy one' ice cream seller's transport. It must have been a magnificent sight to see her pedalling around Windsor Forest.

16th May, to Lumley, 'I have been thinking of your three years in the Home Guard. I hope you are finding your work as Company Storeman congenial. I feel sure that many must

107

have regretted putting someone so business-like in that position. You must constantly be producing documentary evidence that people have signed for things they have mislaid!

'Yesterday I ran into our Battalion Padre, Gregory, as I moved along the Corso from the Arab shoe shine boy to the Italian cake shop Signora. I am sorry to say Gregory has been posted away as a Senior Chaplain, a great blow.'

17th May, 'Other patients include Clarke, Adjutant of the Scots Guards and George Palmer, who was my Signals Officer at Alamein and later. Visitors have included Colonel Charles Sismey and John. A wonderful surprise when John arrived. Robert Cecil had thoughtfully sent a signal to John to tell him where I was, so John was able to spend an evening and morning with me on his way to Cairo. He was as usual full of information and gossip.'

20th May, 'I received a letter from John yesterday, from Shepheard's Hotel Cairo. In it he bemoaned the fact that he has been made G2 and will become a major! I have sent him suitable condolences and a shooting-stick, which will no doubt come in handy at Gezira races!! I am sure he will do his job as Chief Liaison Officer very well.

'To my delight Bobbie Erskine has come in here for a few days complete rest. I have been able to have some very good talks with him about the regiment and his own recent successes. In addition Robert Cecil, his A.D.C. has been about, so I have had good company.

'Today I have been declared fully healed with no need to go to the convalescent camp. I am trying to get a room in a hotel until the Battalion arrives back here.'

23rd May, Oliver wrote to Cosmo Lang who had now retired and was living at Kew. After explaining about his wound, he wrote, 'The enforced leisure has been a great opportunity to do some reading. Harold Nicholson's excellent old book, *Curzon the last phase* and *The Screwtape letters* by

108

my tutor at Magdalen, C.S. Lewis, have been among the most interesting books. The latter is full of good ideas put in a most original and amusing form. I have tried it on both officers and other ranks with great success ... I hope the war may soon be over, so that I may return to the purpose over which you have given me such great help and encouragement.

'John now a Major on the Staff! I am delighted to find myself playing an admiring Reuben to John's very embarrassed Joseph.'

BACK WITH 2ND BN 60TH AND LEAVE IN CAIRO

1st June, 'On my return to the Battalion from hospital I found awaiting me thirty six letters - thirty seven if you include the one Felicity wrote to John and addressed to me (a pity she was quite so frank about her elder brother in it!)

'I spent one day with the Battalion and much enjoyed it. The Colonel was back looking much refreshed. He agreed it was no good starting again as Adjutant and there is no need as I am proud to say Jim Harries, whom I selected and trained, is doing extremely well. The Colonel is making a vacancy for me as 2nd in Command to Roly Gibbs in C. Company, so that I can gain experience from him, until a vacancy for a Company occurs. As Roly is about my greatest friend and a very fine soldier the prospect seems quite perfect.

'The Colonel then sent me away for a fortnight. By great luck I got a plane the next day, 29th May. I was thrilled with my first flight done at a great height. Seeing the great city [Cairo] from the air was the most striking thing, I thought. Coming down the only discomfort.

'Needless to say, I found that John had gone away for the weekend.'

4th June from Cairo, 'First I must comment on your many letters. Bertie Jackson size 4'9" was John's cox at

Magdalene [when John stroked the war time VIII and Bertie made 4 bumps in the 4 days of races] and is one of our very best officers. A really remarkable man. A tribute to Gerry marksmanship that they have hit so small a target twice! He is now in hospital in the Delta with a wound in the foot received about the last day [of the battle in Tunisia].

'John returned here Monday evening, left by air (his first trip!) Thursday morning. We had two perfect days together. I was very proud of 'my minor the Major.' I visited his office and saw a very friendly Sir O.' (Oliver Leese).

10th June, 'I hope to be going back to the Battalion tomorrow, refreshed by a really splendid leave. I have been to the other great city [Alexandria] where I had one of my few pleasant bathes! Strange to say I had never been there before. Pleasanter, but not so good for meeting friends. The W.R.N.S. in their white kit are very attractive! I met Heywood Cutting there. He is an American who was wounded in a very brave way at Alamein with the Battalion, and now has a staff job, as not A.1. Then I returned here and I went down to stay with Alan Holmes at his convalescent camp and found him nearly recovered. It was very good to see him again after two months.'

16th June, from Bill Heathcoat-Amory to Lumley, 'Just a line to tell you how pleased we shall be to get Oliver back again after his wound. He has done a very great deal for this Battalion and as my Adjutant for nine months was literally a tower of strength and the best person to have with me imaginable. His well developed sense of the ridiculous, which you will know about, is worth a company of infantry at certain moments.'

18th June, 'When last I wrote, I thought I was returning from leave to the Battalion the following day. Instead, I had a note from Oliver Leese asking me to do a job, which involved flying to Syria. Very interesting and I loved being in really mountainous country. There was still snow on the hill peaks. Now I have returned from a wonderful week with a cold in my head, and once more hoping to return to the Battalion tomorrow. In the course of my travels I ran into David Graham-Campbell and Martin Charteris [at Haifa Staff College] both looking far better, and Kenneth Crawley almost the first time since the war began.'

26th June, 'I returned to the Battalion to find forty letters. We are quite near my old hospital [Tripoli]. Roly gave me a wonderful welcome to C. Company. George Palmer, previously my signals officer at Alamein and a Magdalen man is in the Company.'

7th July, 'I do enjoy working with Roly. He takes everything so light heartedly. We have been very strenuous with route marches and games. We are right on the sea and it is so hot I bathe daily with pleasure.'

13th July, 'We still lie by the sea and rejoice in good news from Sicily [invaded on 10th July]. It is thrilling that we are invading Europe at last. I suppose John is over there.'

19th July, 'I am beginning to feel quite at home in C. Company now and very glad that I did not return to be Adjutant. Alan Holmes has not yet returned from his wound, I miss him very much. There are only six officers left who started to reform at Tidworth three years ago. Some of course have gone to staff jobs.'

31st July, 'We are still bathing in the same place. Bertie Jackson has returned to the Battalion quite recovered from his wound. [Meanwhile 8th Army was advancing across Sicily towards Mount Etna]. The news from Italy sounds very good at present. I am sure the Italians must long for peace.

'I am wondering very much whether I shall get a chance of going to the Staff College now. It would be a wrench to leave the Battalion, but it would be good for me in the future,

111

if I want to get a good staff job. I would rather command a company in this Battalion. Luckily in the Army one doesn't have to choose.'

10th August, 'Yesterday I received posting orders to report to 7th Armoured Division as Staff Captain. Apparently Bobbie Erskine has persuaded the Colonel to release me and I have no choice but to go. The job sounds a dull one, but may lead to something. It will be good working for Bobbie Erskine again and I have very many friends on his select staff, including many black buttons [i.e. Green Jackets].

'So tomorrow morning the faithful Wells and I set off along the coast road and leave the Battalion after just over three years.' 7th Armoured Division were busy planning to take part in the invasion of Italy.

17th August, 'Well, the 100 mile journey here was eventful. My jeep had a head-on collision with a truck coming in the opposite direction through no fault of Wells, the driver. The other truck was travelling in the opposite direction to us, when the one in front of it stopped quickly. To avoid running into the back of it, or the trees on the roadside, it took a chance in the middle of the road, and we met at 30 m.p.h. each. A horrid experience. I 'came to' bruised and scratched all over, rather badly in the legs. Wells was rather less bad, the third occupant lost a couple of teeth. The opposition had one person badly cut. We all went off to my 48th General Hospital, where we were patched up and Wells and I were not detained. I am still hobbling after six days. My dear old specs were broken after fourteen years.

'This is a pleasant spot by the sea. The best part of the job so far is the people with whom I have to work, especially Jim Stanton (Gloucester Hussars) the D.A.Q.M.G. for whom I work in particular. The General gave me a wonderful

112

reception and I dined very well at his Mess.'

24th August, 'You asked about Alan Holmes. He was wounded in the foot, calf and bottom by an 'S' mine near Medenine while leading his company in a night attack. He returned to the Battalion the very day after I left. A great blow.

'Martin Charteris visited us here the other day. He looks better than usual. He has just become a Lieutenant Colonel as instructor at the Staff College [Haifa]. The outstandingly nice people are Basil Wingfield-Digby and Jim Stanton. The former is Senior Padre and almost a contemporary of mine at another Cambridge Theological College. Jim Stanton has a delightful sense of humour.'

30th August, 'My legs are taking a long time to get right, but I should be thankful nothing has gone septic so far. I can walk quite easily, but they ache at times and hurt if I stand for long. The General has been amazingly thoughtful and kind about it all. I hope you saw his C.B.?'

3rd September, 'No letters have reached me here. I haven't seen or heard from John. These are exciting days and I don't suppose he has much time to write in his job. [In fact, John developed Malaria in Sicily towards the end of July and was told to report to Haifa Staff College in September, when he had recovered]. I am at the moment working with Harry Moore a major of the Fusiliers, who is about my age. A rowing man at Pembroke, Cambridge, and a budding barrister and M.P. I find him an excellent companion. He came recently from a job for which he shared a house with Kenneth Crawley.'

It was the anniversary of the start of the war and he was just off to a special service in the local church. It was also the day that 13 Corps of 8th Army landed on the toe of Italy. The 7th Armoured Division was part of 10 Corps, on loan to the American 5th Army. They were due to land at Salerno on 10th September, two days after the Armistice with Italy.

CHAPTER 11

ITALY. SALERNO LANDING. SEPTEMBER 1943.

18th September, 'A short note to let you know I am very well and happy after a very exciting and interesting time. Unfortunately I can not tell you more than that I personally had a grand-stand view well forward, and that the apples, peaches and tomatoes are plentiful and delicious. My legs seem to be healing quickly now that we get plenty of fruit and no sand.'

24th September. After three weeks he at last received some 20 letters and heard that John was at the Staff College, 'It will give him a good break from this rather bitter war ... I was surprised at your congratulations on my staff appointment. I had hoped you all looked on Regimental soldiering as the place of honour. I count the days when I can return to command the Company promised me by the Colonel.'

25th September, he wrote to his sister Hilaré Ryder, who had a son, Lisle, born in January of that year. Now he had heard that another child was due. 'I do wish you every happiness in your rapidly increasing family. The idea of calling him David Oliver (if a he) is the greatest honour I have ever been paid and I am most touched by the thought.' In fact, in March 1944, a girl was born and was named Susan Myfanwy, and later became a well known artist and portrait painter (see cover picture).

'Lavinia also wrote that she had seen you and your handsome son.' Lisle followed his father into the Navy, and then his uncle into the church, to become a Canon of Worcester Cathedral.

'I didn't welcome the idea of coming to this job and it looked rather like what the Silent Service calls a shore job. However, my views have been altered by finding it is interesting, in very good company, and anything but safe. Life has been very stirring lately. The fruit is wonderful and the country glorious.'

1st October from Italy, advancing north of Salerno bridgehead, 'I have heard tragic news that both Francis Wigram and John Harley have been killed in their magnificent action here. It has upset me a lot, as I had seen both recently and liked them so much.

'How I wish I could tell you more. I was on a special job and arrived the first day [of the landing]. The people are mostly friendly, but terribly hungry. How sad to read of all your rejoicings over P.O.W.s released in Italy. Most of them must be very disappointed. My legs are a bit better, but still very tender.'

10th October, 'So glad to hear George Mann has M.C. [his family lived in the next door house to Lovel Hill in Windsor Forest]. It was a dramatic moment when we heard of Italy's surrender, a few hours before landing.

'Last Sunday, a little cluster of clergy approached me and asked permission to ring the bells in their Campanile. This was given and they greeted their liberators by such a clanging that speech on the wireless was quite impossible. Then the brass band arrived and blasted its way twice round the square pursued by some very young catholics in uniform. The very very young at the end of the column had to run, exhorted onwards by perspiring priests. After two circuits the band could march and blow no further, so they decided to blow only and did it about 10 yards from the liberators. Not only speech by phone, but thought and action were paralysed.'

23rd October, 'I am very distressed at the news of John Loyd's death. He was always so friendly and polite in an old-fashioned way.

'I had my third traffic accident the other day, when the back wheel came off, while we were at the top of a very famous mountain near here [Vesuvius]. No injury luckily, as I haven't got over my August accident yet.'

26th October, 'I received a letter from Colonel Heathcoat-Amory telling me that my M.C. has come through at last. So sorry to have been so long over producing my modest contribution to the Lovel Hill 'Cross' collection. I am really most grateful to the Colonel for a very fine piece of imaginative writing.'

The citation reads, 'Captain Green-Wilkinson has been Adjutant to the Battalion throughout the period under review. Throughout the battle of Alamein he controlled Battalion Headquarters with the greatest efficiency and dealt with every situation with the utmost coolness and good judgement.

'On the night of 26/27 October during the attack by the Battalion on the 'Woodcock' position [next to Snipe, where Vic Turner won his V.C.] Battalion Headquarters came under heavy small arms fire from an enemy strong post and might have quickly become disorganised if Captain Green-Wilkinson had not energetically taken steps to collect the various vehicles, and by his calm and confident bearing steadied everyone, and ensured the necessary communications for the control of the battle.

'Again, at Beni Ulid, on the night of 17/18 January [1943] while the Battalion was carrying out an operation of cutting the road behind the enemy, the Commanding Officer's Reconnaissance Headquarters with the forward party was cut off by a force of enemy tanks. Captain Green-Wilkinson immediately took control of the situation and organised a firm base from which the forward party could be supported. The quickness with which he got the 25 pounders and anti-tank guns into action, was largely responsible for the success of this operation, resulting in the destruction of several German tanks and a large number of M.T. vehicles.

'During the whole period under review, the gallantry shown by Captain Green-Wilkinson in those and other operations, combined with the display of many other soldier-like qualities has contributed largely to any success this Battalion has achieved.'

On 7th November, to Prudence, Oliver explains that he knew about his Recommendation way back in April, since he was the Adjutant. It must have been a tantalising period waiting to hear if the Colonel's Recommendation had been accepted.

Then he asks for his replacement spectacles to be held at Lovel Hill, and await instructions, so he must have known that the 7th Armoured Division was about to be returned to England for the Normandy invasion.

JAUNCICE

14th November. Back to hospital, this time for a bad bout of jaundice.

29th November. After three weeks in bed in hospital he was hoping to be allowed up and go soon to a 'lovely convalescent camp (or rather hotel) across the bay.' [The Bay of Naples].

5th December, 'At last I have been moved to a convalescent home in a comfortable Edwardian hotel in Sorrento. The village is close by and the whole atmosphere of the place is more like the Italy we loved in Rome and Cadenabbia. I feel so weak after 3 weeks in bed, but the fortnight I have been ordered should more than restore me to health.

'Before leaving the hospital I discovered Christopher Loyd was in it, wounded for the second time since he has been in Italy. It was delightful to talk to him, as he is so like his brother John, to whom I was so devoted. Peter Wyld (Coldstream Guards) is here recovering from a wound and in very good spirits.' Peter, an old Harrovian, used to meet Oliver and his family at the Eton and Harrow match at Lords - both were families of six children. He was later to go out to Zambia as a priest in Oliver's Diocese.

117

CHAPTER 12

BACK TO ENGLAND. 1944

There are no records of Oliver's return to England, but we know that Montgomery wanted the 7th Armoured Division brought home for the Normandy landings, and the Anniversary Book mentions that Oliver arrived in England on 8th January, after 2¼ years overseas. As it happened, John landed in Italy on 9th January, after the Haifa Staff course, to work again for Oliver Leese. The General had just taken over the 8th Army from Montgomery. So the brothers' paths no longer crossed each other.

BACK WITH DIVISION H.Q.

Oliver next wrote from Didlington Hall, Thetford, in Norfolk on 3rd February after having overseas home leave, 'For me it was like a very happy dream. What a lot was crammed into 22 days!' Then he described visiting a unit at Hunstanton, which was expecting a new commanding officer. 'My British warm [overcoat] was too much for the sentry, who thought the great moment had come. He turned out the Guard, the reception committee swept down the stairs, the police sergeant opened the door of the car and out stepped Capt. G-W. A tribute to Mr Welsh! [Welsh and Jeffries the Regimental tailor].

'Yesterday evening I went to tea with the Stanton family. The daughter, Anne, aged two was a charming little girl and much appreciated the [toy] dog that I saw in King's Lynn in the morning. Mrs S. very nice looking and worthy of Jim's lecture on married bliss.'

25th February, from Didlington Hall, the Headquarters of the Division, he wrote, 'My future movements are more uncertain than ever as, to my great sorrow, Jim Stanton has been promoted away from the Division. I am glad to say he becomes a Lt. Col., but we shall miss him very much. Harry Moore, now D.A.A.G., will succeed him as D.A.Q.M.G. In the meantime, I do the job down here and then the General wants me to be D.A.A.G. (Deputy Assistant Adjutant General), a major's appointment, which I think I should much enjoy.' He later explained that his appointment deals with reinforcement of men, discipiine, welfare, entertainments 'and most important the Chaplain's Department, with an opportunity to cooperate with Basil Wingfield-Digby.'

19th March, from King's College, Cambridge, 'I am back in my old haunts. I had to spend the night here ... Westcott House was deserted. I ran into David Graham-Campbell's brother, now the Dean of King's College, and he very kindly showed great hospitality to the young man who had so impertinently turned down his offer of a good curacy. [At the start of the War, when Oliver delayed his ordination].

'I have seen quite a lot of the Rifle Brigade this week, Mike Edwards, Chris Milner and Gordon Johnson. It is good to have this contact with regimental life and a bond with John.'

26th March. After a visit to London, he caught a very early train back to H.Q. to meet the District Welfare Officer. 'This was amply rewarded by its turning out to be Salter, John's Magdalene tutor, masquerading as a Lt. Col. in the Rifle Brigade. [John had gone to Magdalene, Cambridge for the first year of the war]. I hadn't met him before and took a very great liking to him.'

13th April, 'Please note the new address, the postage is only 1½d [letters were now to be sent to his H.Q. via the Army

119

Post Office, in preparation for the Invasion of Europe]. I cannot thank you enough for my leave. I really do feel immensely refreshed by it, and know what a number of sacrifices you all had to make.'

On his return to H.Q., he found a letter from John, 'He talks of Luke Asquith being with him at T.A.C. H.Q. 8th Army, and is astonished at England not knowing *Lili Marlene.*'

LUKE ASQUITH ABOUT TO BATHE IN RIVER ON ADRIATIC COAST

CHAPTER 13

NORMANDY. JUNE 1944

Letters written in May, during the preparation for the Invasion, are of little interest due to censorship requirements. The landings in Normandy took place on 6th June and Oliver landed with 7th Armoured Division H.Q. on D + 2, 8th June. His first letter home was written on 11th June, 'Sorry to have not written for so long, but I am safe and well, happy and very busy. None the worse except for a bullet through the back of my car, which I thought was a back fire at the time, so was only worried about the engine. I love this country. The flowers are very lovely and the people rather a good type. I like the Americans more.'

16th June. He had just received a large bag of letters which varied in date from 9th November to 8th June - such were the difficulties of the Army Post Office. He was happy, extremely busy, very cold and very wet, 'Just what I foresaw during all the wonderful weather, while we were indoors!' He was enjoying using the French language again.

18th June. He was very distressed to hear that Humphrey Woods D.S.O. and 2 M.C.s had been killed, 'Who rebuked me for taking cover, when I was wounded. A Lt. Col. at 27 and a very fine, loveable soldier.'

21st June. He reported that it was still very cold and he had a 'hacking cough, and the highest medical authorities have produced some medicine.'

22nd June, he wrote to his sister, Felicity, who with Prudence was a V.A.D. at Winkfield Place Nursing Home, 'You are really more in the front line than I am with these horrible pilotless planes. I wonder when the first patients from Normandy will arrive at Winkfield Place.'

30th June he said that the weather had improved and his 'cough has softened a bit. We are doing very well with Camembert cheeses and butter.'

121

4th July, 'Work is extremely hard at present. I cannot say I like this job and would gladly exchange it for one with a lower rank, but feel I must go on at present.

'So delighted about Hamilton at St George's.' This refers to the appointment of a new Dean of St George's Chapel, Windsor.

9th July, 'Terribly difficult to give you interesting details when life is as dull as it is for me at the moment. I have had a good talk to Basil Wingfield-Digby and our very nice chief doctor, and on the strength of that, asked the General [Bobbie Erskine] for a change of job. This one is too uncongenial in every way. It is a relief to have made a decision. I pray it was a right decision. I am much excited to know what will happen now. I hope something that I can really enjoy.'

11th July, Oliver wrote to Prudence, 'I am so sorry to hear you have got run down through overwork [she had been promoted corporal in the V.A.D. at the Nursing Home] you must indeed have overdone it, as I thought you were quite tireless. It is good news that you are having a rest at Tabley [home of the Leicester-Warrens, Oliver Leese's in-laws]. I am feeling rather better and my cough has quite gone, but I look forward to a change of job, whatever it is. I don't consider 'A' work as soldiering. Endless paper work recently.'

The 7th Armoured Division was being regrouped with the Guards Armoured and 11th Armoured Division in preparation for Operation Goodwood which was due to start on 18th July. This would push south of Caen and give more elbow room, while retaining the eight Panzer Divisions opposing the 2nd Army. Two days earlier Oliver was sent back to England for a rest. On 17th July his postcard said, 'This will surprise you, I am in England. The doctors insisted on giving me a rest, as they feared I would break down from overwork. Already I am feeling very much better, after three days of sleep.' On 18th July he rang his parents from Muswell Hill Hospital.

CHAPTER 14

ENGLAND AND STAFF COLLEGE. 1944

Oliver enjoyed telling the story of his journey back across the Channel. Due to his love of the local Camembert cheese, he bought some to take home and stored it in his wash basin, which had a canvas cover. During the night crossing, when they were all dozing on a lower deck, he realised that, due to a miscalculation, the Camembert was becoming far too smelly. So he decided that he must get rid of it. He took his wash basin up on deck, threw the offending cheese overboard and returned to his seat or bunk. It dawned on him that anyone might jump to the wrong conclusion, when they saw him return with his wash basin and realised that the strong smell of feet had gone. As some were slumbering he could hardly announce what he had done.

Oliver wrote to Bobbie Erskine to apologise for his departure and on 23rd August, he got a reply, 'I am so glad to hear that the sick leave has put you right. You never failed at all as D.A.A.G., but nobody can help getting ill.

'I am very sorry to have left the Division and such heaps of good friends. I am doing nothing at present, but I daresay the rest is doing me good.' He had been replaced by Montgomery who wanted a fresher Divisional Commander for 7th Armoured.

After Oliver's release from hospital, he went on sick leave and visited his sister Deborah in Derby, where she was a captain in the A.T.S., working at the R.A.O.C. Depot. Then on 3rd August he wrote from Garrowby in Yorkshire, 'Richard [Wood] met me at York Station after a rather crowded journey from Derby. Richard looks amazingly well and walks about without any embarrassment.

'This afternoon we are going for a ride. Tomorrow Mark and Diana Meynell arrive [Oliver last saw them on the bicycle ride in Holland] and on Saturday Lord and Lady Halifax come up for the weekend. It will be a great moment to meet them.'

Richard Wood writes, 'Oliver came to stay with me at Garrowby and arrived just before my parents, who were briefly on leave from Washington. They flew up to Yorkshire and landed at the small wartime aerodrome of Pocklington. Oliver, never having met them, came with me to drive with them back to Garrowby. He politely shared the back seat with my mother; my father, in front, whispered loudly to me: "Who is the young man in the back? Is it the Civilian Instructor at the aerodrome?" After that, until he signed 'Oliver Northern Rhodesia', he always added 'C.I.' after his name.

'Both my parents became immensely fond of Oliver and my father, in spite of his snoring during one of Oliver's sermons at Kirby Underdale, used later to question him closely on the problems of South Africa. Charles after atoning for the misunderstanding about the request for a padre in the Desert, became a great friend.'

10TH BN 60TH, TRAINING DEPOT

By the middle of August, Oliver was due to report to the 10th Battalion K.R.R.C. (60th) at Strensall Camp in Yorkshire, which was a training Depot.

16th August, 'I feel very like a new boy writing after his first day at school. I have found some friends here, notably Tommy Trotter, who commanded C. Company in 2nd Battalion for 2 years. I first knew him as my fag master at Sheep's and later he was Adjutant to the Eton O.T.C. Tommy Trotter had a damaged arm. While serving with the 60th in India he was attacked by a tiger and saved his life by pulling on the tiger's tongue.

'I find I was quite right to appear as a captain. It was sad to part with my crowns, but better to have done so before I arrived. I feel terribly sad to be stuck away here, when such great things are happening on the continent, but I must learn to be patient.'

20th August, 'On Sunday I hope to go over to Garrowby to see Richard. He has asked me to say Evensong in the village of Bugthorpe, where the vicar is having a holiday. My first service [taken] in Church since Lent 1940.

'No definite news of my future till Colonel Osborne returns [from leave], but the prospects of getting to France look very remote at present.'

22nd August, 'Colonel Willy Osborne returned today and gave me a most touching welcome. [He had been in command of 2nd 60th before Egypt]. The position is as follows. A month ago my return to the 2nd Battalion as a Company Commander was easy. Colonel Heathcoat-Amory had applied for me, and officers with experience of battle were scarce. Now he has gone, to everyone's regret, and another Battalion has been split up to provide reinforcements. The policy is to send out Company Commanders, who are senior and fresh. Therefore my chances are rather remote.

'Colonel Willy wants me to take over A. Company here. In many ways it is an attractive offer, and it means that I keep my Majority. I shall not put up my crowns again until next week; but I shall have pleasure in telling John that my appointment is back-dated to be continuous, so I am still the senior Major G-W!!

'The problem which puzzles me is whether to try for the Staff College in December. No one ever gets in without backing high up ... on the other hand having been at Camberley might stand in the way of ordination.'

2nd September, 'Tomorrow I shall command my Company on Church parade. Five years ago we were all together at Lovel Hill. What a tremendous amount there is to be thankful for, both nationally and personally, in the five years. John's transformation from schoolboy to veteran major is the best part of it all. I say this even though the little blighter has never written the letter he promised me. Possibly the marvellous move by the 8th Army to the Adriatic is some excuse. Tomorrow I go over in the afternoon to Garrowby and take with me Henry James, one of my subalterns, who was a contemporary of Richard's at Eton.'

15th September, 'I was thrilled to hear news of John's meeting with the PM.' When Churchill visited Tactical Headquarters of 8th Army on the Adriatic coast on 27th August, the officers were introduced by Oliver Leese. It came to John's turn and he was introduced as the son of Canon Green-Wilkinson, in spite of Lumley not actually being a canon. To which Churchill replied, with a chuckle, "Ah! That lends an odour of sanctity to the Headquarters." Oliver continued, 'The 'Odour of Sanctity' will obviously become a classic joke.'

17th September, Oliver was keen to discuss his future with the Archbishop of York [Garbett] as he was nearby. He managed to make an appointment and afterwards wrote, 'I had a most delightful day at Bishopthorpe yesterday. Arriving in time for tea, I had about half an hour with the Archbishop in his study, sitting under Cosmo's portrait. Then went for a walk with Gerald Ellison. [Later Bishop of London].

'On returning, the Archbishop walked round the garden with me. Evensong in the chapel was followed by dinner in the wing where the Crawleys used to live, and more conversation before my taxi picked me up at 10 pm.

'On the question of what action I should take now, he gave me some lines to think on. It was a surprise to find that

126

he, like Ted Talbot, thought I had chosen rightly in 1939. At that time I felt that few approved of what I had done. [In delaying ordination]. I expect the right line to take is to go ahead as if I were staying in the Army till the very end of the war, and leave it to the Church authorities to take any action to get me demobilised, if they think it right. I don't think the Staff College makes much difference one way or the other, and I doubt whether I should get in this time, unless Bobbie Erskine were ready to do something for me.'

14th October, 'It was the greatest possible pleasure to have John here last night. [John had flown home from Italy with Oliver Leese, when he was appointed Commander of Allied Land Forces South East Asia, and was due to fly out to India with him on 1st November. John landed at Hendon on 2nd October three years and two days since sailing from Glasgow]. It was a red letter day for me, and many of my brother officers enjoyed meeting him very much. John seemed thinner than when we last met in Cairo and very yellow. No doubt it is part of a plan to pass as a Chinese. [Due to the mepacrine taken against malaria].

'The Colonel has put me in for the Staff College. I am quite prepared for anything, provided I don't stay here much longer. It is neither a rest, nor an adventure, and it is difficult to see that it is of great use, as the men pass so quickly. As soon as I get to know them they are gone.'

4th November, 'How greatly I enjoyed my brief holiday and it was very refreshing to be at home again and to see John. I have been thinking of him on his great journey, constantly. Tonight he must be at our old haunts in Cairo and tomorrow will be breaking new ground at Basra. It is interesting to see the news announced in the papers today. Oliver [Leese] gets some good write ups. How very impressive that Sidney Kent [his Chief Staff Officer at T.A.C. H.Q.] is now a Brigadier.' In fact, the journey to India was hair-raising. Oliver Leese flew in his Dakota, lent to him by the kind

127

Americans, plus an American air crew. They were shot at over the Channel, nearly crashed into a fighter plane when landing at Brussels (to see Monty), fog cleared in time to land in Paris (to see Eisenhower), just missed the Massif Central when heading for Malta, landed safely at Cairo but in the dark, and finally the pilot had to do a U-turn at Basra on the edge of the runway, to avoid the Euphrates. Oliver's prayers must have saved the day!

CAMBERLEY STAFF COLLEGE

9th December, at last he hears that he has been accepted for the Staff College, starting in January and lasting six months, 'I do hope and pray that it will turn out to be for the best, and up to expectations I have built up since I was first put in for the Haifa Staff College, in October 1942, before Alamein.'

1945

The year starts with Oliver working hard at Camberley Staff College. 'I am extremely busy but also extremely happy,' he wrote to his father on 7th January. He continued, 'Saturday afternoon I went for a walk and ran into the padre, who was a friend of mine in Egypt, P.S. Howard. He is a regular padre, but excellent. He took me to tea with his wife. Adam Fox comes to stay with him quite often.

'R.M.C. (Royal Military College) Chapel at 8 and 11 this morning with Erskine-Crum. A thrilling service and a beautiful chapel. After Parade Service I met Tim Gibbs, Roly's elder brother who got a D.S.O. and lost half his foot at Alamein. He is a Squadron Leader at Sandhurst and took me into their mess. From lunch to dinner I worked, then Tim came here to supper.

'About the two best here so far are Sandy Reid-Scott an 11th Hussar, who lost an eye in Wavell's campaign and has since been his A.D.C. Sandy is a cousin of Jim Stanton and so I knew him in Italy. The other is an American, Lt. Col. Russell, a really good type.

'I am delighted to have found Uncle Louis' name on the wall here as an old P.S.C. (Passed Staff College.)'

It was a great achievement to have reached the Staff Course at last. If he had been staff trained earlier it would have made life easier for him in his various appointments as Technical Adjutant, Adjutant, Staff Captain and finally D.A.A.G.. He was prone to overwork, as we saw from his school reports. Being very conscientious he tackled these jobs which were unsuitable, without complaint. All along he yearned for a Platoon to command and later a Company. It was not to be. As soon as he got sight of one of these, he was snatched away for another staff task. Perhaps all his work and his eventual staff training were of help to him when he had to take on the administration of a diocese and later the Province of Central Africa, in addition. However, he would then, at last, be doing work that was truly suitable, and would be helped by his spiritual life style.

CHAPTER 15

OUT TO GERMANY (BAOR). 1945

By the end of June he had completed the course. It must have been very satisfactorily completed, since he was appointed a Brigade Major.

On 23rd July, he wrote from Purfleet, Essex, 'We left Chobham at an early hour this morning and travelled via London. A very cheerful, pleasant party. Our only responsibility is our own luggage. Moving it about keeps us quite busy. At Fenchurch Street [Station] which must have been designed at the time of the Norman Conquest, the crowds of 'daily breaders' seemed much amused to see twelve majors sweating under valises and tin trunks, as we climbed up the staircases ... We expect to go aboard this evening. The end of a very refreshing and excellent year in England. I hope the next year will be as good in Europe.'

BRIGADE MAJOR, 103 INFANTRY BRIGADE

27th July, HQ 21 Army Group, 'We arrived here yesterday and this afternoon I go on by car to take up my new appointment as Brigade Major to 103 Infantry Brigade. The Brigadier is called Orr.

'The journey was not uncomfortable. A day in Ostend was pleasant. In the evening I went with Carey-Elwes to the 'Cercle Interallié' where we danced with an attractive blonde in brown, who only spoke French, and a very lively brunette dressed in what appeared to be a white bath towel. The latter spoke English.' 103 A.A. Brigade was no longer A.A. and was based on Siegen, East of Cologne.

7th August, 'Brigadier Orr arrived last Friday; he is a Scots Fusilier aged about 40. He seems to be firm, efficient and friendly. A great games player. He is playing cricket for 21st Army Group next Saturday.

'My future is at the moment in some doubt, as 49th Infantry Division have applied for me as G2.'

The Brigadier and Oliver went to a conference held by Division H.Q. at Winterburg ski centre in a luxurious hotel. On the way back they lunched with one of their Regiments. Three Estonian girls had been invited to meet them. 'Their beauty was ravishing, so much so that we took up the carpet after lunch and had a 'déjeuner dansant' - tell John that!' This refers to when John arrived at Sfax in Tunisia, which was the first town the 8th Army entered after the desert. He was given the afternoon off to drive round the town with Bennett his signaller/driver. They were approached by some French girls who insisted on their dancing to a wind-up gramophone, to celebrate their release from the Germans. Unfortunately, when John reported back to Oliver Leese, he admitted to having been dancing. From then on Oliver Leese used to enjoy telling the story of how John had rushed off to a 'thé dansant' the moment they had reached civilisation.

17th August, 'It looks as if I shall stay on here and not move to Divisional Headquarters (49th Infantry Division - The Polar Bears.) I want to stay here as I like Orr very much and it is much more interesting at this level, where one actually meets all the various nationalities, as well as being in direct touch with Regiments.' He then talked about the ghastliness of the Atomic bomb, but realised that it was now possible 'to start on reconstruction quicker, which is a good thing.'

He ended by describing the difficulties of sending off Russians by train for repatriation. 'As the cattle trucks leave, one can't help wondering what awaits them at their journey's end, but most of them seem very cheerful.'

23rd August, 'The religious position is interesting. The R.C.s are strong in one of our three 'Kreis' [districts] and are much the most democratic and Anti-Nazi. I believe they have always been that way inclined in Germany, since they fell out with Bismarck.

'We have been having a drive to get rid of unnecessary souvenirs. The best to date was a land-mine, which the driver of a 3 ton lorry had concealed under his seat. He expressed great indignation when we removed it, as he said he had sat on it for months now and it never went off!

'My French friends have invited me to spend a weekend with them near Koblenz. I expect to be well (or too well) entertained, as they are celebrating the anniversary of the liberation of Paris. They were all in the Paris resistance movement! Parades and a dance are on the programme. I hardly think the French dance after lunch.

'This evening I heard that demob should reach group 23 by Christmas. It depends what is happening, when the time comes, but I hardly feel I shall want to leave such interesting work so soon. The spring would suit me better, and give a reasonable gap before Westcott House in July.' He was to return to his Theological College for a refresher course before being ordained.

11th September. One of the three Estonian girls Oliver had met was called Layta. Now he wrote to his sister Felicity, 'It was sad to read of Winkfield Place [Nursing Home] closing down. I'm sure the patients must be very sorry that they are leaving your care [as a V.A.D.] Don't be disturbed about the Jitterbugs - I have renounced it again at Layta's request, in favour of what she calls the English waltz i.e. slow waltz.

'The chief event, since last writing, has been the move to our new H.Q. at Stift Keppel, an old girls' boarding school

132

about 4 miles from our old home. I am constantly thrilled by it. Parts of it date from 13th Century, including the Chapel (now Lutheran) which has very beautiful stone vaulting.

'Other events of the week have been Italian departures, and an Estonian dance (not at lunch this time!). The Italians went off with characteristic cheerfulness. Their trucks were decorated with pictures of Badoglio - loyalty or lack of information? A corporal of the Pioneer Corps was O.C. [Officer Commanding] train for some 1,500 Ities. He said he spent his life doing this. Usually they got to the Swiss frontier at Bregenz without difficulty. "How do you get back," I asked. "Just chalk up Hamm on the outside of the coach, Sir, and go to sleep inside." I asked him if that worked well. "No Sir," he replied, "Last time I woke up in Nuremburg. While I was away looking for the R.T.O. [Railway Transport Officer] the coach was sent on to Czecho-Slovakia with all my kit and the rest of my party in it!"

'The dance was the greatest fun. The Estonians improved on acquaintance and it really is appalling to hear of what their family went through in two and a half years of making parts for German tanks. Hilda had been a law student and now has a strained heart. Layta was going to be a doctor and now has some disease of the liver. I suppose they are luckier than some in being together as a family.'

20th September, 'I like our new home more and more, and have found the most beautiful walks on the hills close by. Luckily they are covered in oak forest, which is pleasanter than the usual pine forest, melancholy and lifeless. I have just returned from opening a 'Pub' in our village of Allenbach. The beer is quite good, 1½d for half a pint. Incidentally our mess wine cellar is good and absurdly cheap. Champagne (German) is 3/- a bottle and the best Moselle, 2/- a bottle. I suppose the champagne could be sold at about £3 a bottle in London.'

On 26th September he reported that the New Divisional Commander, Gurdon, who had returned from India and was in the Black Watch had spent his boyhood at Aston Tirrold, where Oliver was born, since Gurdon was the grandson of the Rector at that time, Hoskyns. They had warmed the house for the new commander with 'considerable enthusiasm. The Russian Major did his best to embrace the Brigadier and I was obliged to carry him away to his car. A victory for the British Raj!

'Our German cook had cooked for Rommel's mess in the Afrika Korps. Whether it was the lack of sand or abundance of water I don't know, but he has been sacked for general incompetence.'

31st October, he wrote to his mother, 'I am so very distressed to hear of your tired heart and high blood pressure. It is certainly no surprise after all the hard work you have done during the war, but I know how greatly you will dislike the enforced rest.'

12th November, he wrote to Felicity who must have met Lord Haig, and he explained, 'Lord Haig was a fellow liaison officer at the New Zealand Brigadier Clifton's Headquarters at the July battle at Alamein. Because he had a tank, he was allowed to go forward with the Brigadier and got captured. He wouldn't remember me, but would certainly remember his last day of freedom.

'Last Wednesday's party at the Russian Mission to celebrate the Red Revolution was a nightmare from the first mug-full of German gin, which I was compelled to sink in one go, in honour of Stalin.

'Memories of how I described myself (in German) as shooting elephant, rhino etc in Africa, come hazily back. Also an ugly moment when Major Safanow saw me emptying a glass full of gin into a flower pot. Luckily, he hadn't seen the three previous occasions on which I had thus ill treated his flowers. My heart bleeds for them, and I fear they must be dead. The only pleasant memory is of a lucid moment when I discovered that Safanow shared my love of *War and Peace* and *Anna Karenina*.

'The weekend with the French was delightful, the more so because they have their wives with them! We danced on Saturday night and attended Armistice Day parades and a very impressive short service at the War Cemetery. The service was late because the Brigade Major (French) was wearing the Colonel's hat on the parade. The rescue of it put all the French in great heart for the Requiem Mass!! I do love the French in spite of their glaring faults (or rather often because of them!) To my great pleasure, Bill Heathcoat-Amory has asked me to be Godfather to his son, Charles.'

18th November, he described the march past in Siegen where the band forgot the 'British Grenadiers' and stopped too soon. The parade was 'made' for the German crowd by the smartness of the German police in front of the band, 'They were obviously the smartest men on parade, and knew it!'

He then described some of the 'D.P.s' - displaced persons in his area, including three Persians, who were removed to Siberia in the '14-18' War, moved to work in Russia in '42, captured by the Germans, and now wanted to move back to Persia. There was also a 'Hungarian High Court Judge, who claims to be related to our monarch and has papers to prove it! He doesn't want to return to his country because all the people he condemned are waiting for him there. I must see if they will accept him at 'Buck House.' '

On 26th November, he reported on a short leave in Brussels as, much to his regret, all leave to Paris was cancelled for the English troops. He visited 35 Place de L'Industrie where his father had been born. 'The garden and the remainder of the houses look as if they hadn't changed much since '79.' He then described a visit to the opera to see *La Flute Enchantée* where he had a seat in the centre of the front row. 'The opera enchanted me during the first act, the young lady on my right, the second. She would keep pressing sweets on me and I felt the conductor could hear me chewing.'

On 5th December, he heard of the death of the Archbishop Cosmo Lang, which would be a personal sorrow for his father, 'After all your years in his friendship and service ... I too had a great affection for him and shall greatly miss his advice.'

He then described various international parties, ending with an American lunch with 'flashlight photographs of Major Oliver G Watkinson drinking and eating!'

12th December, 'You will be glad to hear that the Persians have been sent home after 31 years of exile.

'We have had two W.V.S. here for two nights with a mobile library. As you might expect, one was a real Gorgon, the other extremely attractive. You may well imagine our schemes to dispose of the former.

'My cigarette case has broken, but I have a new silvery metal one, with a map of England on it. This type were made in thousands as souvenirs for the German troops, when they invaded U.K. A very inaccurate map!'

19th December, 'It is splendid that you will have John with you for Christmas.' He had returned from Ceylon in an aircraft carrier in September and was now at the Regimental Depot in Winchester, under Bill Heathcoat-Amory, Oliver's former Colonel, of whom he was so fond.

He then reported the latest event 'at the Russian Mission. The 2nd in command was taken off under arrest for kidnapping an attractive young German, under the excuse that she was a war criminal and had hanged thirteen Russians herself. A strange form of courting! No sooner was he safely in the 'cooler,' than a Russian Colonel arrived and said my friend Safanow was recalled to Berlin. This apparently warranted an immediate party. Alas there was no flower-pot! All I can claim was that the Russian Colonel had to retire a good half hour before I did, but my head is only just recovering from the gin. I shall miss Safanow, whom I respected and liked. His successor is called Captain Singagin or some such horrible suggestive name.'

1946

15th January, 'Life has been so busy and gay recently, that letter writing has been difficult. Polish dances, a visit by Americans to us, a visit by the W.V.S. (less chaperon this time!) and an occasional bit of work, keep me pleasantly busy.' At the end of December, he met Krystena, a displaced Pole, at Heidenberk barracks, Siegen. They became great friends, dancing and playing chess frequently before they parted on 2nd February. They kept in touch by letter throughout his life.

Oliver continued, 'A visit to Garmisch and skiing are now off, as my job seems likely to wind up sooner than expected. With luck I should be home by the end of February.

'I went to a wonderful light opera, sung by the Poles, which was enriched for me by the explanations given by Lt. Whisky, their schoolmaster. For 'Brigands,' he said 'Brigades' throughout. I nearly walked out when he announced that a filthy looking man in a long dressing gown was 'Chief of Brigade.' The man I clearly identified as the fiercest 'Brigade' turned out to be the organist, so I must have missed something in the plot.'

1st February, 'I expect to leave here on 15th February and should be Mr. G-W about a week later. There is hardly any work to do here now, except to attend endless farewell parties. I must stop to have an early bed after brushing up my German for the Polish dance tomorrow night. Essential to get the wording right for the tender farewells!! To my great pleasure the Brigadier has asked me to conduct a service in our chapel on the last two Sundays. No sermon but fairly good attendance.'

10th February, 'I should be home for good on 19th or 20th a very exciting thought. Last week I paid a farewell visit to H.Q. B.A.O.R. with the Brigadier. A four hour journey each way, anyhow, much longer in rain and floods. While there I ran into Pam Harrison, the very charming W.V.S. mobile librarian,and took her to dine and dance at their club. I was glad to find her as mobile on the dance floor as in her library.'

So Oliver was demobilised on 19th February 1946 and thus ended his military career, lasting six and a quarter years. At the age of 32, he was able to pursue the career he had planned to lead for so long. His army life had given him valuable experience in dealing with his fellow men.

CHAPTER 16

ORDINATION - SOUTHAMPTON 1946

After Oliver's demobilisation in February he visited Richard Wood at Garrowby for Palm Sunday in the middle of April and returned south in time to see the Constable Exhibition at the Victoria and Albert Museum, accompanied by his mother, father and artistic sister Felicity. All this is recorded in the Anniversary Book, so we know that he then went back to Westcott House for a refresher course starting on 24 April. He took his M.A. at Oxford on 15th June and on 29th June, St.Peter's Day, met Spencer Leeson, Headmaster of Winchester College, to discuss the possibility of becoming his curate when ordained. Spencer Leeson was due to become the Rector of St. Mary's Southampton.

In August Oliver wrote to Felicity from Westcott House. 'I am so glad Cressida and you have exchanged letters and do hope you will be able to sketch Adam some time.' Cressida Ridley was the widow of Jasper, his fellow officer in the 60th. Oliver became very attached to Cressida and hoped that Felicity, who was particularly good at sketching children, would draw a picture of Adam, her son, but unfortunately Adam became ill, when the drawing was due to be undertaken. It may have been drawn later. Oliver continued 'The Chaplain has been more amiable until this morning. Actually I have been very busy so far, unknown to him, with sermon, deacon's exam and coaching the VIII on the river. I am afraid we lost the race this afternoon by one and a half lengths. Two of the crew had gone sick and we lost the toss, so had to row on the outside of the bend. We really did quite well.

The new arrivals here this term are very good men, including two who were here in 1939.'

The

COMPANIONS

of the.

SOCIETY OF SAINT FRANCIS

OF ASSISI.

Signature .... *Olivia Green-Wilkinson*

Officiant .... *Francis Tyndal-Biscoe SSF*

Date .... *9ᵗʰ May 1947.*

Place of Admission .... *The Friary of St Francis*
.... *Batcombe.*

OLIVER'S CERTIFICATE AS A TERTIARY FRANCISCAN

On 22nd September Oliver was finally ordained a
Deacon at Winchester Cathedral and took up his appointment
as curate under Spencer Leeson. But before this on 10th
September Spencer wrote to Oliver 'Dear Oliver ... I always
think of you like that, so I should find the more formal address
difficult. You will be very welcome on 19th, high tea about
6.45 and we will expect you again on 22nd same time.
Evensong is at 6.30. We have got fixed in and all is ready for
you. You will indeed be welcome.' He had recently arrived
himself and continued:

'There is no end of promising stuff lying around here. I
am digesting a lot of ideas, which I shall want to discuss with
you. Thank you for your thought of me on Saturday.'

Before the Ordination Oliver had a letter from Algy
Robertson S.S.F. The Society of Saint Francis, welcoming
his request to become a 'Priest Tertiary'. He also heard from

140

Adam Fox, 20 Dean's Yard, London S.W.1. The Rev'd Canon Adam Fox had been a Fellow at Magdalen, Oxford in Oliver's time and was now Sub-Dean of Westminster Abbey. 'I am very glad you wrote to me - I shall think of you in Winchester Cathedral on Sunday and afterwards too. St. Mary's, Southampton, would be a very good start and you will learn a lot from Spencer Leeson. I am so glad that you are going to be ordained. It is very rewarding in ways one couldn't have guessed and in some ways exciting. I feel I ought to give you some good advice. I think the most useful thing I have learnt is to avoid speaking or writing strongly "because I feel strongly". Wait until the feeling dies away or crystalises with thought. I rather believe you learnt this long ago.'

Richard Wood wrote after the Ordination 'I could not help feeling how happy you must be to start at last. You must have undergone as long a preparation as anyone, with the military part perhaps not the least valuable.

'I look forward to the possibility of spending a day in Southampton in early December. I hope to spend several days with the Franciscans at Cerne Abbas and thence make my way to Mark Meynell in Sussex.

'I go back to Oxford on 6th October to take over the humble duties that you once performed in Magdalen J.C.R.' [Junior Common Room as President].

'I long to see you, now you are "revved up".'

Richard, now Lord Holderness - the name of the constituency that he served for so long in the House of Commons - has lately added, 'After Oliver had resumed his ecclesiastical life and begun with his curacy in Southampton he came often to stay with Diana and me, first at Welburn (near Kirkbymoorside); more often - and sometimes with Prue and Felicity - at Flat Top. Any hospitality we offered was a poor reward for Oliver's invaluable service as my Best Man in Westminster Abbey [on 15th April 1947]. Of course the routine duties were perfectly carried out, but he did far more. The bridegroom was badly in need of moral support, which he cheerfully supplied; and when, in a rare moment of consideration for anyone else, I asked him how his parents planned to get to the wedding, he answered with a Delphic smile. Not until long afterwards did he tell Diana and me that we had forgotten to send them an invitation!

'We paid him several visits at Southampton. Oliver described life in the unpretentious house of his kind landlady. Diana questioned him closely about his evening meal! She herself seldom drinks tea and wondered if Oliver could get a glass of water if he wanted it. Oliver was amazed: 'People like my landlady never drink water.' He did later admit that she had some other little failings. With his tea one evening he found a small spoon inscribed: 'Stolen from Brown & Johnson'. The lady said without shame: "Yes, I remember. My husband picked that up!"

'On our visits to Southampton, Diana and I particularly enjoyed listening to the peal of the bells of St. Mary's. On one occasion, just off the boat from Le Havre, we were summoned to breakfast with Oliver and the Leesons. Some time later, when both Spencer Leeson and Oliver had been consecrated, and Spencer was seeing him off at Peterborough station, a small boy was said to be overcome by the sight of these two splendid figures in purple cassocks and exclaimed in wonder "Cor, two of them."

'Oliver particularly enjoyed Mrs. Leeson's report after they had moved to Peterborough. "Spencer is in very good form and positively oozing with matiness."

'Oliver came to Yorkshire to help us celebrate Diana's 21st birthday. In the absence of a party we decided to go to the cinema in York. It was still the days when a live cinema organ played jolly tunes while the man with the projector was changing the film. Oliver disappeared when the interval began and I imagined he had gone to the loo; but a few minutes later a message was passed to the organist from behind a nearby curtain. When Oliver returned, the Manager stepped on stage and told the audience how lucky they were that the Honourable Mrs. Richard Wood was among them. Would they all join in "Happy Birthday to you" in her honour? Diana, thoroughly embarrassed, instead of keeping quiet (in which case she would have remained unrecognised) began to belabour Oliver and me, so that everyone in the stalls knew clearly whom we were honouring.

'All the Green-Wilkinsons were enthusiastic and accomplished family historians. Diana and I were delighted by Oliver's account of his mother's having her money cleaned each day; and of her following his father in great anxiety when he never reappeared from the gents' loo on Waterloo Station. [Lumley had descended the long flight of stairs to the loo, but at the bottom step the ligament in his knee gave way and he collapsed. It was then that Myfanwy seeing his distress, wanted to go down the steps forbidden for a woman. A Railway Policeman was there to restrain her, but as luck would have it the man turned out to be one of her evacuees during the war, who had been billeted on Lovel Hill - so all was left in his capable hands!]

'Among the memories I most enjoyed was Oliver's stern chaperonage of Prue, who on one occasion briefly managed to avoid his watchful eye. He suddenly remembered his duties when he spied her from a balcony on a warm summer night and shouted into the darkness: "Prudence, come back at once."

'He never shared Bob Ryder's love of the sea or understood exactly how he should behave on board. Once, when he was handed a bucket full of dirty water and asked to

SAILING WITH RYDERS ON *FORESIGHT*

PLAYING WITH HIS NEPHEW RICHARD

throw it overboard, not only the water but the bucket went into the sea.

'When his nephew, Richard, aimed a toy gun at him, Oliver announced: "I'm dead." Richard was not to be fooled: "If you were," he said sensibly "you couldn't speak."

Oliver lodged, to start with, at the Leesons, until he found lodgings with Mrs. Minns. Audrey Leeson, their daughter, now Mrs. Nevin, remembers Oliver well. She could always tell when it was Oliver speaking on the telephone, as a finger would appear round the corner of the telephone room, which went up and down to emphasise the points he was making. Audrey also remembers the slight embarrassment, when her elderly grandmother thought Oliver was her fiancé. It is a small world - John discovered that he is now painting in a small group run by Lindsey Nevin, Audrey's daughter-in-law, who is married to a Housemaster at Winchester College.

Sister Alison, who has now moved from St. Mary's Convent, Wantage, to Leeds, explains that she joined the Leeson staff in September 1948. 'By that time the three clergy members of staff were well established - Canon Spencer Leeson as Rector, Oliver as senior curate and in charge of St. Nicholas's, Dock Street (known as the Dock Street Mission) and Ian Weathrall who was based at the other end of the parish which had belonged to Holy Trinity, a church which no longer existed apart from the church Institute and hall where I had a bed-sitter.

'One interesting thing about us as a staff was that all of us were working in a parish for the first time. Spencer Leeson had recently stopped being Headmaster of Winchester College, Oliver had been in the Eighth Army and Ian in the Indian Army. This made for a freshness of approach to the running of the parish. Spencer was a superb delegator so we all had ample responsibility.

145

'Oliver lived in the Dock Street district taking a room in a house with a certain Mrs. Minns, who was a widow and had, I think, lived in the area much of her life. Oliver used to have many amusing anecdotes about her. The only one I remember concerned various items in the house such as forks or spoons inscribed 'stolen from: such and such a hotel. When Oliver commented on this, the explanation was 'My late husband often used to bring me things like that.' [which confirms the amazing story of Richard's].

'Oliver's sense of humour is one of the chief things I remember about him. He often had amusing incidents to share when all of us met at least twice a day at St. Mary's for Morning and Evening Prayer. He was also a devoted pastor, much loved by the people of the Dock Street Mission and elsewhere in the Parish.

'It was a parish with old traditions as there had been a church on the site of St. Mary's for many centuries. Most of the houses dated back to mid-nineteenth century. The area had experienced a good deal of bombing during the war and St. Mary's itself had been bombed and gutted. The tower had been repaired and the bells re-dedicated shortly before I arrived, but worship had to take place in the Chantry Hall over the road.

'There were a good many superstitions among the local people. One was to do with women being 'churched' after childbirth. Anyone who went shopping, did her washing, or called on her neighbours before 'being churched' was viewed askance by her neighbours. This meant that women turned up to be churched at all sorts of odd times. It was a standing joke among us as a staff that churchings turned up whenever Oliver was around!

'One thing which Oliver and I had in common was that both of us were Franciscan Tertiaries, i.e. members of the

146

Third Order of St. Francis, closely linked with the Franciscan Friars based near Cerne Abbas in Dorset. We used to attend and sometimes arrange meetings with other tertiaries in the area.

'My memories of Oliver are of a priest for whom I had an enormous respect and someone who was a delightful friend and companion whose lighter side never got eclipsed for long.

'I don't remember exactly when Oliver left Southampton to go to Pretoria but I suppose I can't have had more than 18 months on the staff there during his time.

'I myself was 3 years on the staff of St. Mary's Southampton. By the time I left in 1951 (Sept.) all the original team had dispersed - Spencer Leeson to be Bishop of Peterborough, Oliver to Pretoria and Ian to Delhi.'

Ian Weathrall writes from Delhi where he still lives.

'I remember Oliver with great affection. He had a great gift for thanking people profusely, even for quite small services rendered. His strong sense of commitment stood him in good stead in the ups and downs of life in Southampton's dockland.

'Once on a never to be forgotten Sunday School outing to the Isle of Wight a head count was taken on the return journey - we found we were one more in number than when we had set out in the morning. A wretched child from Portsmouth on a similar outing had made friends with one of our boys so joined our group. When we landed at Southampton, although tired after an exhausting day, Oliver insisted on taking the child home to Portsmouth and that on a Saturday night!'

Oliver was ordained Priest on 1st June 1947 and he recalls that his first mass as a Priest was at the Chantry, Southampton, at 8 a.m. on 3rd June. Later that year on 10th December his mother and father attended the unveiling of the War Memorial at the Dock Street Mission.

Early in 1948 Oliver visited the Franciscans at Cerne Abbas and on 29th June he assisted his father and Jock Henderson (later Bishop of Bath & Wells) in the marriage of his brother John to Prudence Pipon. As there were now two Prudences in the family, the younger one became known as 'Pip' among the family.

The following year was a sad one for the family as Myfanwy died of a stroke in February. In the summer they sold Lovel Hill and moved to Ennismore Gardens in London. Lumley was keen to return to the London of his youth, but he found it not so satisfactory for an elderly citizen. He had been a great theatre goer and kept every programme of all the plays he had seen during his lifetime - it was quite a collection. While he was living in the country, he would go to London for a week and see two plays a day from the 'Pit'. This was a standing area at the back of the stalls, at a very reasonable price. Shooting sticks were forbidden, so when Lumley was elderly he found an umbrella, which was designed as a shooting stick and enabled him to relax for a few minutes from time to time, without being spotted.

Oliver spent his first night at Ennismore Gardens on 28th July and attended a Cromwell Day service with the family on 3rd September, no doubt since the family are descended from Jane Desborough, Oliver Cromwell's sister.

Then on 27th September his father died suddenly and peacefully in London. The funeral on 1st October was at St. Paul's, Knightsbridge, taken by Bishop Mervyn Haig and Dr. Alan Don, who had been the senior chaplain with Lumley to Archbishop Cosmo Lang, and was now Dean of Westminster.

Almost at once, after the funeral on 4th October, Spencer Leeson left Southampton to be Bishop of Peterborough, so Oliver became the priest in charge of the parish until the new Rector, George Hales, arrived on 30th January 1950.

Mrs. Leeson had written to Oliver on 28th September 'I can't tell you how grieved I was to hear of your father's death: it was a terrible shock to you all and how much he will be missed. I shall never forget the beautiful way he took the service at Dock Street. I am so glad he had your company up to the end: he must have very much enjoyed your leave and you will have been glad to have been with him. But poor Oliver, what a lot you have had to go through this year. I do feel for you most deeply and for your sisters.

'I am so glad we shall get a glimpse of you on Sunday, it is good of you to come [before they left the parish]. People have been tremendously kind and we shall need almost another van to remove our gifts. The paralysing climax came last night, when the Ruridecanal Conference took place. I crept in (without a hat and very untidy) and sat at the back for the service, hoping to get a glimpse of the presenting of the stoles, when Mr. Evans came up and insisted I should sit at the table in the Chancel with Spencer and Mr. Evans - all this without a hat and then to crown everything a flashlight photograph.'

Then she explains the complications of their move and how little will be left in the Rectory for Oliver to use. 'You may prefer the vestry or chateau Minns. I wish I could leave the gas cooker for you to brew yourself hot cuppas, but I cannot alas do that. Mrs. Mac is going to hold the fort until she hasn't a chair to sit on - then she is coming up to Peterborough.'

The departure of the Leesons was a great loss to Oliver, which could not be fully replaced by the new Rector, George Hales and his wife Diana. George had been Chaplain to the Sherwood Rangers in the Desert when Diana Holderness's father, Col. E.O. Kellett, had been commanding, before he was killed soon after Mareth.

Oliver had been admitted as a Postulant Tertiary of the Society of St. Francis on 12th December and then on 22nd

January Bishop Mervyn Haig, Bishop of Winchester, came to preach at the Dock Street Mission. It is interesting to see that Oliver preached at his father's old Parish, St. Peter's, Bournemouth, on 12th March.

It was now time for Oliver to move to Pretoria. Plans were under way before Lumley died, as he had taken a keen interest in the service times at St. Wilfred's, where Oliver was to work. Oliver had kept to his promise to return to South Africa.

On 7th May he preached a farewell sermon at St. Mary's and also at the Dock Street Mission, before leaving Southampton on 11th May. He then had a busy month preparing for his departure overseas. He visited Cerne Abbas on 26th May and was made a Novice in the Third Order of St. Francis of Assisi three days later. On 2nd June he made a farewell visit to Richard and Diana at Bishop Wilton, accompanied by his sisters Prudence and Felicity. He sailed from his beloved Southampton in the *Carnarvon Castle* on 15th June, arriving in Cape Town on St. Peter's Day, 29th June 1950.

A letter from Oliver appeared in the St. Mary's Parish magazine written on 1st July in Cape Town, while waiting for a train to Pretoria. 'My heart is full of gratitude to you all ... It was indeed a sad parting for me and I miss you terribly, but I feel that the sadness was transformed by the joy of sharing in a fellowship stronger than the separations of six thousand miles. That was the thought which helped me, as the ship drew away after your wonderful send off at St. Mary's in the morning and the Docks in the afternoon.

'The voyage lasted for exactly a fortnight ... and was a very busy time for me, because in addition to being chaplain, I was elected a member of the Sports Committee. I was able to teach my fellow passengers a good deal about socials from

150

our ways. They seemed unaware that the left and right ear had to be put in and out in the Hokey-Cokey and many had to be taught the simplest of old-time dances.

'I found there were 87 children on board. We held a very lively children's service for them, arranged parties for them and wrote introductions for their families to the parishes to which they were travelling, if they were going out for the first time.

'I was met at Cape Town by a South African friend, who took me to stay on his farm. He had to introduce me to a wife and three children who had appeared since I last stayed with them in 1937. The view from his farm across the Table Bay to Cape Town, lying under the mountain, is extremely beautiful.

'Now I am about to set out on the 36 hour journey to Pretoria and the beginning of my ministry in South Africa. It is an inspiring and humbling moment, when my thoughts turn naturally to St. Mary's and the Dock Street Mission, with deep gratitude.

Your sincere friend.'

+ Oliver N. Rhodesia

CHAPTER 17

PRETORIA 1950

Oliver wrote to the family on 1st July giving details of his arrival at the Cape 'We docked at 6 am. I got ashore about 10 o'clock to find to my horror that de Villiers had been waiting with a car for me for over an hour. It was good of him. He took me off to de Grendel, his farm on a hill on the other side of Table Bay. There I met Ena his very nice wife and his three children. It was ridiculously like staying with Richard and Diana [Wood]. A farm house with a wonderful view, constant pic-nics, talk about Parliament and a stream of questions about religion. I'm sure you would all like them so much.

'To-day I left de Grendel and took a room at the Helmsley Hotel in Cape Town. After lunch I set out to visit Michael Gibbs, the Dean of Capetown, of whom I had heard from Father Algy Robertson at Cerne Abbas. His house turned out to be in the same street by sheer good luck! Have spent the rest of the day with him and his very nice wife. The Dean is more like Bishop Hamilton [Dean of Windsor] than anyone else I can think of. After supper we went to see his curate John Aubrey who was at Westcott House after me. He has a charming S. African wife, who asked me if I had a brother called John! Apparently her best friend was a girl John had met in Cape Town on his way to Egypt in 1941!' He ended his letter, 'Tomorrow I catch the 10 am. train with a lovely journey through the mountains. The thought of Pretoria at 9.20 on Monday is very thrilling.'

He arrived at St. Wilfred's Parish on 3rd July and was due to take over from Maurice Clack, while he was on leave in England. In the August edition of St. Wilfred's Parish Magazine Mr. Clack wrote from London asking the Parish to look after Oliver and spoke of the joy in meeting old friends 'a few of them seem to have changed much since we saw them last before the war.'

Oliver also wrote to the Parish thanking them for 'an equally wonderful reception from you to that send-off from Southampton ... I hope you will continue to be patient with the mistakes of a beginner.

'The beautiful dignity and homeliness of St. Wilfred's church has impressed me more and more. It is now nearly a year since the Church was completed ..... we shall be observing our Dedication Festival on 10th September.

'On all hands I see daily the signs of the Rector's devoted work in this parish. We must make up our minds that with God's help, he will return to find the life at St. Wilfred's as happy and vigorous as when he left it.

God bless you all
your Priest and friend.'

He preached his first sermon to Africans at St. Michael's church in Pretoria at the end of August. Then he had to broadcast a service on South African Broadcast Company Radio from their Pretoria studios on 15th November. By the end of that month it was time for Oliver to leave St. Wilfred's and move to his work at St. Alban's Cathedral in Pretoria. He was to work as a Junior Canon on the Cathedral staff under the Dean, Freddie Amoore.

But back in August he had written to say 'Last week I met Father Trevor Huddleston, a Mirfield Father from Johannesburg, who is head of the Community in South Africa. To my delight I found he was at the 'House' [Christchurch Oxford] in my time. I knew him then quite well and he is a great friend of Bimbo [John] Rickards who was also at the House. I had expected to meet an oldish man as the Superior. He is the father Vincent in *Cry the Beloved Country* and the whole book is about his Mission.

'I have visited the Pretoria Zoo. Their showpiece is a

white rhinoceros called Zuluana. Unfortunately I referred to her as Juliana, which caused an uproar amongst the Hollanders here!!'

On 21st January Oliver wrote from Irene Hotel Pretoria where he was staying, while working at the Cathedral. He went for a farewell lunch for Bishop Parker and 'was introduced to the prettiest (and richest) girl I have yet seen in S. Africa, who somewhat startled me by saying "I used to be in love with you." This was Georgina [Albu, the Bishop's niece who had met Oliver in 1937]. In case you are now hopeful of a rich match I must explain that Georgina is to marry on February 8th!! However the reunion with Sir George and Betty Albu was the greatest fun.

'The election of the new Bishop takes place on Thursday in the Cathedral, all clergy and representatives of the Laity voting. My choice is the Bishop of Barbados. In strict confidence, Jock Henderson was asked to stand for election, but refused to leave St. Paul's Knightsbridge.' Jock Henderson had assisted in the marriage of John to Prudence Pipon and later became Bishop of Bath and Wells. In the end Bishop Robert Selby Taylor was chosen, thus leaving a vacancy in Northern Rhodesia.

There is a letter to Felicity written by Oliver on 26th April 1951 in which he said 'You may be interested to know that I have given a pew to St. Wilfred's church for the Lady Chapel and have had a metal plate with Daddy and Mummy's names, 1949 and R.I.P. placed on the end of the pew. Mummy of course never knew about St. Wilfred's, but you will remember the great interest Daddy took in the church, when I returned to the flat in September 1949, writing down all the services to see how they fitted in.

'I have had a very busy week. Two funerals and two weddings on top of everything else. One girl, aged 19, niece of the Cathedral Organist was married to an R.C. in his church at 2.30. last Saturday. At 8 p.m their car, driven by him, turned over. She was killed outright; he was almost untouched. The funeral was at the Cathedral last Tuesday. A vast congregation, including the R.C. family and bridesmaids from the wedding. All very difficult. The poor husband and widowed mother (her only child) are both very upset.'

Also in the letter Oliver commented on the skill of Felicity in a 'Smash and Grab' raid in Sloane Street. She was passing Dibdens the Jewellers, as it was attacked, and took the number of the get away car. Several years later she was able to identify the robber in an identity parade, and convinced the judge that, as a portrait artist, she was capable of remembering a face. The man was convicted and Felicity received high praise from the Judge.

He ended the letter 'Ted Peel has written from Matlock Bath where he has been spending a holiday in Derbyshire near Mollie. She may be out of hospital by October. They are apparently NOT married yet.' This must have been tantalising for poor Felicity, as she had fallen in love with Ted, when Oliver first introduced him to the family before the war. Hilaré had been thought by the family to be the most suitable match. Anyhow, Felicity never gave up hope and eventually married Ted, when he was a Chaplain and Housemaster at Rossall School in 1958 - a twenty year patient wait.

During June of that year Oliver wrote a lengthy thesis entitled *The Present Relationship between Holy Baptism and Confirmation*. He sets out the historical background to the present Baptism and Confirmation and discusses the problems as experienced in England. This was based on the summary by the Bishop of Winchester of answers to the questionnaire submitted by the Deaneries of his diocese. Oliver had taken part in the discussions in the Southampton Ruridecanal chapter before leaving England.

One paragraph of the thesis is of particular interest as it

illustrates his approach to faith:

'There can be little doubt that the theology of Holy Baptism has become considerably confused during the many changes throughout the centuries in the practice of baptism. This theology requires to be thought out anew in face of the intellectual and pastoral needs of the day. It is characteristic of God's ways in leading us into all the truth by His Holy Spirit that theology should grow in face of such demands upon the Church, that God should use the circumstances in which we find ourselves to provoke us to thought, to discussion and controversy and thence to a deeper truth.'

Alison Willis, who had been on the church staff at Southampton with Oliver, moved out to Pretoria in September 1951 and has written:

'I went out to South Africa to work in the township of Lady Selborne, joining the Tumelong Mission there. Four of us lived there in the township which was seven miles from Pretoria. Of the four, three of us were Franciscan Tertiaries and this gave an added link to Oliver who was in the centre of Pretoria on the staff of the Cathedral.

'Oliver quite frequently came out to Lady Selborne to spend his day off with us on the Mission. One of us there was in charge of a nursery school for two hundred African children under six. Oliver was immensely popular with these children and they became really excited when he visited them. He played all sorts of games with them such as making funny faces or doing action games for them to copy. He had a real gift with them and it didn't seem to matter in the least that he didn't speak their language.'

On 16th September he told John 'This is a busy week. Harold Beardmore, an ex-Naval Officer, is away on leave. I am taking his services at his church in Arcadia (!) this Sunday and also his service in the Central Prison in Pretoria at 1 pm.

He is a genius at this work. I found 175 men crowded into a room for this voluntary service. Their singing reduced me to tears. It was all what a service in the Army should have been, but rarely was in my experience. I go again next Sunday!'

Then on 15th October the bomb-shell arrived in the form of a confidential letter from Geoffrey Cantuar, Archbishop, to Oliver in Irene Hotel where he was living in Pretoria. The letter from Lambeth Palace was dated 12th October:
'Dear Mr. Green-Wilkinson,

Perhaps the close association of your father with Cosmo Gordon Lang and with Lambeth will dispose you to take a letter from the present Archbishop with patience and quietness, even if its contents are somewhat startling.

As you know, the new Bishop of Pretoria has come from the diocese of Northern Rhodesia which is under my jurisdiction, and it falls to me to appoint a new Bishop there. I have consulted fully with the diocese of Northern Rhodesia and have received a very clear description of the special conditions and needs of that diocese. Here, I have been advised by a strong committee with direct knowledge of Northern Rhodesia and the other dioceses thereabouts. The committee now puts your name before me with the strong recommendation that I should invite you to accept appointment as Bishop of Northern Rhodesia. Some individuals who know you, and whose judgement I have special reason to trust, join in this recommendation.

This may be regarded as startling in view of the fact that you have only been in Holy Orders five years; but you were ordained above the usual age and are now, I believe, thirty-eight years old and you have had a varied experience all of which has played its part in fitting you for a call such as this.'

He then refers to Oliver's various activities, mentioning his service in the Rifle Brigade instead of the 60th! He continued:

'Northern Rhodesia requires a Bishop who, in addition to the necessary spiritual and pastoral qualities, is fitted by wide experience to deal with a Church half European and half African, to deal with mining people as well as with Government civil servants, and who, besides presenting the faith of the Church faithfully to them can by his wisdom understand the conflicting trends of opinion and be able to exercise an influence in the political conflict of opinions between the Colonial Office, Europeans and Africans, helping to soothe jagged nerves and encourage co-operation. The right person will learn to meet these demands and you have the initial advantage that the native problem in Africa has always been one of your special interests.'

The Archbishop ended by saying:

'I shall feel abundantly satisfied and happy if you are able to accept and I would add that in all matters I, as your Metropolitan, would be at your disposal with such help and advice as I could give and that before very long one can hope for the formation of a Province of Central Africa whereby you would have the strength and encouragement which would come from other members of the Episcopate within that Province. So I commend this matter earnestly to your prayers and pray that you may rightly hear and follow the guidance of God.

Yours sincerely

Geoffrey Cantuar.'

The next day Oliver received a letter from Alan Don the Dean of Westminster:

'My dear Oliver,

By the time this reaches you you will have received a letter from the Archbishop of Canterbury about the Bishopric of N. Rhodesia.

I can well believe that this bombshell has struck you all of a heap and that you are torn in twain - You may well feel on the one hand that as a man under authority you ought to go where you are sent; on the other hand as a priest of only five years standing you may naturally plead that you are too inexperienced for so responsible a task.

My purpose in writing is to let you know that Dr. Broomfield, the Secretary of U.M.C.A. took me into his confidence and showed me a letter which Bishop Leeson had written about you in this connection. I told Broomfield that from what I knew of you and your career I had no hesitation in endorsing all that the Bishop had said and that I was prepared wholeheartedly to support the suggestion that your name should be submitted to the Archbishop of Canterbury for nomination to the Bishopric.'

Alan Don ended this letter:

'My advice, for what it is worth, is that you should trust the judgement of the Archbishop and his advisers and take the plunge. N. Rhodesia needs a man with just the qualifications that you can bring to it - and how much more important is the shepherding of that vast territory than would be the care of a parish in England or a Suffragan Bishopric at home!

I know, dear man, how many misgivings you will have - but I pray that you will take your courage in both hands and say to the Archbishop! 'Here am I - send me.' May God guide you to a right decision.

Yours affectly,

Alan C. Don.'

Then five days letter a letter was written by Spencer Leeson, Bishop of Peterborough adding his support for the appointment and said 'to tell the truth it was I who set the ball rolling, and I do not apologise! I knew nothing of N. Rhodesia, except what I have learnt at the U.M.C.A. Council, but I do know you.'

From Oliver's previous letters we knew that Oliver's one ambition was to be a Parish Priest and had no ambition for higher responsibility. As in the Army his one wish was to command a Platoon and then a Company, so it must have been an agonising decision to accept the call to the Episcopate. Here it had to be his choice - while in the Army he had to accept the various appointments ordered.

Oliver had also received a letter from Canon Broomfield, who was General Secretary of the Universities' Mission to Central Africa (U.M.C.A.) giving his full support to the appointment and reminded Oliver that his new Bishop in Pretoria, having just come from Northern Rhodesia, would be able to tell him all about the Diocese.

By 25th October the Archbishop sent a telegram 'Letter deeply appreciated - desire consecration St. Andrew's Day Westminster Abbey - Propose announcement Tuesday morning. Please cable consent to both propositions.'

Alan Don then wrote 'I am delighted to hear that you have offered what you call "unconditional surrender:" I feel sure that you have been guided aright. When the Archbishop asked permission for the consecration in Westminster Abbey, I naturally agreed with alacrity: it will be lovely to think that you will be raised to the Episcopate within the walls of Westminster Abbey, and will thereby join the long list of Bishops who have gone forth from the Abbey to the ends of the earth in years gone by.'

When the news was announced he received many letters of congratulation and support. He specially appreciated a letter from Trevor Huddleston of the Community of the Resurrection in Johannesburg, saying 'I can think of no one of whom I should be more certain that the episcopal office was right than yourself. It will demand everything you've got, and the ideal of Franciscan Poverty can so well be practised in a Diocese like N. Rhodesia. It has been a joy to know you even for this

160

short while, and you will ever be in my poor prayers.'

On 11th November Oliver had a farewell from Pretoria Cathedral and his sermon was broadcast. He confided in Alison Willis, that when he told the Dean of Pretoria Freddie Amoore, that he had been invited to become the Bishop of Northern Rhodesia, Freddie thought he was joking. Alison states 'Oliver was highly amused at this, though it was mildly embarrassing. As Oliver remarked to me, he was the only priest in Pretoria in an assistant priest's position, rather than having a parish in his own right.'

Oliver told us the story of his attendance at Synod after the Archbishop's letter had arrived, but before the appointment had been announced. He must have entered a discussion on Baptism, no doubt based on his thesis written that summer. One of his friends sitting behind him chaffed him saying "Sit down Oliver, you've only just been Baptised yourself." Little did he realise that he was talking to a Bishop elect!

Back in England on 25th October the G-Ws were busy electioneering in support of their brother-in-law Bob Ryder, who kept his seat at Merton and Morden. After suitable rejoicing they all went to Trafalgar Square to hear further National Results coming in. By 4 a.m they all returned to Ennismore Gardens including John who had joined them. Four hours later the post arrived with the news of Oliver's appointment. Hilaré said in a letter to Oliver: 'I heard surprised whispering at the door, as I was half awake and when I called out, there was a perfect explosion into the room! What thrills us most of course is the idea of seeing you again.'

The letter from Oliver said, after discussing the prospects for the General Election, 'I have just written to the Archbishop of Canterbury to accept the Bishopric of Northern Rhodesia. It is just a week since he made this very surprising and humbling offer. I feel many misgivings about it all, especially as I am so inexperienced in Native mission work, but those whom I have consulted here advised me to accept and our

161

new Bishop has infected me with love for his old Diocese.'

So in an exhausted state after little sleep there was much family rejoicing. But one election result which particularly pleased Bob was to hear that Richard Wood had increased his majority from 9,000 to 17,000. Better than most results in the country. Prudence reported to Oliver that it had been heard from a neighbour that 'Richard is considered a 'Saint' when he goes round speaking.' She went on in her letter 'Tomorrow we start working at the T.& S.R.M. [Transvaal and Southern Rhodesia Mission]. Sale-cards to be sent out. Shall we have to switch over and work for another Mission? We shall miss Mike Furse.'

Oliver wrote on 6th November to Prudence confirming his arrival at London Airport at 11.45 on Wednesday 14th November. He discussed his robes being prepared by Wippell in Tufton Street and asked for 'the more reddy purple for the cassock.' He also mentioned friends to be added to the ticket list for the Abbey, ending with Mike Wilson and Margaret his wife. 'Mike is in superb form about the Consecration and said, "with Bishop Mervyn [Winchester] in the slips and plenty of Franciscans in the outfield!!" '

The Consecration was on Friday 30th November. All that could be written on the Service Sheet after Oliver's name was 'Lately working in the Diocese of Pretoria,' while his co-consecrand was The Venerable Arthur Chadwell 'Archdeacon in the Diocese of Korea.'

The sermon was given by Father Algy Robertson, Minister General of the Society of St. Francis and the Gradual was rather appropriately the hymn:

Jesus calls us! - o'er the tumult
of our life's wild restless sea
Day by day his sweet voice soundeth,
saying, 'Christian, follow me.'

CHAPTER 18

NORTHERN RHODESIA 1952

After Oliver's Consecration he was able to spend a family Christmas at Ennismore Gardens before departing to his Diocese in January. While in London in December he met Fr. Semenya on arrival from Pretoria.

The following charming letter was printed in Pretoria in gratitude: 'I deem it is my pleasant duty to say to all my friends in Pretoria, I have had an enjoyable trip (by sea). In London I have seen the greatest wonder which the world can show to an ordinary African like myself. The city is covered with churches and stone forest houses. Its inhabitants are a display of real Christian brotherhood and a fullness of life, which does not exist in some parts of the world.

'My companion and I were crowned with blessings by the presence of Bishop Parker at the Cape Town Docks and Bishop Wilkinson at Waterloo. The latter took us to lunch - an historical first London lunch.'

Oliver left London on 9th January and arrived at Bishop's Lodge in Lusaka on 13th. It had been an eventful journey as he explained in his letter to Prudence of 12th January from Nairobi:

'We returned from Dijon with one engine out of order. A new plane was provided, which took us very well to Rome by midnight and Cairo by dawn. Then to an airport 20 miles from Khartoum for lunch. There the engines went wrong. About 5.30 p.m we were sent in to dine at the Grand Hotel. Halfway there the bus broke down! That eventually recovered and we enjoyed a splendid dinner on B.O.A.C. by the Nile. We flew away at mid-night to Entebbe in Uganda for breakfast, and a breakdown by the plane from 5 till 10. The Captain made a personal apology to each one of us before we reached

MAP OF NORTHERN RHODESIA
(LATER ZAMBIA)

164

Nairobi nearly a day late. My plane had left for Lusaka.' No seats were available till 20th but eventually he was given a seat earlier and ended the letter 'It is a wonderful thought that tomorrow I should be in my diocese.'

Now, to set the scene in Northern Rhodesia, we give the notes written by Canon John Houghton, who had been in the Diocese since 1942:

'Oliver was the fourth Bishop of Northern Rhodesia/ Zambia and the last expatriate to hold that office. But, though an expatriate, he became a Zambian citizen when Zambia became independent. So he died a Zambian. His seeking Zambian citizenship was typical of him. It was a sincere gesture, designed to identify himself with the young republic as it began its independent existence - a gesture much appreciated. Not many Europeans made such a gesture. The law required that, for a British person to become a Zambian, he had first to renounce his British citizenship. Among Anglican clergy, only three did that. Oliver was one; Denys Whitehead and I were the other two.

'It is interesting to compare the lives and achievements of the first four Anglican Bishops of Northern Rhodesia/ Zambia. The first was Edward Hine. He had been Bishop of Zanzibar. In 1907, to mark the Golden Jubilee of the Universities Mission to Central Africa, in response to David Livingstone's challenge in 1857, it was decided to attempt the establishment of the Anglican Church in the huge country of Northern Rhodesia. By 1910 the plan was put into effect.

'In purely human terms the project was fraught with difficulties. Bishop Hine had only two priests and one layman to begin the work with him. Northern Rhodesia was two and a half times the size of the British Isles. Initially the work was begun at Livingstone, at Mapanza in the Southern Province, and at Chipili in the Luapula Province.

'In 1912 Bishop Hine went down with Blackwater fever at Chipili. Blackwater fever was then almost invariably fatal, but the Bishop survived. (I have a fellow-feeling for him, for in 1946 I went down with the fever at Mapanza. I too survived after being in a coma for ten days. Only later did I realise that, during those ten 'missing' days of my life I had passed my 30th birthday). In 1914 Bishop Hine, still very ill, resigned. He had served Africa for 25 years, his service in Zanzibar crowned by his heroic pioneering work in Northern Rhodesia.

'Alston May succeeded him and was Bishop from 1914 to 1940. He died and is buried at Chipili. World War I broke out at the very beginning of his episcopate, a fact which greatly compounded his difficulty in getting new priests to serve in his huge Diocese. He travelled incessantly and had no home of his own anywhere in the Diocese - just two rooms in the Rectory at Livingstone and two more in the Rectory at Ndola. He made Holy Trinity Church at Ndola his Pro-Cathedral. (Bishop Hine's Cathedral had been St. Bartholomew's Church at Mapanza). Bishop May's episcopate lasted from the outbreak of World War I to his death at Chipili in the second year of World War II.

'Robert Selby Taylor, a priest in the Diocese, was chosen to be the new Bishop. The circumstances of war meant that he could not be consecrated in England. Instead, his consecration took place at Michaelmas 1941 in the Cathedral on Likoma Island in the neighbouring Diocese of Nyasaland (Malawi). Exactly ten years later, in 1951, Bishop Robert was translated to the Diocese of Pretoria. He went on later to become Bishop of Grahamstown and finally Archbishop of Cape Town.

'His decade as Bishop in Northern Rhodesia called for infinite skill and wisdom to provide the Church with a constitution which counteracted the colour bar of that era. The setting up of the highly controversial Central Africa Federation also occurred while he was Bishop.

'Much progress was made by Bishop Robert in the building up of Africans in the ministry. Another development in his time was the decision to make Lusaka the headquarters of the Diocese. Bishop Robert was also involved in the first discussions in 1950 on the possibility of creating a Province of Central Africa, which would include Nyasaland, Northern and Southern Rhodesia. The plan was finally approved in 1952 and naturally involved Oliver, who had been consecrated in Westminster Abbey as Northern Rhodesia's fourth Bishop.

'The Archbishop of Canterbury had acted commendably quickly in finding a successor to Bishop Robert. His choice was Oliver. I remember that the first news we had of the appointment was the report of it in the Bulawayo Chronicle. We learned from this that he was an Old Etonian and an Oxford graduate. We were further interested to read that, as a young layman, Oliver had spent a year in Africa, including six months working on a farm near Lusaka. So Pretoria, to which Bishop Robert was translated, furnished Northern Rhodesia with his successor. That report also told us that the new Bishop was the son of the former Chaplain to Lang, Archbishop of Canterbury; it added that Francis Oliver Green-Wilkinson was a Tertiary or Third Order Member of the Anglican Franciscans.

'Everything we learned in that report about the new Bishop delighted us and we looked forward eagerly to his coming. Meanwhile in Lusaka at the Diocesan Office, where I was filling in, I opened a new file on the cover of which I wrote in capital letters BISHOP FRANCIS. A little to our surprise, we soon learned that the new Bishop was to be known as BISHOP OLIVER. His devotion to the Franciscans was real nonetheless. Some years later he arranged with the Society of St. Francis that they would open a small House at the Fiwila Mission. He hoped that vocations to the Franciscans there might be fostered among Africans. To his and their disappointment this did not happen. So, after some years, the Franciscans left for Dar-es-Salaam.'

Oliver wrote on 2nd March and ends his letter: 'To-day (Sunday) I set off at 5.30 a.m, to drive 43 miles to the big Government Teacher Training College (for the Africans) at Chalimbana on the Great East Road to Fort Jameson. I celebrated for the forty Anglicans at 7.30 and preached to the whole College at 10. Then lunch and inspection of the site for the new Chapel before returning here for tea. This was a fairly regular monthly duty for Bishop Robert and a pleasant one. The College is beautifully situated with a view of hills, so rare here.'

On 20th March Prudence arrived at Bishop's Lodge to help Oliver and they were both welcomed to U.M.C.A at Chipili mission station on 24th April. Other notes from his anniversary book record that (The Rev.) Rees Phillips arrived on 5th June and the first Diocesan Synod was held at All Saints, Lusaka on 27th June.

Oliver reported: 'The Conference and Synod went off quite well and I enjoyed it all. There was remarkably good feeling between the Europeans and Africans. Prudence was superb in entertaining her 18 guests, with 35 to lunch on three days and 110 for the tea-party (including the Governor). The African staff worked splendidly.

'To-day Prudence, Rees and I went over to the farm which Alan Hewitt now manages. I had not seen him since he was my manager at Makeni in 1937.'

Prudence received a letter on 5th July from James Mwela, writing from St. Mark's College, Mapanza where he was teaching. He thanked her and the Bishop for 'your warm hospitality during my long stay with you in Lusaka. Your bounty was most appreciated by us all, making us all feel quite at home. It was indeed good of you to come to Rhodesia. You have no doubt succeeded in giving the Bishop a good start at this stage. He has indeed impressed everyone, the African priests in particular. They seem to have gone back to their work with renewed vigour.' Prudence wrote a note on this letter: 'O. was so very pleased by this, as he values Mwela's opinion.' There is also a photograph of him, wearing his new O.B.E.

In August Oliver wrote to his sister, Deborah: 'I am feeling surprisingly fit after my four days 100-mile tour by bicycle from Fiwila. Cycling on African track in the bush is a new sport to me, for which one has to keep wide awake - for stumps, streams, snakes etc. The weather was surprisingly cool and at nights it was cold for sleeping in schools. The country was hilly, rather like Scotland, especially when one gets one's feet wet wading through burns. Wild flowers were lovely.

'Now Prue and I are staying at what is really a country parish with an African Rector - no Europeans within fifty miles, as far as we know.' [This was written from Kakwe Lesa, near Mkushi, Broken Hill].'The Rector is delightful and the Church, in which I celebrated and confirmed 35 this morning, is one of the best in the Diocese. We were met with songs and dancing, followed by the usual list of complaints from teachers and catechists. The better the former, usually the longer the latter!!'

Oliver met his neighbouring Bishops of Nyasaland (Malawi) and S. Rhodesia in Salisbury in September, no doubt to discuss the proposed new Province of Central Africa. On his way back by air the flight was very bumpy. 'Unfortunately' Oliver wrote 'I sat next to the Assistant General-Manager of Central African Airways (Mr. Oliver). This meant carrying on a bright conversation, while feeling for the paper-bag. We touched down not a minute too soon, so that I emerged pea-green and gulping, but with a clean paper-bag. It was a pity

Prudence's invitation to Salisbury came too late to get her a seat.' Perhaps she was lucky.

The Nave of the Pro-Cathedral at Ndola was blessed by Oliver on 2nd November and Michael Wilson was instituted as Rector. Michael was a close friend and Margaret, his wife became a good friend of Prudence's. They now live in retirement in Winchester and worship in St. Swithun and St. Lawrence where John and his wife, Pip, attend. Their Rector, David Scott, was also in Zambia for a short time - a small world.

Michael and Margaret have written a lovely story about Oliver. 'He was driving along a country road to the Belgian Congo, as Elizabethville was under his care. He noticed an elderly African walking alone, so he stopped to offer him a lift. He sent the African catechist, his travelling companion, to invite the old man to join them in the car. After some discussion the catechist returned, saying that the man declined the offer, because he thought that the Bishop planned to take him over the Congo border, where he would then eat him. Oliver loved to tell this story. He had heard of Africans eating missionaries, but this was the first time he had heard of this reversal of roles!'

The story sounds amazing, but the day that John was told it in Winchester he went to a party with Robert and Sally Dick-Read. On telling the story to Robert, he came up with a similar strange event. Robert once entered a village in the Congo, only to find it was deserted. He eventually discovered that the inhabitants were hiding for fear of being eaten up. Apparently, some time before, a European sculptor had come to the area. When the Africans saw the stone figures, word got around that they were made of ground-up African bone.

On 30th November Oliver dedicated St. Philip's Church at Luanshya. In Oliver's Anniversary Book all Dedications and Blessings of churches are listed. They are set out for reference in Appendix B, and indicate the large number of new churches built in his time.

In his letter of 7th December to John's wife, Pip, Oliver ended: 'Lusaka has been shaken by the wickedness of a girl at the Girls School who, when her turn came to say grace, spoke as follows: "Please God while I close my eyes, may my food grow twice the size." Fortunately, the Headmistress reported the crime to the Rector and not me; or I should have been shaken - in quite the wrong way. The Headmistress, Miss Goring, comes soon to dine, and I shall be sorely tempted to use this Grace!'

On 16th December Oliver wrote in the Anniversary Book: 'Letter from Father Algy Robertson S.S.F, proposing Franciscan Missionary enterprise in Northern Rhodesia.' To Oliver's great delight he was to get support from the Franciscans, and Canon James Robertson has written of Oliver:

'He was indefatigable in his care for the clergy, and his many contacts with the Franciscans and the Community of the Resurrection enabled a regular flow of Retreat conductors, from outside the Diocese, build up the kind of devotional life of which he was himself an exemplar.'

James Robertson has also written of Oliver's arrival in Northern Rhodesia: 'For those of us on the Diocesan staff of N. Rhodesia in 1951, the news of Oliver Green-Wilkinson's appointment as Bishop, to succeed Robert Selby Taylor on his translation to Pretoria, came out of the blue. We had known nothing of the choice process and none of us knew of him. Gradually the news of his pre-war spell, farming in the Southern Province, his splendid war years, his curacy under Spencer Leeson and his short period in Pretoria, filtered through and we longed for his arrival.

'The Diocese had been dominated by the influence of the Universities' Mission to Central Africa and there was a

171

BISHOP'S LODGE
THE CHAPEL IS IN THE CENTRE WITH CHEQUERED WALL

ST. JOHN'S SEMINARY
IN THE GROUNDS OF BISHOP'S LODGE

172

growing contrast between the work centred on the four major Mission stations and the line-of-rail parishes and Copperbelt. Bishop Robert had been deep in the U.M.C.A. ethos and Bishop Oliver had come from a different ecclesiastical background. At the same time the state and nation were moving to sharper political polarisations, local government was being developed by the Colonial Administration, and our ecclesiastical links with Nyasaland and S. Rhodesia were growing stronger.

'I had resigned from U.M.C.A. in 1950, as had Mina my wife, and had accepted work as a Diocesan priest at Mapanza. It was from there in early 1952 that I paid my first visit to Bishop Oliver in Lusaka. I had a difficult pastoral and disciplinary matter to discuss with him and I was immediately struck by his capacity to listen and give counsel. I began to learn of his Franciscan spirit and youthful bearing, punctuated by gusts of merriment.

'I was due for leave in mid-1952 and, at the instigation of Archdeacon Smith, who was his senior advisor (tradition of the elders), he wrote and asked me to use my leave to train as a post-graduate teacher, so that the Diocese could be reimbursed by grant-aid in its major school work.Older staff were soon to leave the Diocese. I had taught for many years in my curacy, so I agreed.'

Oliver spent his first Christmas in the Diocese at Msoro mission station in the east of Northern Rhodesia. He described the day to John:

'We have just listened to my broadcast talk being relayed and hope to hear the Queen at 5 p.m, when the programme has (after three hours) reached a higher level! The midnight mass was lovely, but the crowds came this morning, as the villagers don't like venturing out at night for fear of lions and elephants! At the service of nine lessons and carols there was a treble soloist worthy of King's Chapel. This is very rare among Africans. Usually they produce good basses. Their real skill is being able to harmonise, naturally without music to read from. We have had a good deal of rain which is welcome. Unfortunately my house is newly thatched and, as the thatch has not settled, the rain comes in by bucketfuls all over the place. I kept dry in bed, thanks to a raincoat and Prudence's present of a golfing umbrella tied to my mosquito net!'

1953

Oliver wrote to his brother, John, on 24th March after he and Prudence had returned from Mongu in the Western Province, where they had attended the annual Umboka. This was when the Paramount Chief Mwanawine moved by barge from the swamped Zambesi river to higher ground. Oliver adds the amusing coincidence that 'Daddy's Anniversary Book records that on 20th March, 1929 he sat on Queen Mary's left at Bognor, while I in 1953 sat on the left of the Paramount Chief at tea on the Royal barge on the Zambezi! The Royal barge' Oliver added 'is paddled by Princes of Royal Blood.'

In 1929 Lumley, father of Oliver and John, had been at Bognor with Cosmo Lang, who was recuperating from illness, as was King George V. It was then that he lunched at Craigweil and the book records that Princess Mary and Princess Elizabeth were also present.

Oliver continued: 'While at Mongu we went for a night at an out-station and found, as usual in Africa, a charming girl who knew you. I gather that you knew her in Ceylon in 1945. On our way back from Mongu Prudence and I were the only passengers in our little plane. The pilot wished to show us some hippos. This he did by diving several thousand feet and almost flying upside down. We did see many hippos in the flooded water, but I haven't recovered from the feeling!!'

Prudence wrote on 1st June about preparations for the Coronation celebrations: 'I have just been tying up Oliver's Loyal Address in a roll with red, white and blue ribbon for presentation to-morrow. He wears his gaiters for their annual outing and, for the ball to-night, he wears his black cassock piped with crimson and red buttons. So with his shoulder cape and miniature medals he looks like a Christmas tree! He says the cassock colouring is just like the 60th Mess Kit!'

Oliver said on 29th June: 'Prudence and I are now on our way to Bulawayo for a Bishops' meeting and the opening of the Exhibition by the Queen Mother. Our start was very eventful. At 5 p.m yesterday I received a telephone message that Mrs. Morris, wife of the Priest-in-charge at Mapanza, had been taken ill and was expected to die. Awful moment to know what to do. In the end I left Bishop's Lodge at 3.30 a.m, drove to Mapanza (250 miles) by 9.45, where I found poor Mrs. Morris had died. I was glad to have come as Harry Morris was dreadfully upset and there were a number of things I could do. At 2 p.m. I caught the train at Choma, finding Prudence on board.'

From Chipili mission on 23rd July Prudence wrote: 'Margaret and Mike (Wilson) were here when we arrived as they have been up north taking services at outlying bomas. They both seem very settled out here and Mike is starting cricket in Ndola! Poor Oliver is having to deal with all sorts of troubles up here. The Bemba tribe are an excitable lot and thoroughly enjoy an argument. It is their nature to spend hours going round and round a point. Very wearing for Oliver at first, but he can cope so much better now.'

'It is very sad to think of Prudence leaving on Tuesday' Oliver wrote on 9th August. 'I shall miss her continually and especially on my tours. The long journeys were the times when we were best able to talk about the family and to read your letters. On Wednesday I set out for over three weeks in the

Eastern Province, a tour in lovely hills which I usually enjoy. It is very good news that we now have a permanent Doctor at St. Francis Mission hospital, the temporary one, Eileen Welcher, having agreed to stay on. The blessing of the Cross on the Cathedral site was an impressive service last Sunday. We had a good crowd of Africans and Europeans.'

The building of a Cathedral for the Diocese became as much a concern for Oliver as the building of churches in it. A local newspaper wrote: 'No plans have been drawn yet; no stone hewed nor bricks burnt: but on Sunday the act of faith for this country's first Cathedral was made, the first prayer said and the first hymn sung by the first congregation. On the site where the finished building will rise there now stands the symbol of the Christian faith it will preach. The Cross, hewn from one of the great teak forests of the Territory. His Lordship said there would be many difficulties to be faced as the task of building was prepared. There might be times when temptation to give up was great and hope of completion small. The Cross stands on the summit of the hill which sweeps up from the town area to the Ridgeway.'

Oliver travelled to the Eastern Province on 12th August accompanied by Canon Rogers from Fort Jameson and Vera Hassall, a Mothers' Union worker. They had been staying at Bishop's Lodge for the blessing of the great Cross on the Cathedral site and were given a lift to Fort Jameson and Msoro respectively.

In his first circular letter to friends, Oliver wrote: 'I set out from Lusaka on this tour with a sad heart, because the day before I had said good-bye to my sister, Prudence.' She was returning home by sea after eighteen months in Northern Rhodesia, which was longer than originally planned. He then described the journey: 'The party was completed by my driver, Joram; my cook, Mackenzie, who added distinction to the party by wearing his chef's hat all the way, although he was going

176

on holiday; and a vast quantity of luggage, hospital comforts, kanzus, church box etc. Together we bowled merrily along the Great East Road for nearly four hundred miles.Many people think of N. Rhodesia as being flat. It is true that our country does in parts enjoy very poor physical features, but the Great East Road is like a scenic railway. There is a famous notice on the road which warns travellers of dangerous bends for the next 120 miles. The bends are both horizontal and vertical, the driving is difficult, the test on the stomach severe, but the mountain scenery is very beautiful and the crossing of the great Luwangwa river, flowing rather muddily into the Zambezi, opens the gateway into the beloved Eastern Province.

My first visit was for a fortnight to Msoro Mission which lies about 50 miles from Fort Jameson and the Great East Road. I had spent my first Christmas in N. Rhodesia on the Mission station itself, so on this visit my time was spent chiefly in visiting the three African parishes of Nceka, Mbapongwe and New Mzenje, each under the care of an African priest. In comparatively recent days it would have taken six weeks to complete a tour of these parishes on foot. Now the Mission has a Landrover, it is possible to do the tour in twelve days. The Priest-in-charge, the Rev. Cyril Mudford, showed the greatest skill in packing ourselves, the African priest in whose parish we were travelling, our cook, William and all our kit into the Landrover; and then driving us over hill and drift, soft sand and rock without one breakdown. Each night was spent in a different village, usually sleeping in the school. I held six confirmations during the journey and each day there was a celebration of Holy Communion. The villagers were very generous in their welcome. At Nzeha we were given so much rice that it was difficult to find room for it in the car; and at one time the shuddering of the car over the rocky track was punctuated by the squawking of four chickens which we had been given. In this area (and elsewhere in N. Rhodesia)

177

there is a great need to build new churches. It was therefore very good to see at Jumbe (in Nceka parish) a good brick church being built to God's glory. Humanly speaking, this good work is due to the inspiration of the clergy, the active leadership of the Chief and the generosity of one of you who gave a cheque for £10, just sufficient to supplement the money raised locally.

'I hope to be able to dedicate this Church at the beginning of December, in honour of St. Joseph. The foster-father of Our Lord and the Carpenter should be an inspiring patron for the village. I have never understood why so scriptural a saint should be considered to be a Roman Catholic and have been so sadly neglected in the dedication of Anglican churches. At any rate we now hope to have one Church of St. Joseph in N. Rhodesia. Do you know of one in the whole of England?

'During our tour we travelled along the beautiful hilly valley of the river Luwangwa and saw many buck, hippos and elephants. Our best view of the latter came one evening when we were sitting at dusk by the river. Three elephants appeared on the opposite bank, came down to the river to drink and then waded across to land on our side not more than 25 yards from us. After the tour I spent a couple of days in Msoro itself.

'At Fort Jameson it was good to see the progress in the work of restoring the lovely brick tower of St. Paul's Church from the ravages of white ants. After a visit to the Angoni villages and a Sunday in Fort Jameson itself Canon Rogers took me off to the Boma (or Government District Headquarters) at Lundazi, 120 miles to the North. Our visit here had a special interest. As we sat down to dinner a White Father walked in with the news that a plane had crashed many miles away in the bush, a Government Rapide with the Commissioner of Police and three other police officers on board. A party set out at once in the night to help them. Fortunately, all were alive, though the Commissioner is still

178

in hospital suffering from the injuries then sustained.

'There is a good story about the crash. The plane tipped up and all the occupants were thrown out into the night. After a time they shouted to each other to enquire after injuries. One man replied that he must have broken his back because he could not stand upright. "Try unbuckling the bucket seat attached to you" was the helpful reply. He had been thrown out, complete with his seat strapped to him. From Lundazi we sped back to Fort Jameson with news of the crash and then went on the 50 miles to St. Francis Mission Hospital, Katete.

'You will have read about the blessing of St. Francis Hospital and the dedication of its very beautiful stone chapel in the presence of about a thousand Africans and Europeans. It was a memorable and inspiring occasion. Here I will only pay tribute to the vision of the hospital's Founder, the Rev. Dr. Francis Trefusis, and to the skill of its builder, Mr. Hubert Jebbett.

'The Rev. Isaac Mungwa is now established as Chaplain to St. Francis Hospital and seems to be very happy in his new work. For my return to Lusaka I had the company of the Rev. Filemon Mataka [later to become Bishop] and his family. I am glad his wife is the better for her visit to Lusaka Hospital.

'St. Francis reminds me of the wonderful prospect of a visit from Father Joseph Botting of the Society of St. Francis. I hope that he may be with us for at least eighteen months. My own friendship with this Society of Anglican Friars goes back to the visits of Brother Douglas to preach in our school Chapel, in particular to the day when he forgot his engagement to preach and arrived at the last moment by plane on the playing fields.'

After the tour at Msoro Oliver related his adventures to the three women missionaries, including Vera Hassall. She was so inspired by his story that she was reminded of St. Paul's missionary journey in the Acts of the Apostles (Chapter 15,

St. Francis Hospital, Katete, Eastern Province

Crossing the Luapula River

verses 36 ff). She then wrote the following description of Oliver's journey in the style of the New Testament, 'part in fun' as she described it 'but also to show how hard he had to work and how much he loved everything he was doing, his attention to every detail and to every person. He really loved people, respected them, prayed for them and thought the best of them.'

'And after some days' Vera's description began 'the Bishop said unto Cyril: "Let us return now and visit the brethren in every district where we visited last year and see how they fare." And Cyril was minded to take with them Alfred also, who was called Jeff. But the Bishop thought not good to take with them him who had a lot of building to do and who had charge of the womenfolk. And Cyril was obedient to the Bishop and chose Leonard and so they departed in the Landrover.

'And they went through the region of the Tsetse Fly and came to Nceka, having picnic-lunched on the way. And as they went through the villages they delivered them the decrees for to keep and the next day the Bishop confirmed many. And from thence they went to Kakumbi, taking with them Patrick, and there they slept the night. And when morning was come they called together the few faithful and after they had said Mass they came to Katemo where the teachers received the medical box with thankfulness.

'And having departed from Katemo they returned to Kakumbi and here Patrick departed from them. And when they had loaded the Landrover again they assayed to go into Cilongozi and the people suffered them not. But when they found there was no road, then had Cyril to put the Landrover in four-wheel drive and they did pass through a muddy stretch and other times he had to swerve round fallen trees. Now when they had passed through Kalefya and Cimbwa they came to Cilongozi, having found Isaiah at Cimbwa. And there they

181

found many brethren who received them very warmly, but the tsetse fly troubled them again.

'And from thence they passed to Ciwale where the Bishop confirmed many. And other times did the Bishop stop and confirm the aged. And having approved the building of the Church at Ciwale they continued on their journey. And passing by Sandwe they came to Sasare and, hearing that there were certain Europeans in that area, they stopped to enquire. But a certain platinum blonde took them in and assured them that there was no wealth there. And after taking leave of the platinum blonde they passed to Lundu where they camped and confirmed all the faithful who came to them. And they came also to Cindamba.And on the Friday they set off for Mzenje and, finding Misael at Cilwa, they continued on their journey and made a straight course to Mzenje. But here the wind was against them so that the dust was great and the Bishop caught a cold. And here the disciples had gathered together to see the Bishop bless the church and induct the new elder, who troubled us greatly over the loss of his gun.

'And passing on from thence we came the next day to Petauke where we met white and black brethren and burnt our tongues with curry and did eat ice-creams to cool them; and after that we set off at a great speed towards the Great East Road, for the Bishop had determined to sail past Katete, for he was hastening, if it were possible for him, to be at Msoro for Sunday afternoon tea. And so it came to pass that they escaped safe to Msoro, rejoicing in the knowledge that the churches had been strengthened and the numbers increased.And they rehearsed all things to the women assembled.'

Vera Hassall says that Oliver was very amused by her report and impressed by how well she had listened to his account of the travels. She also added some kind remarks about Prudence: 'I have never known her to be angry or depressed.

She was full of life and a tremendous asset in the life of the Diocese.'

In the middle of December the promised Franciscan, Father Joseph Botting, arrived, to Oliver's great joy.

He wrote to his sister 'The visit to Chipili was wonderfully happy and peaceful; not one complaint or demand for more pay.' He ordained Christopher Kaoma, Priest at St. Michael, Chipili, and stayed with him over Christmas. Later he cycled with Fathers John Kingsnorth and Joseph Njamu to Mutipula where there was a Christian Chief and a new church. He blessed All Saints Church there on 30th December, and his letter continued: 'I enjoyed the visit, especially a day on cycles with Father Joseph and the good teacher, Jason, when we went to visit a village called Cimbalanga. We went along the valley of the Luongo, country surprisingly like the Broads in Norfolk. On our return Jason brought us to a ferry about 5 p.m. It was a dug-out canoe. He tried to get 3 cycles and 4 men on it, but it turned over near the bank. He then went off with the cycles, leaving us on the bank enjoying the river, water lilies and birds. After ten minutes we thought the ferry-crossing of a 50ft river very long. After an hour we were convinced he was drowned and we were lost. After an hour and a half the ferry returned and we had a half-hour trip up the lovely river in the dusk.' The ferryman thought they knew how far he had to go round the bend in the river, and thought they would enjoy the waiting!

1954

On 17th January Oliver wrote to Prudence, who was due to have an operation on her thyroid gland at Westminster Hospital in February. He was then about to fly to Nairobi to stay with the Barings, the Governor. 'Father Joseph has just gone off to Ndola to make plans for Lent in the Copperbelt.

THE PICNIC
(LEFT TO RIGHT: OLIVER, VERA HASSALL, PEGGY HATHERLEY,
ALFRED JEFFERY, MOLLY LAMBERT AND CANON ROGERS).

THE HAT GAME AT MSORO

Then he goes for three weeks to Mapanza. His health is much better.' Oliver refers to all the interviewing Prudence was doing on his behalf in England and ends: 'I am overjoyed and deeply impressed by your wish to return to N.R. It seems that God is really calling you to work here. Joseph Njamu told me that people in the vaillages near Chipili were asking him when you would return. Everywhere I go there is the same question from Europeans and Africans. I have always longed for your return and felt sure it would be right for you. Do come as soon as you are really well.'

On 20th February Oliver wrote to his sister-in-law, Pip: 'I am thrilled at the thought of a new nephew or niece. I wish I could pay you a visit as I did after Penelope's birth. [In March it was to be a nephew, Simon Oliver]. The Bishops' visit went off very well on the whole. May Smith and the staff did very well. My first sherry party seemed to go well, but I don't intend to have another. As host you don't get to know people any better. I spent all my time with the sherry and the nuts. There was a sensation when the sitting-room door fell off its hinges, eaten away by white ants! Bishop Paget [later the Archbishop] said instantly: "That is a charge on the Diocese, not the Province."

'I took the Bishops to Lemba Farm at Chisamba, 40 miles north of Lusaka, for tea. They were much impressed by the Friesland cattle and pasteurising plant. I love the place.'

In May Oliver wrote to Prudence:'Thank you and Felicity so much for your offers of help out here. I agree that Felicity might prefer to come out after my leave [in England] when the weather would be better and she could come for longer. If you are really well again, I can only say "Come as soon as possible after the children's [nephews' and nieces'] holidays." In fact Prudence returned to Lusaka on 22nd October; and then flew back to England with Oliver for his leave in June 1955. Felicity decided to go out to Africa with

Prudence in the autumn of 1955 after their home leave - more of that visit later.

On 30th May Oliver wrote to his brother: 'Please thank Prudence for letters. She did so well with young Pitt that he has accepted my invitation to come out before I made it. I am glad he sounds so promising. I dined at Government House yesterday to meet Sir. G. Huggins, P.M. of the Federation [Northern and Southern Rhodesia plus Nyasaland]. I was interested in him, but charmed by the new Governor [Benson] and his wife.'

On 27th June he wrote: 'The Diocesan Conference and Synod were more difficult than last time, but all went with goodwill. The garden party with the Governor present was fun, though colder than last time and very few flowers out. Synod was rather troublesome over the Cathedral, where the method of selecting an architect ended in their giving to me the entire responsibility for choice - together, of course, with the blame!'

Then came what Oliver used to call "the Botting Bombshell." In a letter to John, dated 27th June, he wrote: 'I must share with you a most serious blow. Father Joseph Botting came out last December on a mission to help the Diocese for about 18 months. I did mention in a previous letter several personal disappointments over him. I returned last Thursday to find him wearing civilian clothes. He announced that he could continue as an Anglican no longer and was becoming an R.C. at once. This he did by leaving for Salisbury, S. Rhodesia by car with a Jesuit yesterday. The result is that there is no priest for the large African mission of St. Peter in Lusaka. Also Father Joseph was due to conduct several retreats this year.

'When I broke the news to the African congregation this morning it was obvious they could not understand such a good priest wanting to change to Ma Roma. They clearly

186

thought that Joseph had eloped with a very attractive young teacher, whom he rashly brought to stay here and to church. In fact she came to discuss becoming an Anglican Nun!! Never a dull moment is our Diocesan motto. So far the Franciscan Community have sympathised with me.'

The sequel to this story came in a letter to Prudence dated 23rd September written in the train to Livingstone at Mazabuka station. He started by wishing Prudence 'God speed and a very happy voyage on the *Braemar*. The farewell will be sad, but I hope the thoughts of so many looking forward to your arrival will sustain you. God bless you in this new venture.' [She eventually arrived on 22nd October.] He continued, 'Just had lunch and found Stephen Easter, Railway Missioner in the Diner. I like him so much. Joseph Botting's permit to stay in S.R. has expired and, alas, he has returned to the Copperbelt to find work in the mines in order to support his mother. The Jesuits don't seem to have given him a good welcome!'

In October Oliver saw Mr. Prain, Chairman of a copper mine and discussed the building of a Cathedral, to obtain his support no doubt. James Robertson continues his reminiscences: 'Our return to Mapanza in 1954 was accelerated by the death of a colleague at the Mission station and at Christmas that year Bishop Oliver came to keep the Feast with us. The Midnight Mass was in St. Mark's Chapel and he celebrated. I assisted and at the beginning of the Gloria I noticed the servers were jumping and slapping themselves. Then I noticed the Bishop was in difficulties too. It came to me that the powerful incense had disturbed a huge swarm of bees in the South East corner of the roof and they were attacking the whole sanctuary party in the candlelit darkness.

'I remembered that the altar was all prepared in the parish Church of St. Bartholomew, half a mile away. At the end of the Gloria I stopped the liturgy, explained to the congregation of Sisters, staff and the boys and girls of the College and schools our predicament and asked them to move quietly to the Church. The procession of the congregation in the darkness, silently, lit only by stars and hurricane lamps as it snaked to the new sanctuary was something that Oliver never forgot. It was the only time he sang Midnight Mass part at one altar and part at another. He had been badly stung and confided in me later, gusting with laughter, "I never thought that martyrdom would ever take that form".

The year ended with a cryptic note in the Anniversary Book '31st December swam river Ngonga.' It is not known why exactly he had to swim the river. Not for pleasure, it is certain. The river is near Mapanza, as we learn from John Houghton's book *Borrowed Time Extended.* He was sent to work at Mapanza, when he first arrived in Northern Rhodesia in 1942. He writes 'While Fathers James and Fiennes reigned supreme at St. Mark's College, Father Adams and I were the two parish priests for the district with its twenty outstations. We took it in turn to tour the district. We cycled or walked..... with a Scotch cart drawn by four or six oxen. I came to know and love that countryside very much indeed. It boasts three rivers, the Munyeke, the Ngonga and the Mutama. We were too fearful of bilharzia to swim them. But when they were in full spate in the rains and had to be crossed, I used to strip, make one crossing carrying my cycle over, a second crossing to carry my clothes.'

1955

The Rev. Bernard Higgins was installed Rector of Livingstone on 6th February and nothing else appears in the Anniversary Book until the great visit of the Archbishop of Canterbury Geoffrey Fisher and his wife on 13th April. They landed at Livingstone and moved to Lusaka for the launch of the appeal for the proposed Cathedral of the Holy Cross on 17th April. After visiting Kitwe they flew from Lusaka to Fort Jameson (now Chipata) some 400 miles to the East. 'Here there was time only for a halt of little more than an hour' John Houghton wrote in *The Eagle,* 'to meet European and African delegates from a radius of some sixty miles. They came from Fort Jameson itself, where St. Paul's Church is nearly five years older than the Diocese; from Msoro, oldest and largest of the Mission districts and from St. Francis Hospital, Katete, the largest and finest venture of the Diocese in the field of medicine.'

So the Archbishop's visit ended and he flew on to neighbouring Nyasaland (now Malawi) and then to the inauguration of the new Province in the Cathedral at Salisbury. After the Archbishop had left, Oliver was visited by Bishop Eric Hamilton, Dean of Windsor, who had flown out for the inauguration of the Province which took place on 8th May.

It was time for Oliver, accompanied by his sister, to return home on leave after three and a half years - not that it was to be all holiday for Oliver. It was reported in the *Eagle* 'As readers may see from the list of some of his engagements, the Bishop's leave is to be a strenuous one and it comes at the end of a most strenuous tour. New churches have been completed and dedicated at Chingola, Luanshya, Lusaka, Katete, Jumbe and Fort Roseberry. Both churches at Ndola have been enlarged and great progress made with the saving and restoring of the church at Fort Jameson.

'The Seminary (next to Bishop's Lodge) has been made Provincial and doubled in size.The Cathedral site has been finally secured and marked with its great Cross, and the Cathedral fund launched. Negotiations regarding the teacher-training move to Chalimbana have been accepted. The Province of Central Africa has been born. Two African priests

189

have been ordained and a third ordinand is now nearing the end of his Deacon's course. Truly there is much for which to thank God, as we look back over these past years. And all will join in tribute to our Bishop for the unflagging zeal and wisdom with which he carried out his duties as our father-in-God.'

James Robertson refers to the teacher-training in his reminiscences: 'At that time a major Report on African education in N.R had advised Government to end the support of many small Teacher Training Colleges run by the voluntary agencies and concentrate on five major centres. The missions belonging to the Christian Council of N.R. were allotted two, the Roman Catholics one, Local Government one, and Central Government one. There had been for a long time an Anglican Chapel at Chalimbana, the Government College. In negotiations with the Director of African Education, Bishop Oliver asked me to move there, with our students in 1955. The grant aid continued and enabled me to be Anglican Chaplain and to lecture as a Staff member. In 1956 he asked me to relieve the Diocesan financial burden by accepting Government conditions. I then became Principal, continued as Chaplain, and also supervised the Ecumenical chaplaincy arrangements. I record this because it illustrates Bishop Oliver's imaginative response to changing historical circumstances within the Diocesan tradition.

'This same gift was apparent in his policy of bringing many key people to the Diocese as a result of his links with the Church of England. The result was a consequent enrichment of the tradition enabling the emergence of a diversified Anglican Diocese. He had built on Bishop Robert's early work in preparation for a Central African Province, linking the Dioceses of both Rhodesias and Nyasaland. The climax came with the visit of Archbishop Fisher in 1955 to the Diocese, prior to the formal inauguration of the Province in Salisbury (now Harare). This visit put the seal on the move from a 'missionary diocese under Canterbury' to a sense of autonomous membership of the Anglican Communion. In Salisbury I remember Oliver coming up to me after the formal election of Bishop Edward of Mashonaland as a first Archbishop. He was bubbling with laughter. "Guess what?" he said, "We are thinking of calling him Ted Fed." Those who remember the disaffection in the years of the Federation of Rhodesia and Nyasaland and the sensitivities of the northern dioceses will understand.'

EMMA DRESSED UP AS A BISHOP
WITH HER PARENTS, RICHARD AND DIANA WOOD

CHAPTER 19

LEAVE IN ENGLAND - 1955

On his way home Oliver visited St. Albans Cathedral, in Pretoria, his earlier home as a humble Priest, and then went to Bishops Court at Capetown, before returning to England in time for the 60th Rifles Bicentenary on 25th July. It is noted that Queen Elizabeth II inspected the Regiment at St. Cross. She also inspected the Old Comrades and spoke to Oliver. As one old comrade chaffed afterwards "I ask you, what can you expect, when the Queen spots a veteran wearing Bishop's gaiters, she is bound to stop!"

In between his appointments he was able to cruise with his brother-in-law Bob Ryder and sister Hilaré in their boat the Foresight from the Hamble. He was also able to achieve his earlier dreams of a visit to Assisi. Oliver and Felicity travelled to Perugia by train, where they met Richard and Diana, who were in their tent nearby. When they stopped at Paris, in the early hours, Oliver descended from his sleeper to the platform, with a coat thrown over his pyjamas. He always enjoyed some exercise at a stop on a railway journey. An African stop would probably last some little while, but to Oliver's consternation the train suddenly moved off, leaving him on the platform, and Felicity alone in the train. Luckily he soon discovered that the train was changing platforms and he was able to rejoin his sister.

The visit to Italy, which included Perugia 16th August, Assisi 19th, Isola Maggiore on Lake Trasimeno 22nd and Pisa on 29th is enriched by Richard Holderness' comments: 'A longer and even more memorable time that we spent with Oliver was a delightful week when he was on leave from Africa. He and Felicity, not yet married to Ted, based themselves in a hotel in Assisi, while Diana and I slept in a comfortable tent in the foothills below. On several evenings we mounted to Perugia, where Oliver developed a great liking for the Passegiata, a parade at dusk of all the Perugian young up and down the town's main street. Oliver was determined that I should enjoy this to the full and pleaded with anyone who attempted (very naturally) to obstruct my car.

"Mio amico, multo mutilato nella guerra."

'Oliver's Italian was limited, but he had completely mastered this phrase and it generally worked. Less successful was his ordering luncheon at a small restaurant on the edge of Trasimene lake. When he commanded, for two of us, "Due green beans" the waiter roared with laughter. Oliver felt he had done his best and was greatly offended.

'It is glorious country, soaked in memories of St. Francis, whom Oliver habitually honoured in England with regular visits to Cerne Abbas. During our short holiday, we also did our best to pay him honour, with a celebration of Holy Communion one morning in our 'camp' and Evensong in quiet meadows on several occasions. Oliver and I had long theological discussions. I remember being surprised by his stern views on the subject of fasting. I had always thought him, although a traditionalist, sensibly liberal and was therefore amazed when he advised me that I must on no account swallow any water I needed in the night before making my communion, but must merely use it to rinse my mouth. I am horrified to think how shocked Oliver would be about my growing laxity over the years.

'In spite of this unexpected strictness, he was a natural choice as one of Emma's godfathers. He and she were soon on excellent terms and her letters to him were a suitable blend of respect and affection. They always began 'Darling Bishop Oliver.' On one of his winter visits to England in 1962 he agreed to confirm her, together with three other girls, in Kirby

Underdale church. Apart from some doubt whether we should get to the church on a particularly wintry evening, Emma looked very happy. The other three girls were much less so. When they heard that they were to be confirmed by a Bishop from Africa, they naturally expected him to be black and were bitterly disappointed to find that he was not!'

Oliver's niece, Susan Ryder, who is now married to Martin Bates, has written about his visits to the family from Africa. It was during one of these visits that she painted his portrait - one of her early works - as on the cover. She writes:

'When Oliver came to stay it was usually for a few weeks - we would be his base in London for the Lambeth Conference or he would join us for a week or two on the boat and of course occasionally he would be with us for Christmas. Then everything would be twice as much fun, partly, I think because my mother so adored him. We were all caught up in the excitement and pleasure of his visits. He generated such a wonderfully happy atmosphere, bringing out the best in everyone - with shouts of laughter and gentle, teasing; though when he persuaded my father to eat a 'joke' chocolate while fasting before Midnight Mass and it turned out to be full of mustard - it wasn't quite the gentle tease Oliver had intended.

'I remember the division of the contents of Ennismore Gardens when the family flat came to be pulled down. Deborah chose to have cash instead, so that left the five Green-Wilkinsons to take it in turns, starting with the eldest Oliver to choose what they wanted - first with the furniture, then the paintings, silver, books and rugs. I remember, as a child, being so sorry and worried for Oliver, who never chose the obviously valuable or beautiful, but hunted instead for anything with a dog on it. It so diffused the situation to see his collection of doggy pictures, books and china greyhounds!'

Pip, his sister-in-law, also remembers that moment, when Oliver proudly took his niece to see his collection. All

194

she could say was "I just feel sorry for you!" John remembers the distribution. Apart from being impressed with Oliver's Chairmanship of the gathering, he was amused at the heated arguments among the family as to why they themselves should not have a particular valuable item!

Susan continues, 'I also remember the wonderful stories he used to bring back from Africa. The story of a leopard who had been shot and dumped in the back of a jeep with an African boy, who after a few miles, could be heard tapping on the partition between the front and back of the truck, saying "Leopard feeling better now." Or the tale of the Bishop who was being driven through the bush, miles from anywhere, when the car broke down. The driver tried tinkering with everything he could think of; but nothing worked, night was falling, finally the Bishop suggested in a rather embarrassed way that they should try praying for help - so they knelt by the car and prayed. "Now" said the Bishop, "try the ignition again" - and it started. "Good God" he said in amazement - and then Oliver rocked with laughter.'

After his visit to Italy Oliver went to the Friary at Cerne Abbas on 4th September to attend Father Algy Robertson's last retreat. He also visited Cuddesdon Theological College, where his father had been trained and the Community of the Resurrection at Mirfield on 19th September.

While he was in England he planned to have his leg seen to, as it was painful for him to stand for long periods. He went to see a Specialist in October, Dr. John Hunt at St. George's Hospital. While he was there he was informed that his Grandfather's leg was held by the hospital as a training exhibit. It had been amputated early in the century to avoid gangrene. This was probably caused by a bad kick from a horse, when the General was in India during the Mutiny.

It is not often that you are confronted by your Grandfather's preserved leg! A minor operation was found necessary on Oliver's leg, but before this took place on 10th November at St. Mary's Hospital under Professor Robb, he attended the re-dedication of Lambeth Palace Chapel. He recorded that he sat with the Welsh Bishops and met Her Majesty and Princess Margaret afterwards.

Before Oliver returned to Northern Rhodesia he also recorded that on 6th December Father Denis Marsh S.S.F. spoke to him on the telephone about N.R. Undoubtedly about a replacement for Joseph Botting.

He was keen to be back as soon as possible after his operation and to be in his Diocese for Christmas. So he flew out via Nairobi, with a short visit to Sir Evelyn Baring and arrived back in Lusaka on 15th December. Meanwhile his sisters Prudence and Felicity were travelling out by sea and reached Lusaka before him.

OLIVER IS MET AT LUSAKA AIRPORT
BY TED EASTON, CANON SMITH,
JOHN HOUGHTON, PRUDENCE AND FELICITY

CHAPTER 20

RETURN TO NORTHERN RHODESIA
AND FELICITY's VISIT

Oliver had invited Felicity to come out with Prudence and to stay for six months in Northern Rhodesia. She wrote many letters home which are very descriptive of the country seen through an artist's eye and give a good idea of the life Oliver led. This visit was two years before Felicity married Ted Peel, who was a Housemaster at Rossall public school. Later he became Chaplain of Cheltenham College.

Felicity and Prudence arrived in Cape Town on 6th December 1955 and Felicity wrote to Hilaré Ryder on 12th December from the train while travelling to Lusaka:

'I have fallen in love with the Cape! It is simply lovely there. If you can picture the heavenly smells in Spain, the twinkling lights of Oslo, with the coast roads of the South of France, plus the surf of Devon and Sugar Loaf mountain of Wicklow and ranges of beautiful mountains all round - you have got the Cape!!'

This was the enthusiastic description of an artist. Then later she wrote: 'The first part of our journey was lovely and very beautiful, like wandering through the mountains in Scotland, only on a vast scale. It was the Hottentots. The Karroo was dull, the Orange River fairly full. At Francistown there was a moth-eaten ostrich by the line and the rivers are completely dry.

'From now on we shall be in Southern Rhodesia. We had a magnificent sunset last night and the cloud formations to-day are lovely and quite different to those you see in Europe.'

They arrived in Lusaka on 13th December, surprisingly only half an hour late, to be met by five clergy plus May Smith with Lydia and John Forester. Oliver had not yet arrived by air as he was visiting the Barings in Nairobi.

Geoffrey Fiennes was at Bishop's Lodge recuperating from an illness while having treatment three mornings each week at the hospital. He had just heard that he would need six more weeks of treatment which was depressing for him. There was also Rees Phillips at Bishop's Lodge. Felicity wrote: 'Rees Phillips is a dear, so easy and full of amusing stories and terribly proud of the Seminary next to Bishop's Lodge - and rightly so.' She continued: 'Prudence is absolutely wonderful and completely in her element. Rees and Geoffrey love her stories and being organised! Prue has a tremendous reception from everyone in Lusaka and I'm continually shaking hands with new people. Everyone knew we'd arrived as it was in the social column of the "Northern News." So I can't disguise myself as a parlour maid here!'

The last sentence refers to when Felicity went to stay in 1949 with Hilaré and Bob Ryder in Oslo. Bob was Naval Attaché and Felicity was very timid. She heard that there was to be a large dinner party her first night in Oslo but, as there was a shortage of staff to serve the dinner, she readily volunteered to serve at it. During the evening a guest turned to Hilaré and said: 'I thought you told me that your sister was coming to Oslo.' Not a word was said about the parlour maid hovering behind him at that moment!

Felicity also wrote: 'Lusaka I like very much. It feels gay and alive and I love the many different styled bungalows built amongst the attractive trees, all on the Riviera style. It is far more impressive to me than Bulawayo, though it has no sky-scrapers. It has some very large, smart shops. The municipal buildings and the Cenotaph impress me very much, but the Post Office is old and grim - just as Oliver saw it in 1936!

'The whole of Bishop's Lodge has been redecorated inside as a surprise for Oliver. The noise of the crickets etc. are so loud I now understand why Oliver and Prudence found London nights so quiet!'

Oliver arrived on 15th December at the airport, only

five minutes drive from Bishop's Lodge. Rees, Geoffrey Fiennes, Ted Easton, John Houghton and the Smiths were there to meet him. 'It was lovely to see him and he is in terrific form' Felicity wrote 'and well rested, though he agrees his leg is not exactly 100%; but he is able to forget it now. After tea we helped him to unpack. Then we three said Evensong in his dear little chapel of St. Francis. Oliver got a great welcome from the boys and he is thrilled with the paintwork the Diocese has given him as a surprise. He loved his stay in Nairobi.'

At a photographic exhibition in Lusaka Felicity met Alan Hewitt. 'He looks fierce and short. I can imagine how he must have been a little difficult when Oliver's boss (in 1936).' At the end of December Felicity wrote: 'Geoffrey can be very silent, but sometimes he is in splendid form and enters into everything and comes out with amusing remarks and jokes. We dined with the Eastons. Ted Easton never stops talking and telling stories. Joan Easton is sweet - one of the kindest and very nicest out here.'

On New Year's Day Oliver broadcast a message of goodwill at a very troubled time, requesting courage from God and courtesy between all people in Northern Rhodesia. Part of the message reads as follows:

'Do you remember the story of the prophet Elisha's servant at Dothan? It happened in the early morning and made the young man full of fear. The servant had gone to sleep in his village feeling quite safe, but when he awoke he found that the village was surrounded on all sides by the hostile army of Syria, so that he cried out for fear. But Elisha. the man of God, had no fear because he saw things as they truly were, as God sees them. He prayed to God that his servant's eyes might be opened. When this prayer was answered the young man saw all the power of God, the angel host surrounding Elisha. Then the servant knew that those that were with them were more than those that were against them. With a good courage

199

he saw things as they really were in God's eyes and knew that the enemy were delivered into their hands.

'I think that story should give us courage at the beginning of a new year, when there are many troubles to fill our hearts with fear for the future of 1956. Let us pray that God will open our eyes to see His presence and power around us.'

He continued: 'God has shown His love for all men by the birth and life, the death and resurrection of Jesus Christ. As God has loved all His world, so we are to love all the world around us, to show courtesy and goodwill to all men. Do you know the story of St. Francis who lived in the village of Assisi in Italy many years ago? During 1955 it was my good fortune to visit his village and hear much about his life. It was a life full of courage and joy and peace because St. Francis really believed that God loved all the world which He had visited and redeemed. St. Francis showed this courtesy or loving respect for all that God had made. He showed this courtesy to water which makes clean and refreshes; and to fire which gives us light and warmth. He showed this courtesy to animals when he tamed a hungry, fierce dog in Gubbio and when he preached to the birds about God's care for them. Above all, St. Francis showed that wonderful courtesy, that loving goodwill to all men who were made in God's image, of whatever type they might be. Although many men in his days were afraid of lepers and were cruel to them, St. Francis treated them as brothers and looked after them. He loved all men, rich or poor, because God loved them; and so his life was full of joy and peace.

'Can we not resolve that, by God's help, we will try to show that same courtesy and good will to all whom we shall meet during 1956.'

He ended by saying: ' May God bless us all in the coming year so that we may grow in the good way of courtesy and goodwill to each other.'

200

1956

Felicity's letter of 2nd February to her sister Hilaré described a typical day at Bishop's Lodge:

7 a.m Mass at St. Francis Chapel here and at the Seminary where nineteen students have just arrived;

8 a.m. Breakfast;

8.30 a.m. Prue gives out stores to dear Mackenzie;

9.15 a.m. Prue and I plus Joram go to Lusaka, dropping Geoffrey at the hospital every other day for his exercises;

10.30 a.m. Back home, having picked up Geoffrey from the hospital. Morning tea, at which two Seminary Wardens, Rees and Edward, appear. Oliver and Kay Quiggin, his secretary, have theirs at their desks. Vistors sometimes appear and expect tea, so it can drag on till 11.30.

After this I try to arrange the flowers, which I have picked at 7.30 before the sun is too hot. Zinnias are vast and last longer. I may file Oliver's letters for Kay, as all the letters when he was on leave need filing too. I love Kay; she worships Oliver and she works very hard to save him money and collect for the Cathedral funds. She sings in the choir. Hilary, her husband, is a Lay Reader and a great pillar of the Church. He sang Mozart on the wireless last Sunday. In the afternoon Geoffrey and the Wardens sleep on their beds. Oliver (if free) reads, under a tree in the garden with his hat on, papers or a theological book. Prue housekeeps, while I file. She should rest, but she won't;

4.30 p.m. Everyone appears for tea; then if Oliver is free he suggests a walk - either a short round or sometimes jump in the car and drive to an attractive ridge and have a walk with a view;

After this Oliver goes to his desk while we bath.

7 p.m. We join Oliver for Evensong in the Chapel;

7.30 p.m. Everyone drinks. Oliver always appears last with a lamp in his hand!

8 p.m We shift into the other half of the sitting-room to

have dinner.

Then back for coffee;

9 p.m. Oliver goes to his desk;

9.30 p.m. Oliver says Compline;

10 p.m. Prue and I go to bed.

In the March issue of the *Eagle* the Diocesan magazine Oliver ended his letter: 'Every Bishop outside Britain has a number of Commissaries who represent him in various ways in England especially over the recruiting of staff. It is with great sorrow that I write of the death of one of my Commissaries, Dr. Spencer Leeson, Bishop of Peterborough on 27th January. He was my Rector when I was a curate at St. Mary's Southampton and has been a continual source of strength and help to me since I became your Bishop. Our sympathy goes to his wife and family and the Diocese.'

Earlier in his letter he gave interesting advice on prayer, which is reproduced in Appendix E 'Oliver's thoughts on prayer.'

On 2nd March Felicity wrote to her brother John: 'Prue and Oliver went to Broken Hill last weekend, so I went to stay with Oliver's old boss, Alan Hewitt and his wife Elizabeth, who I know well, as she stayed with us at the flat in London. I enjoyed it very much. It was much hotter as lower, near the Kafue River. The farm is for sale 50,000 acres at 30/- an acre - so going very cheap! ... Prue, Oliver and I drove up to Ndola yesterday. It was great fun and our first long trip together (200 miles). We stopped for elevenses at the vicarage at Broken Hill and a picnic in the heart of Africa en route. We left at 9.15am and got here at about 4.00pm - P. and I sang Tinno Rossi, Robeson and other old favourite records on our way, while Oliver dozed or read at the back. He felt he was back at Lovel Hill he said! My great excitement was seeing 2 large monkeys walk across the road.

'We had tea with Mike and Margaret Wilson, she is very sweet. He is vicar here and Oliver is staying with them. I am staying with Col. and Mrs. Hamburger. He is a local magistrate.

They are very kind and showed me round Ndola. It is wonderful how they all try to keep up the 'culture' out here. They have 'French mornings' when groups of them meet, sew and talk French all the time. They also have musical evenings and I heard Bach's St. John's Passion on my hosts' wonderful radiogram.'

Prue had gone on to Chingola to stay with the Pawles, while Oliver and Felicity moved onto Kitwe where she met Donald Weston the new vicar, who she says ... 'is a dear. We like him so very much. He stayed with us at the Lodge for 2 weeks for Financial meetings. He is always glad to hear news of Freddy, Dorothy and Ethne [Pelham Clintons, their cousins]. We go on to Luanshya on 5th where we stay at the vicarage together and then to Mufilira for three nights; finally to Chingola. Oliver drives Prue home, while I stay on with the Pawles and go home by train, a night journey.'

Felicity wrote to Hilaré on 7th March from Luanshya: 'We read your letter to Oliver on our way up to the Copperbelt on 1st March. He loves hearing family letters and is good, like Daddy, about showing us letters he has had of interest to Prudence and me. We always have special prayers for family on their birthdays, or any of Daddy's Anniversary Book events ... I just wanted you to know that I am simply thrilled with this place and the Copperbelt as a whole ... there are some of the kindest people here in the world! ... Everything is done for both black and white ... all the wives are thrilled with their modern bungalows. The size of the house goes by size of family, not seniority, except for the very heads ... the dam I was taken to, looks just like Southampton Water, as Canon Hewitt said with yachting, water skiing and fishing ... Even during strikes the 'feeling' is good they say. I think Mr. Prain must be like Spedan Lewis [Founder of John Lewis]. Even the Africans have their swimming pool, cinema and club and electricity in their houses! ... They don't seem to expect a slump out here, its an amazing feeling of prosperity. I wonder how long it will last?!'

Felicity to John on 8th March from Mufulira: 'After Ndola we went to Kitwe, where I stayed with some very nice people called Hunter. The young wife is Canadian and the two children Sheelah 10 and Mike 7 were so sweet and thoughtful and were thrilled to hear about England ... Here I am staying with the mines senior scientist and his wife... The Gribbles are new - in fact the service of his induction was today - his wife Jean is 26 and a dear ... There was a 'bunfight' here after the service from 9.00 - 10.00pm for people to meet Oliver. Everyone is very friendly and it is much more like a village than a town ... you should see the beautiful trees all covered with red flowers and yellow ones, with blue hills in the very distance ... This place is more woody than Kitwe.'

Felicity to Hilaré 18th March from Chingola staying with the Pawles: 'I may go to Chipili (mission station) on my own as Oliver does not go until August or September. Prue and I hope to visit Elizabethville for a couple of nights, while Oliver tours with Archbishop Paget in June ... Prue, Oliver and I start off on Maundy Thursday for my first mission station at Fiwila. We stay with the Cranes, who leave for good in May. It will be lovely to meet Brother Stephen and the lepers. There are beautiful views, with steep hills and cave drawings. Oliver will be taking the 3 hour service ... We go to Mapanza 13th to 27th April (famous for its snakes and ticks!). Oliver flies to Fort Jameson next weekend (40 miles from the hospital at Katete). I can't afford the flight so I may get a lift from Canon Adams. He is such a dear and full of stories.

'I've talked to Oliver, against Prue's wishes, about her resting, egged on by Mike Wilson, who says that he and Margaret (like everyone else) always do. Mike has been on at Oliver to do so, but he says he feels worse, if he does go off to sleep. So I hope Prue will rest in future, when she can.'

'I'm sitting under the potato tree (blue flowers) in Nan Pawles garden. I've been to church opposite at 7 and 9 and it

204

was packed - it is a beautiful modern building. This and Kitwe (Donald Weston's) are my favourites so far. Though I love Luanshya, which has a copper altar and surround for the hangings, which is blue material from the coronation (straight from Westminster Abbey!!). All the Copperbelt churches have beautiful copper bowls for the fonts too.

'I have loved my tour of the Copperbelt. The towns amongst the woods are most attractive - Oliver says 'like the New Forest'. I saw very little of Oliver as I never stayed with him except in the vicarage at Luanshya. I enjoyed driving from one town to the other with Oliver and stopping for half an hour or so on our way, for Oliver to write his next five (or more) sermons! Poor Oliver, they work him so hard on these tours and he has no time to himself. He dashes from one service to the other, then meetings, problems and socials. He was in splendid form, even at the end of it, to my surprise - but of course he will have to catch up on two weeks' letters when he gets back to Lusaka. Fiwila and Mapanza should be more restful for him.'

From Fiwila Mission Station Felicity wrote to 'Hip' on 4th April. (Hilaré was known as 'Hip' and Felicity as 'Lit' among the four youngest of the family). 'We set off' Felicity wrote 'on Maundy Thursday and drove the 90 miles to Broken Hill, then turned off along a winding sandy track through woods (as usual out here!) for 125 miles to Fiwila. Rather like driving through Windsor Forest, only smaller trees, on a sunny day. We had a picnic lunch and crossed seven rough log bridges, and were pulled by Africans across one river on a pontoon. No cars or traffic of course to pass and the last 17 miles here are rougher still with tall grasses well above your bonnet and you plough it down as you go!

'We were given a great welcome, arriving at 5 o'clock, and the whole school, boys girls and masters, marched up and greeted us when we had just started tea, and Oliver made a speech. This is a really beautiful place. Prue admits it's the most beautiful of the lot. Picture this mission house, built like a cloister (3 sides only) with a paved courtyard, on the side of a hill with a wonderful view of hills beyond. This part is very like Scotland - you even get mist low down on the hills and in the valley some mornings. As I sit writing I can see into the courtyard, through the arch and over the paving, with the sundial and little fountain, a most wonderful view of the blue, blue hills in the distance. There are geraniums, carnations, roses and marigolds against the walls and steps of the cloisters, which stand out beautifully against the distant hills. (I've tried to paint it, but can't do the view justice).

'Prue is staying in the village with Eileen Brown (here while Miss Trentham is on leave) just below this. The leper colony (100) live a little lower still. This is a very peaceful place and I'm glad to say has a holy atmosphere too, in spite of its many problems. On Easter Day we climbed up the mountain behind the cloisters, with lovely wild flowers and heath among the huge, flat, grey rocks. Through the trees a beautiful waterfall and stream rushing down over the boulders just like a burn in Scotland. We didn't get as high as the cave drawings unfortunately.

'On 2nd April, Prue's birthday, we drove along the valley and climbed to another waterfall with Oliver and with dear Brother Stephen. Eileen and Christopher Lay are here. He is a R.A.M.C. orderly, just arrived to help brothers with the lepers, especially those with no feet.

'There was an amusing incident on Saturday when Oliver baptised forty including some lepers; and then confirmed sixty. Those to be baptised (no babies) carry candles and have white sheets draped round their shoulders. Oliver started by flicking the Holy Water all round and then has to flick it over himself. Of course this meant his glasses became covered in water and I could see him smiling as he took them off and started mopping his specs, causing a delay! Still, in two hours he had finished both services, but it is amazing that Baptisms are saved up for him, as it means standing by the font which makes him tired. He has bought a shooting-stick, but never uses it. I must say I hadn't realised how terribly hard his mission trips are, though he considers it a rest and a change.' Kenneth Francis says that Oliver was always relaxed when he was going on *ulendo*, which he much enjoyed - in shorts, shirt and pectoral cross - with Joram driving.

On 25th April Felicity wrote to Hilaré from Choma while staying with the Bruce-Millars. 'I have enjoyed my visit to Mapanza mission immensely - such fun and I love the five sisters. Oliver, Prue and I plus Joram and Dominico drove south for Choma, via the Kafue River and through the lovely hills to this flat bit of farm country. We stopped for tea, 10 to 11 a.m, at the Duckhams at Mazabooka, where Prue once went to church on a tractor! Then we stopped at Monze to see a tiny little church, built and looked after tenderly by a dear little enthusiastic African.

'We arrived at the Bruce-Millars at 3.15, had tea and left Prue with them. Then Oliver and I went on about 30 miles to Mapanza. We got a great welcome. The five sisters work so hard and are so happy and good. I had Sister Maria's sweet little house - a few misgivings the first night, as lots of snakes here. A puff adder had turned up in the vestry and terrified John Houghton the week before. It makes a noise like a motor bike. Ticks are terrible here and can cause fever and bad poisoning. Poor Oliver has had them badly. I removed about three from his back one night after his trek. He could hardly sit and came up in blisters - such tiny things too.

'I had breakfast (in silence) after chapel with the five sisters; and morning tea with them. The lunch and dinner with the five bachelors, (Oliver plus Father Twell, Canon Adams, Dick Maxwell, Geoffrey Fiennes and Edward Robinson). Imagine my horror when Oliver and Twell went off for a trek for four days and nights and I was left with Geoffrey, Dick and Edward. Canon Adams disappeared too, into Choma hospital with an abscess on a tooth. They were very kind and Dick took me with Oliver and Twell to Lugwalo, an out-station about 20 miles away in real bush, where Oliver started his trek after a confirmation. We drove along footpaths, amongst trees and past isolated villages. It was very wild and difficult to find. Then we suddenly got to this out-station, where we were completely mobbed, and singing and dancing went on while we shook hands, two at a time. It was getting dark, so I only had half an hour there. Dick got lost twice driving me back.

'St. Mark's College (at Mapanza) and Chapel are most impressive. It has a feeling of tradition and the buildings are almost like Eton! The Chapel feels a bit austere, but the magnificent heavy doors and mouldings by Geoffrey; and the screens make it a lasting thing. So many buildings out here have a non-permanent feeling about them.

'The scenery is pretty flat and dull, the only attraction being palm-trees against the sky line. I loved the Sisters' chapel and St. Bartholomew's where we all met for Evensong at 7, followed by a chat outside by lantern-light. Then the Sisters and Bimbo, the dog, would go off to bed and we would go to have our dinner. I wish you could see the hospital, women orderlies carrying the babies in Moses baskets from one house to another on their heads!

'On Sunday 22nd we drove to Choma for a great service, the dedication of the now mixed denomination church. Oliver preached one of the three sermons. We all went back to tea and supper at the Bruce-Millars, said Evensong, followed by a sing-song as Dick Maxwell played the piano, before they went back to Mapanza leaving me with the Bruce-Millars.'

6th May, Felicity to John from Bishop's Lodge: 'We loved your story of Richard thinking he'd caused Oliver's leg-trouble with his pop-gun. [See Richard Wood's story of Oliver being shot by his nephew!] The sisters at Mapanza loved it. On our way home we had to stop at Choma hospital for Oliver to have his tick-bites dressed and to have penicillin injections.

'Bishop Robert [Selby Taylor] of Pretoria is now staying

to see his old haunts. I have always heard of him as brilliant and silent, so I was horrified when Oliver and Prue flew off to Kitwe for a Cathedral ball for two days. Actually he is quite chatty once on a subject, and rather a dear.

'To-morrow we celebrate Oliver's birthday by Prue and I taking him and Bishop Robert to dine at the Ridgeway, followed by the first performance in the New Theatre next to the hotel, to see *The First Born* by Christopher Fry, which is going up to compete at the Copperbelt drama festival. Lusaka usually wins. It was superbly done and very hard not to forget they were amateurs.'

12th May, Felicity to Hilaré from Katete: 'On 8th May Canon Adams appeared at 8.30 a.m and we had a great send-off for our 400 mile drive here! What a lovely drive it was. Perfect weather, lovely hills and twisting roads. I've heard so much about the escarpment, so I was wondering what it was really like. But only for one mile of the road there is a real drop one side and sheer cliff the other, but for a hundred miles you are warned DRIVE CAREFULLY FOR THE NEXT 100 MILES and it is rather like a scenic railway and you can't go more than 25-30 mph.

'Canon Adams has only just been passed fit enough to go to Fort Jameson for six months' relief duty. He's had coronary thrombosis and angina. Oliver warned me to try to prevent him driving, so imagine my horror when Leonard, the African driver, said he felt dizzy, had fever and couldn't drive! Canon Adams drove most of the 200 miles to the Kachalola Hotel where we spent the first night. A beautiful spot. You have a magnificent panorama of ranges of mountains disappearing into the distance, which is Portuguese East Territory. Luckily Canon Adams was in good form, but I was terrified he'd collapse. I offered to drive. If Leonard really was dizzy and weak we might have all gone over the edge!

'Next morning we left at 8.30 a.m. Leonard was better and drove the rest of the way here - a faster road and we got here by 12. We got a great welcome. The Doctor, James

Wright, his wife and two sons are on local leave and due soon to leave altogether. There are two male orderlies and 19 African girls training as nurses. The hospital is far more well-equipped than the Lusaka one, so different to the "Crimean" conditions in the Mapanza and Fiwila clinics. Even so, Ursula and Margaret mourn at the lack of perfection and hope to have it up to Westminster Hospital standards, I'm sure! It pains them when they can't afford to give people the right expensive drugs.

'All the services here are said in Nsenga, but we have Compline at 7 p.m for Europeans, taken by Mr. Jebbett. They produce attractive bricks here and the Chapel is built of stone, which is white with almost a crystal look. The Altar built of it looks almost like mother of pearl.

'I spent the morning with Rosamund Hatchwell. Her husband is a new District Officer. She has a lovely view from her house of hills close to her. Her in-laws own the Southgate Hotel in Winchester. You do realise out here how much the missionaries are up against not only the work, conditions and climate, but also each other! Luckily the feeling here is as perfect as possible. The fact that there are so few Europeans, even the best of them get on each other's nerves after three years together.'

Felicity wrote on 31st May to Hilaré from Lusaka: 'The day after to-morrow is the great Church sale. Last year they made £700. I can't think how they make so much money out here. Everyone works like beavers: it puts our London sales to shame! Poor John, you shouldn't have given him my long letters to read. I know he can only cope with Air letters. He called my Copperbelt one a book!

'I simply loved our visit to Livingstone. Prue and I were staying with Mr. and Mrs. Schonland from Pretoria, who had known Oliver there. They have two daughters, one of whom is married; the second Oliver admires and has started Ballet. She looks most attractive in photographs. The daughters were away but Mr. and Mrs. Schonland treated us as family and showed us the Falls from every angle. Mr. Schonland's brother is brilliant and is assistant director of Atomic Research at Harwell. We also had lunch at the Falls Hotel with Oliver, Rector Higgins and his wife. I was most impressed by the Falls after walking the length of them in the Rain Forest. We were drenched by the spray. At Danger Point, just above the Boiling Pot, when all this hurtling, thundering water pushes itself through the narrow gap, the spray falls down on you like a cloud burst. We were standing ankle-deep in rushing water - worse than any wave over us in *Foresight* [Hilaré and Bob's boat].

'I wish the Falls were still called the Smoke that Thunders. It describes them so exactly. In spite of continual work, Oliver is in very good form and was leaping about the garden just now, saying he wants to get the Deck Quoits fixed up on their now weeded tennis court as he'd love a game.'

John received a letter from Prudence, dated 4th June, in reply to his: 'Yes, Oliver knows Trevor Huddleston very well; they were at Oxford together and then they met in South Africa. He is Oliver's Commissary in place of Bishop Leeson.

'We are about to be very busy with Provincial Synod. That means eight representatives from each of the four Dioceses plus the four Bishops. They start arriving to-morrow. When you have a two day conference out here, it always entails entertaining people for a week, as those coming from the bush want to take the chance to shop; and others who travel by air or train have to wait for a connection! Felicity and I worked out the menus for the whole week, and then the kind and generous Crosses gave us a whole sheep, so we have to rearrange. I wish I had known earlier.'

On 9th June Prudence wrote to Hilaré: 'To-morrow we have great services, including one on the Cathedral site, when the Archbishop will preach. On Monday evening we go to a party given by the Mayor for the Synod and then on to dine at the Ridgeway Hotel with Harry Grenfell. Then on to the New Theatre for a special performance given by his sister-in-law,

211

Joyce Grenfell.

'The week touring round the Copperbelt with the Pagets [Archbishop] should be fun as no responsibility for me beyond looking after and introducing Rosemary Paget.'

Felicity wrote to John from Ndola on 24th June (8 p.m in the train): 'Prue and I are just going back to Lusaka from Chingola. We were driven the 60 miles to Ndola and should leave here in 15 minutes and reach Lusaka at 6.30 a.m. Oliver and the Archbishop and Mrs. Paget plus niece arrive by car from Chipili mission to-morrow afternoon.

'I've stayed ten days with the Pawles at Chingola while Prue toured the Copperbelt with the Archbishop. Kitwe was their base. When they came to Chingola I was taken by Nan and Roger Pawle to see Joyce Grenfell again. Oliver was taken by Donald Weston too and was in my row. Prue was taken by her host and hostess and was a few rows behind us! There was no room for us when the Pagets went to Chipili, so Prue and I went to Elizabethville in the Belgian Congo for a night with Nan Pawle. It is extraordinary how different the atmosphere is there. You might be in Belgium and it is totally different from Northern Rhodesia. They even have pavé on the roads in places, but most of the roads are poor compared to Northern Rhodesia. Donald Weston drove me over to Rees Phillips' wedding at 80 m.p.h. on the tarmac roads in the Copperbelt, a bit too fast as there is a speed limit!'

Here it is worth mentioning that Rees Phillips and Celia Hanford had a considerable problem in obtaining permission from their Bishop, and indeed the Bishops of the Province, to get married. As members of U.M.C.A. they had promised not to get married, among other promises such as leading a life of simplicity. Rees' additional problem was that, as Warden of the Seminary for training clergy (alongside Bishop's Lodge) it had just become a Seminary for the Province, so all the Bishops were concerned. There was no separate building for a Warden and a wife would need the extra cost of an allowance.

Oliver was told of the attachment in February 1954 and

was involved in much secret correspondence with the couple until it could be announced in June 1955. He showed his concern for their happiness, balanced against the strict rules of U.M.C.A. and his duty as the Diocesan. He was able to negotiate a happy outcome when Rees returned to Africa from leave as an employee of the Province and Celia had completed her turn as Sister Tutor at St. Francis Hospital, Katete and a replacement for her had been found.

Celia has written explaining that Oliver had known Rees at Oxford when he was a Librarian at Pusey House and, after the war, at Theological College. Oliver had invited Rees to go out to his Diocese as Warden of St. John's Seminary. Rees became ill and for a time was in Lusaka Hospital. Eventually May Smith, a nurse and wife of Canon Smith, suggested that he might have typhoid. He eventually arrived at St. Francis Hospital to convalesce. There he met Celia and in December 1953 they fell in love and Rees proposed marriage.

It was all kept secret and Oliver asked them in February 1954 to pray about the problem for two months and "if you believe God to be guiding you to marriage" to let him know by the end of April. Celia then wrote to Oliver, convinced that it was the will of God, and offered a small sum to help towards the cost of a Warden's House, and asked for no extra marriage allowance.

The secret was well maintained and, when she was in Lusaka as a Synod representative, she attended a social function. Mina Robertson, acting as hostess for the Bishop, introduced her to Father Phillips without realising their attachment. Celia then carried on a polite conversation with Rees. Eventually in June 1955, a year before they were married, the engagement could be announced.

Oliver married them in Luanshya from her sister, Monica's house and they honeymooned at Shiwa Ngandu, Sir Stewart Gore-Browne's palatial house and estate, before going

213

on to stay with the Gamwell sisters at Abercorn on their coffee farm. There she was to meet Prudence and Felicity before Felicity flew back to England.

Before leaving Lusaka Felicity wrote to Hilaré on 29th June: 'This will be my last letter to you from Lusaka! I'm full of very mixed feelings. It will be thrilling to see you again, but saying good-bye to Prue on 18th July will be horrible. I shall hate leaving Northern Rhodesia. We hope you will be the next to come out; how about next Spring? It will give Prue and Oliver something to look forward to. Prue and I have just got back from the airport, where we saw Oliver off to Livingstone for a missionary conference over this weekend - my last, what a shame!

'Prue, Oliver and I have been quite alone here this week for the first time since I arrived, which is lovely. Rees is on his five weeks' honeymoon, Edward Pitt is in Salisbury with his mother, and the Archbishop and Mrs. Paget with niece left on Tuesday.'

On 8th July Prudence and Felicity were due to fly to Abercorn to stay with the Gamwells, where they would also see the honeymoon couple before the couple left for Shiwa Ngandu. On 18th Felicity would fly home to England, leaving Prue to be joined by Oliver on 22nd. Felicity wrote: 'Then on 25th July they will start for Lusaka, staying at the famous Sir Stewart Gore-Brown's home that Prue is longing to see. The two clear days at Abercorn are Oliver's promised two week holiday this year!!! We have a busy week ahead, including a day with Elizabeth Hewitt and her children, who are taking us for a picnic lunch by the Kafue. She told us to-day they are moving to Ndola. The farm has been sold at last and Alan did not want to go on with the new owners. Otherwise, mostly teas, dinners and farewells. I must say they are a lot of nice friendly people out here.'

Oliver wrote to Felicity in London on 16th September:

214

'The Cathedral is much in our thoughts at the moment, for Friday was the Patronal Festival and last Monday we appointed the Architect. It is Richard Hope of Ndola. I hope he will do well. He is certainly very keen and is going back to England in November to study Church Architecture. It is rather remarkable that the choice, on good design, should fall on the Churchwarden of Ndola, who was recently elected President of the Institute of Architects in Northern Rhodesia.

'Amazingly fortunate we were with the weather and the peaceful year when you were with us. Just off to the Copperbelt and Chipili. The former seems quiet, but the show of strength by the Government should do good. They have declared a State of Emergency.'

Having just mentioned Rees Phillips, there was another priest in Northern Rhodesia called Ray Phillips, who adds his story below. It was two years ago in January that John, with his wife, Pip, attended a series of lunchtime talks in Winchester. Before the talk began he was approached by a Priest who recognised him as a brother of Oliver. Ray had arrived in Winchester to be Chaplain at St. Cross Hospital. The talks were given by the Rev. Colin Morris, the well-known Methodist speaker who had also been in Zambia for a number of years and was an admirer of Oliver and his ecumenical activities.

Ray remembers: 'Accepting an invitation to join the Rector of Kitwe, Fr. Donald Weston, as his assistant priest, meant acceptance by the Bishop. Bishop Oliver was in the UK at the right moment and I kept an appointment with him at the old U.M.C.A. Headquarters in Great Peter Street. It was quite easy even then to see the care and kindliness of the comparatively young Bishop which was to be my continuing experience of him over the years that followed. That first meeting was early in 1956.

'July of that year saw me aboard a Union Castle Line ship bound for Cape Town; and then the three-day journey by train to N. Rhodesia. At the lengthy stop in Lusaka, the Bishop

215

was there to greet me and commend me on my way with the promise of a visit to Kitwe in the near future to license me.

'Over the time of my first year of duty, the Bishop came on the normal pastoral visits and was always the most charming and easy of guests at the Rectory - a bachelor household - and the three of us were often invited out to meals. On one such visit, Prudence was also with us; an evening dinner-party went on a bit long, and Bishop Oliver was beginning to nod off! Prudence came to the rescue with a rather sharp sounding cough and the Bishop almost automatically jumped to his feet saying: "Well, we really must be going now. Thank you so much." And home we went!

'Father Donald Weston was made Archdeacon while I was with him in Kitwe. This was probably on the cards when he had been given permission to seek a curate. He became very close to the Bishop as friend and adviser. It was therefore very sad indeed for the whole Diocese when Father Weston died in an accident caused by his falling asleep at the wheel of his rather fast car on the last leg of a rather long journey. Bishop Oliver conducted the funeral service, of course, and was most moving in the words of the panegyric - he was using words which he had found from his own heart and which were of consolation to everyone present as well as himself. He immediately showed his care for me by sending Canon George Hewitt to Kitwe to help me and the Parish through some very sad days. My first leave followed within a few months and, in response to my own request, I was promised a move to a Mission Station. So to Chipili I went early in 1960.

'The staff on a Mission Station always enjoyed having visitors and not least, of course, in the person of the Bishop. He would come once or twice a year, and spent Christmas at one of the Stations. The pastoral visits were very busy with Confirmations at the Station itself or out in the villages. Using the Landrover on one such occasion, we literally came to a river we couldn't get across. The main supports of the bridge were still in place, but the wooden cross pieces had all been

216

borrowed for firewood! Nothing daunted, the Bishop took the initiative. He and I walked on to the next village and borrowed bicycles for the rest of the journey. The Confirmation took place as planned.

'On a rather longer journey by Landrover to a sub-station, Chibondo, all went well on the outward leg, but on the return the Landrover sank into mud and we were stuck. It was the same road we had used that morning. On the insistence of the Bishop we endeavoured to extricate ourselves. I was at the controls and engaged the four wheel drive while the Bishop pushed from the front, reversing out of mud sometimes doing the trick. However, with four wheels spinning in the mud, the Bishop was liberally sprayed from head to foot! I hastily attempted to wipe it off, but he calmly told me to leave it to dry when it would be easier to brush off. He looked a bit of a mess while a messenger went to summon help. We arrived back at Chipili tired and hungry some few hours later than expected.

'His visits were always highlights of the year and I soon got used to the Bishop disappearing as soon as he had arrived on the Station. He was to be found in the Church, no doubt commending himself in prayer for the task ahead, and in thanks for his safe arrival. The journey in those days included the crossing of the Congo Pedicle and the Luapula River.

'From time to time, of course, problems arose. The staff on a Mission Station did not choose themselves as colleagues. Thus there were differences of opinions and, dare I say, quarrels. Very sadly there were occasions when one of the African clergy went off the rails. At Chipili a young Englishman, commended to us by a priest on the Copperbelt as someone who would work for his keep, did indeed work well for some months. However, on one occasion when I trusted him with my rather large bundle of keys, he absconded with a rather large amount of money. He got well away and was never traced!

'These items are mentioned because Bishop Oliver was always very understanding and always backed up the Priest-

217

in-charge. Assurance of the Bishop's prayers was always gratefully accepted. He was truly a man of prayer.

'A very good friend of the Mission Station was Miss Phyllis Hall, whom I had known as a member of the congregation in Kitwe. She was an inspector of schools in what was then the African Education Department. Having been posted to Fort Roseberry (now Mansa) she, together with another Government worker, Miss Stella Penley, spent weekends with us at the Station when there was not to be a service in the town. Phyllis and I became engaged to be married and, after long leave in UK, were delighted to have Bishop Oliver, by then Archbishop of Central Africa, to marry us. The whole arranging of the marriage had been taken over by Canon Eaton, then Rector of Kitwe: thus it was that in Kitwe that we were married. The Bishop took great care and interest in us and in a short time was able to take very seriously the preparation for us to be married. It was a very special occasion with a Nuptial Mass followed by a Wedding Breakfast. Married clergy were not usually posted to Mission Stations-thus the vacant Parish of Broken Hill (now Kabwe) became our new work.

'The Bishop was always available for the pastoral concerns. He stayed with us frequently and was especially delighted to share with us in the Parish 50th Anniversary in 1968. Bishop Trevor Huddleston, then Bishop of Masasi, was our Guest of Honour during a week long celebration. A highlight of that Jubilee was the Ordination of two members of the local Church community as Deacons, Bishop Trevor preaching and Bishop Oliver ordaining.'

Early in December 1956 Oliver ordained Francis Msokosela as Priest at St. Peter's, Lusaka. There are a num ber of ordinations mentioned in his Anniversary Book, which will be found at Appendix C; while Institutions of Priests are listed at Appendix D.

1957

In February Oliver wrote to Felicity: 'I have recently been by air to the Copperbelt for the Institution of Father Sillett [as Rector of St. George's, Luanshya]. So far he seems to have made an excellent impression upon the parish and the mine. The Church was really crowded out with people from all over the Copperbelt. I like him very much indeed. One of his great friends is Peter Wyld; and we have plans to try to get him out here for Bancroft.'

When Oliver eventually approached Peter, he said he couldn't come because he had lost a foot in the Italian campaign. Peter tells us that Oliver promptly pointed out that the loss of a foot would be no problem, as he had been visited in Lusaka by someone with no legs. So Peter came out and was of great help to Oliver. Later, when Prudence was in a Nursing Home near Oxford, he used to visit her regularly from his nearby parish of Eaton. (Yes, he was an old Harrovian, but it was not spelt Eton!)

Oliver continued his letter to Felicity: 'Rachel Sillett seems to be first-rate and I hope she will become the school doctor for the whole Copperbelt. This afternoon we go to the airport to say good-bye to Harry Grenfell on his final return to England. We will miss him greatly.'

About this time Caroline Forester, the young daughter of great friends of Oliver and Prudence, now Mrs. Fisher, writes of Oliver's love of children:

'I remember Oliver very well with his fairish, neat hair, in his purple cassock, and his distinctive voice. He and Prue always seemed so full of fun.

'When my parents, plus Roz, my younger sister, had had lunch or tea with them, somehow Oliver ended up suggesting he should read Rosey and me a story. We nearly always wanted *Winnie the Pooh* and when Pooh goes visiting and gets stuck in a hole, it always ended in chaos as Oliver became incoherent and incapable of reading as he was laughing too much! So we of course laughed, but more I think because it was so funny seeing Oliver in hysterics. He was wonderful!

'Then, when at lunchtime we asked "What's for pudding?" Prue and Oliver always replied "You're having *wait and see."* It became quite a ritual whenever we ate with them.'

The Revd. Dr. Charles Elliott, now Dean of Trinity College, Cambridge, was in Northern Rhodesia. He was working at the University, so was not part of the Diocese and did not see much of Oliver. However, his wife has reminded him 'how excellent he was with the children - we had two under five. He always enjoyed playing with them. If he came to the house, he would be sure to bring some toys with him to entertain the children. This would be remarkable in any Bishop: it's particularly remarkable in a Bishop who had no children of his own and might be expected to feel uncomfortable with them.

'We also remember the extraordinary hospitality that Oliver and Prue practised to all and sundry with whom they came in contact. Although I did not work in the Diocese they invited us to eat with them and always with the children. That played a big part in making us feel welcome - in the country, in the Diocese and in Lusaka. We were always immensely grateful for the encouragement that Oliver gave us.'

11th July was a red letter day when Queen Elizabeth the Queen Mother laid the Foundation Stone of the Cathedral. It was a great day for the Diocese. Prudence described some of it in a letter: 'I was bang in the middle, so I could see the Queen Mother arrive at the High Court and walk up the red carpet. There were a few speeches and her reply before she unveiled the plaque. She was then presented with some scissors, which was Sir Peter Bell's idea, but we are not sure of the significance. She then looked anxiously around asking for something. Mummy would have approved as she wanted a penny (for luck)!!! There was then a mad dash by the public across to the Cathedral. Oliver had to be nippy to robe in the temporary High Court and be there to receive first the Bensons and then the Queen Mother. I had a brown ticket for the choir. It was a perfect day with a cool breeze. I was told that before I arrived the stone had crashed on the ground! Thank heavens it didn't break. Oliver's address was just right. The model of the Cathedral was on show and people are very pleased with it. The Queen Mother took ages going and talked to all Oliver introduced.'

John Houghton has also written about the Cathedral:

'A great milestone in Oliver's episcopate was the decision to build the Cathedral in Lusaka - a great undertaking brought to fruition in 1957 when Queen Elizabeth the Queen Mother laid the Foundation Stone on one of the two visits she paid to Zambia. The Cathedral of the Holy Cross in the years that followed, as well as being the Mother Church of Anglicans, became in many ways a national shrine, the centre for many great occasions of national significance. It was there that the great service was held when Zambia became independent on 24th October 1964. And every year since then the Independence Anniversary has similarly been observed.

'Oliver's relationship with President Kaunda was always warm. Twice the President came to address the Anglican Synod. Incidentally, it was in Oliver's time that Synodical Government of the Church was developed with Synods meeting regularly. Bishop May had convened one Synod in 1927. Bishop Taylor convened two in 1946 and 1949. But in Oliver's time they became regular occurrences every two years or so.'

John Houghton has also written two amusing stories which are appropriate at this moment:

THE QUEEN MOTHER AT THE LUSAKA LAW COURTS

OLIVER AND THE REV. JOHN HOUGHTON ESCORT THE QUEEN MOTHER
FOR THE LAYING OF THE CATHEDRAL FOUNDATION STONE

'When the Queen Mother laid the Foundation Stone of Holy Cross Cathedral in Lusaka in 1957 I was one of those who had the honour of being presented to her. So we presentees stood in a short line on the Cathedral site. Oliver stood at the Q.M.'s right side and, as we stepped forward, he introduced each of us to the Queen Mother. Immediately preceeding me was Canon George Hewitt. He had first come to N. Rhodesia as far back as 1916 and worked here till 1933. Then he returned to Lusaka in 1945 for a second tour of duty. Oliver introduced him to the Q.M. and I was fascinated to hear the little conversation which ensued. Said Canon Hewitt: "I used to be a neighbour of yours, Ma'am." "Really." said Her Majesty "Where was that?" And Canon Hewitt replied "Snibbleits." Or at least that is what it sounded like. Puzzling to us, but not to the Q.M. She clapped her hands with delight and said "Ah! yes, Snibbleits!" All was explained to us later. Many years ago before the Q.M. married her family home was in Hertfordshire. And just a mile or so away was the ancient church of St. Ippolyts where the young George Hewitt was the incumbent. So 'Snibbleits' really was a bond between them.

TOO MANY ARE WONDERFUL

'It was the same George Hewitt who made a speech at Synod. The subject under debate was a perennial one - the shortage of clergy. Speaking of his fellow clergy George Hewitt said: "One or two of our priests are young; a few of them are middle aged; and some of them are wonderful for their age." Then after a pause he added "And too many of our priests are wonderful." '

In September that year Richard Wood, as he still was at that time, paid a visit to Northern Rhodesia. He was later

Minister for Overseas Development and has written: 'I got to know Prue well when I went with a Parliamentary delegation (which included Jim Callaghan) to the then Northern Rhodesia soon after Oliver was enthroned. Members of the delegation were allowed the choice, on arrival in Lusaka, between visiting a Game Reserve and visiting one of Oliver's Missions. I longed (with the others) to see the animals, but loyalty to Oliver compelled me to a Missionary visit. Oliver called it a choice between the lions and the Christians and commended me on making the right decision!

'This was the first of several visits I paid to Zambia, as it soon became. Oliver, Prue and I made a number of expeditions together. On one of his visits to Yorkshire, I had reproved Oliver for despoiling the countryside with a banana skin. Outside Lusaka he cheerfully threw one over his shoulder. When I again complained he said in triumph: "Ah, that's the benefit of the white ants here."

'They did, however, have their disadvantages and Oliver used to emphasise to me the importance of an effective ant-course both in Bishop's Lodge and in the fine Cathedral he was then beginning to build.

'I am ashamed to remember another occasion when I reproved Oliver, this time for attacking a wasp that seemed to be doing him no harm as we lunched together in a little summerhouse. The next morning I was appalled by a report that Oliver had collapsed in the night, as the result of a sting from the wasp, which had been doing its best to defend itself but on this occasion with possibly disastrous consequences.

'Prue, apart from making Bishop's Lodge as pleasant to live in as anyone could have achieved, was an excellent organiser of picnics and, with the help of a sacking bag hung next to the engine fan as we drove along, made sure that we always had a supply of ice-cold water when we stopped.

224

Zambia, whenever I was there was always dry and dusty and generally extremely hot. On one very dusty drive to or from the Mission Station of Mufulira Oliver opened the letters just arrived from England. One ended with the sentence which delighted him and was later often exchanged between us: 'With all good wishes on life's dusty way.' '

While Richard was in Lusaka, Oliver dedicated an altar on the site of the Cathedral and asked Richard to preach at the service.

OLIVER RECOVERING FROM THE WASP STING ON HIS FOOT

1958

Canon Alfred Webster-Smith was very much involved with the building of the Cathedral and he has written describing how he was persuaded to return to Africa: 'I left the Masasi Diocese in 1951 fully intending to return after my furlough. Instead I was told that U.M.C.A. wanted a new Home Secretary, with recent African experience, to help prepare for the Centenary Celebrations which were on the horizon. So I stayed in England and served in this capacity. It enabled me to meet all the U.M.C.A. Bishops and so it was that I first met Bishop Oliver, who was in England at the time and who would come again in the Centenary year.

'At our first meeting he wasted no time in hoping that after the Centenary I might join his Diocese. He was patient with my constant refusals to say yes but, as I was to discover when I came to know him well, when faced with a problem he never gave up until it was solved!

'When he arrived at the beginning of the Centenary Celebrations, I remember him coming into my office with a wide grin on his face and, with the boyish enthusiasm which I was soon to find was characteristic of him, saying "Is it to be N.R. when all these celebrations are over?"

'So I was booked for the Copperbelt, but before I left these shores a letter came which cancelled the first plan and explained that I was to be Priest in charge of the little church of All Saints in Lusaka "One day" he said "There will be a Cathedral there." So to Lusaka I went with my family.

'It was not long before I realised that the enthusiasm was genuine and from first to last he followed each stage of the enterprise. No week ever passed without his meeting me on the site, often with the Architect or the Foreman, no other white faces! I remember well the day when the site had been levelled, he called the whole Committee (black and white) together and, after a prayer for God's blessing on the enterprise he turned the first sod.

'When at long last the time came for careful preparations to be made for the opening day, there were long discussions as to the names of invitees and such matters. In such meetings and indeed always, Oliver gave me the impression that he was conscious of the Guiding Hand of the Holy Spirit. I think it hardly an exaggeration to say that he never preached a sermon without making clear how conscious he was of God's guiding hand. Although my closest moments with him were concentrated on the Cathedral, I was conscious that I was fortunate in serving one who was guided in all he did and strengthened for service.

PRUDENCE AND OLIVER AT BISHOP'S LODGE

227

CHAPTER 21

TO LONDON FOR LAMBETH CONFERENCE 1958

Every ten years the Anglican Bishops from all over the world come to Lambeth Palace, on the South bank of the Thames for discussions. Lumley had been much involved in 1938 as Cosmo Lang's Chaplain. Now Oliver attended the conference in 1958 as a junior Bishop. He and Prudence arrived early by air in time to marry Ted Peel to his sister Felicity at St. Paul's Knightsbridge and also to join his brother and family for a few days holiday in Exmoor over Whitsun. They stayed at the *Ring of Bells* at 'chilly' Challacombe as he used to call the attractive hamlet. Sadly the Inn was burnt down soon after, no doubt when trying to be less chilly! He had a busy time before the conference and was able to see his nephew, Lisle Ryder, rowing in the Procession of Boats at the Eton 4th June Celebration, as he had done. He preached at Christchurch and Bournemouth, his father's old parish and preached the University sermon in the Magdalen Oxford Stone Pulpit, as his father had done.

The Lambeth Conference was opened on 3rd July with a service at Canterbury Cathedral. Between the meetings, he was able to go to Buckingham palace to be invested with the C.B.E. by the Duke of Edinburgh. Before he returned to his Diocese he had the honour of preaching in the presence of the Queen at the Royal Chapel in Windsor Great Park.

James Robertson has described the importance of the Conference to the Diocese:

'He thoroughly enjoyed his first Lambeth Conference in 1958. His sharing of these experiences wherever he travelled meant a great deal to those whose horizons were almost totally in Northern Rhodesia. Telling of their being required to stand up in Lambeth giving the name and diocese he relished his South African colleague who brought the House down with the statement: "I'm Savage from Zululand."

Canon Robertson has also paid tribute to the hospitality given at Bishop's Lodge:

'His own home at Kabulonga in Lusaka, with sister Prudence as his companion and hostess, was a haven for innumerable guests over the years. As a team providing hospitality they were biblical in their generosity. That piece of ministry by both is something which cannot be too greatly praised. I remember their merriment on receiving a telegram. It was at the time when the Belgian Congo was in turmoil and many Europeans fled to the south through N. Rhodesia. The telegram read something like 'Kenyans reaching Lusaka Sunday afternoon. Grateful for hospitality.' It took several minutes to decipher 'Kenyans' as 'Kenyons' that being the family of a priest from the central diocesan mission station at Fiwila.'

1959

During the following months there were many Churches dedicated, and Priests instituted, as listed in the appendices. In particular we should note from the Anniversary Book that Canon Webster-Smith was Instituted at All Saints Lusaka on 28th June. The same day Father Francis S.S.F. arrived so the Franciscans were again represented in the country. In August the Chapel of St. Francis of Assisi outside the East end of the cathedral under construction was blessed. The Chapel was given in memory of Lord Dulverton, a family friend, and Father Francis preached.

He had been sent out to Northern Rhodesia for three months to evaluate the prospects for work in Africa. In the History of the European Province of the Society of St. Francis titled *This Poor Sort,* it mentions that Francis was convinced that there was a role for S.S.F. brothers in this Diocese. So in 1962 he was allowed to return to work at Chipili mission station. Life was difficult in many ways, as Petà Dunstan explains in the History. The visits to the bush villages by bicycle could be dangerous, with rivers to be crossed by canoe or log bridges. Francis' dog was killed and eaten by a crocodile.

While he was at Chipili Oliver visited him and stayed with him in his cottage. There were many snakes in the area. One night, while Oliver was writing late at night in his room 'a snake came in through a small hole. He made the Sign of the Cross in Blessing over it and it graciously retired!' A charming story told by Father Francis, who is now living at the Hermitage of St. Bernard in New South Wales. He also explains that the Fathers now call themselves Brothers.

We also read in the book that he had other problems at the Mission Station, where the life style was not in the humility that he expected. When he wanted to do some of the menial tasks himself, the Africans considered this as criticism of their work and were resentful. He was even accused of racial prejudice!

The feelings at that time between Africans and Europeans, with the build up to Independence, could be difficult. It is mentioned in *This Poor Sort* that Colin Morris a Methodist Minister on the Copperbelt had declared his support for Zambian independence and as a result a Methodist chapel had been damaged (we have already heard how John met Colin Morris, when he was speaking at Winchester recently).

At this time The Rev. John Gore (now a Canon in West Yorkshire) came out to Northern Rhodesia and recollects:

'My earliest recollection of Oliver was when I first arrived in Northern Rhodesia in April 1959. He had written to say that he would not be in Lusaka when I arrived, but that he would be on tour in the Southern Province. He wrote, however, that he would do his best to meet the train when it stopped at Mazabuka station. Sure enough, when the train came in, I saw a tall, slim man in khaki shirt and shorts - but with a pectoral cross and an amethyst ring - clearly the Bishop. He was very welcoming. It was my first encounter with the 'Church' in Central Africa.

'Oliver used to visit each of the Mission Districts once a year for an extended visit. He would stay for a few weeks touring, confirming, interviewing all his clergy. My memories of Oliver stem mostly from these visits, since I spent little time in Lusaka four hundred miles away.

'Earthy stories are always the best! There are, of course, no toilets in the villages. People just wander off to some quiet spot in the surrounding bush. Oliver was a man of fixed habits, and regularly at the appointed time after breakfast, he could be seen walking off with a determined air into the bush, with a toilet roll tucked under his arm. Often, however, he did not wander off far enough, and his hat could be seen appearing above the tall grass!

'On another occasion, setting off from a Mission Station after his visit, a house-boy came running after him, shouting that the Bishop had left his book behind. It was his toilet roll!

'Oliver was a man of prayer. Often out on tour, everything would be ready for the service - except for Oliver. He would be deep in prayer - and nothing would ever cut that short. The service would have to wait.

'He was also a man of great humility. One of my most terrifying experiences at that time, as a young priest, was to be asked to hear the Bishop's confession!

'The Priest in Charge of Msoro Mission Station, Cyril Mudford, could be difficult at times (he mellowed considerably in old age!) On one occasion, I overheard Oliver saying rather sharply to Cyril, "I am the Bishop, Cyril!"'

'Oliver loved being at the Mission station, and had a fund of good stories to tell at the dinner table. He also loved parties, and was particularly good at charades. I remember him bringing the house down on one occasion, acting the part of a certain Harley Street doctor the U.M.C.A. used to send missionaries on leave to see, a man of odd and sometimes alarming manner.

'Being out in the bush for a few weeks with Oliver was a lesson in how to live a disciplined, dedicated life, but still remain human. He could see the funny side of things, and was a good companion. I wish I could remember the many things that amused him and made him laugh, but I can't - it was all a long time ago. But he was always the Bishop, and he had a very high view of episcopacy.'

1960

In January Oliver met Harold Macmillan when he was visiting Lusaka and in April the Archbishop of York, Michael Ramsey, came out for the Double Jubilee celebrations. It was a busy year for visits as the Queen Mother was out to see the Kariba Dam in May and Lord Mountbatten was in Lusaka in October.

During the Queen Mother's visit she asked Oliver if she could attend a Communion Service in his tiny chapel in Bishop's Lodge. Prue wrote, 'We had never dreamt of her coming. Thank goodness I did not know beforehand, because I would have spent hours having the Chapel polished. She and her Lady-in-Waiting, Mrs. Mulholland, came creaming up the drive in the Rolls with standard flying and police escort. It was a glorious time of day, so fresh and sunny. We three were the congregation. At the end, when Oliver had left and we were still praying, I looked across to see if she was ready to rise and I saw her peeping at me. It seemed strange that she was looking at me for guidance.

'Coming out she remarked on how peaceful it had been. I still can't really take in that she has been to Bishop's Lodge, all these miles away from home! She is so enthusiastic about the Cathedral.' Prudence continued: 'The Standing Committee of Synod have discussed the Cathedral tenders and Mr. Mitchell is to be the contractor. He was Mayor last year and has a local firm, although he is South African. I was glad to hear that James Mwela likes and admires him, as I felt he might not be good on race relations.'

1961

The Rev. Kenneth Francis who is at present Vicar of St. John's Felixstowe has said that, when he was Sub-Warden of the Seminary he knew Oliver and Prudence well. He found Oliver to be very 'shockable.' He certainly was anxious to ensure decorum. When Kenneth was living in a bungalow in the grounds of Bishop's Lodge near the Seminary, his fiancée a teacher lived nearby. She was asked to help prepare lunch at the Seminary, when the Provincial Bishops were inspecting, with a view to having a combined project for Ordinands. The visiting Bishops disapproved of Judith lunching with Kenneth, while she was helping out. So Oliver had to request that a chaperone was present for appearance sake.

Kenneth was at Bishop's Lodge and nearby from 1961 onwards and has told us one or two of Oliver's stories. He mentions that Lumley in a forgetful moment, in old age, said for grace before lunch "Oh Lord open thou our lips."

'One of his favourite tales was that of a Noble Lord who wished to pass on his inheritance undiminished to his son. In the sixties it was possible to escape death duties if you made over your estate by deed of gift to your heirs and successors seven years before your death. A certain Noble Lord made over his estate to his elder son in this way, but

OLIVER WITH HAROLD MACMILLAN,
THE PRIME MINISTER, VISITING FROM LONDON

MICHAEL RAMSEY, ARCHBISHOP OF YORK,
VISITS LUSAKA FOR THE DOUBLE JUBILEE OF THE DIOCESE

unfortunately died suddenly two or three months before the required seven years was up. The family met in hurried conclave to decide what to do and agreed, that since no one outside the family knew of the death, that they would put the body into that recently acquired, modern gadget called 'the freezer,' until such time as seven years from the deed of gift had elapsed. So they put his Lordship's body in a plastic bag and put it in the freezer. Two or three months later, when seven years since the date on deed of gift had safely elapsed, they took the body out of the freezer, defrosted it and called a doctor. The doctor said that he was quite satisfied that his Lordship had died from natural causes, but regretted that since he had not seen his patient for two or three months, there would have to be an autopsy and a coroner's inquest. Two days later the doctor called again. "The Pathologist's report confirms my own conclusion," he said, "His Lordship suffered a massive coronary thrombosis. There is one puzzling feature in the case, however. The month is now January, but there were fresh strawberries in his Lordship's stomach." "Oh, the explanation of that is quite simple," hastily replied the elder son and heir. "You see, Doctor, we have one of those new modern gadgets called a deep freeze ..."

'Another one of Oliver's favourite stories concerned a confirmation visit of his to Msoro Mission in the Eastern Province of Zambia. He had to conduct Confirmation Services in at least four different Bantu dialects throughout the Diocese; in Chitonga at Mapanza, Chilala at Fiwila, Chibemba on the Copperbelt and Chinsenga in the Eastern Province, so never became entirely proficient in any of them. At Msoro Mission where he went for the Confirmation service in question the local Language is Chinsenga. At Msoro there were at that time two large boarding schools, one for boys and one for girls. Confirmation services, therefore, usually included several hundred young people at a time. In the rite of Confirmation used in U.M.C.A. Dioceses it was the custom for the Bishop to make the sign of the cross on the forehead of each candidate in oil. A little bread was, therefore, always put on the credence table so that the Bishop could cleanse his thumb and hand when he had finished confirming all the children. On this occasion, when he had confirmed all the candidates, Oliver said to the servers: "Letani mitanda." What he should have said was "Letani mtanda." The servers disappeared, and no bread arrived, so Oliver cleansed his hand as well as he could on the sleeve of his alb and continued the Eucharist. As the consecration bell was ringing, two servers staggered up the central aisle of Msoro Church carrying a thirty foot ladder. Mtanda means bread. Mitanda means a ladder. The Bishop has asked for a ladder, and if the Bishop demands a ladder, a ladder is what he must expect to get!'

Kenneth Francis also writes:

'In Chinika Church, Lusaka, one of the Churches of which I was Priest in Charge, a large community from the former Belgian Congo, now Zaire, suddenly started worshipping with us. They said they were 'Kimbangists.' They told us that they had looked round all the churches in Lusaka, and that the Anglican Church was the most like their own, so they wanted to be admitted to communion with us. This was a matter which I had to refer to Oliver as Bishop. A meeting was, therefore, arranged in our sitting-room at Chaplain's Cottage, which was just a hundred yards from Bishop's lodge, and Oliver duly arrived to meet the Kimbangist Delegation. The problem was that the Kimbangists all spoke a dialect from the Congo totally unintelligible to us. Their leaders also spoke a little Chinyanga, but Oliver did not speak Chinyanga. He hit on the happy idea of trying them out in French, realising that many Africans from the Congo had learned French from the Belgians before Independence. French worked. Oliver suddenly became a Monseigneur, a title that obviously delighted him! We managed to discover that the Kimbangists were an African sect who had defected from the Roman

Catholic Church in the Congo, following a leader, now dead, called Simon Kimbangu. It appeared that they were all basically orthodox, still utterly opposed to rejoining the Roman Church, but desirous of becoming Anglicans. Oliver accepted the fact that they had all been baptised, but was only concerned that they should be confirmed by a Bishop before being admitted to Communion. "Vous etiez confirmé d'un Evêque?" "Oui de vous même, Monseigneur," replied the leader of the Kimbangists. "By me!" replied Oliver in his best French, totally astounded, "How did you come to be confirmed by me?" "I was working at Mapanza Mission," he replied: "You came there for a confirmation, so I came forward and you confirmed me." "Quelle surprise!" said Oliver, but after such an admission there was no way that he could refuse to receive the Kimbangists into the Communion of the Anglican Church. The following Sunday he came down to Chinika Church and received about forty Kimbangists en bloc.'

The only items of interest in the Anniversary Book at the end of this year are that Donald Arden was consecrated Bishop in the Church of the Ascension Likwenu, Nyasaland (now Malawi). There is also a strange note '17th December: Message from Michael Cantuar received at Ndola.' Could this be about the coming election of a new Archbishop for Central Africa?

1962

This was an important year for Oliver. First of all he wrote to his brother in strict confidence 'When I wrote to Mrs. Eric Hamilton to sympathise with her over the death of her husband the Dean of Windsor, I was greatly touched to hear in her reply that Bishop Hamilton had wished me to be his successor as he was due to retire this year.' This was not to be as he was 'Needed in Africa.' He ended his letter 'I am happy to have been even thought of for such an interesting and historic place!'

Then Oliver was elected Archbishop of Central Africa, by the Bishops of the Province, while still remaining Bishop of Northern Rhodesia. He was installed as Archbishop in Salisbury Cathedral, Southern Rhodesia on 29th July.

Finally the great day for the Cathedral was on 14th September, when the first Service was held and Alfred Webster-Smith was installed as Dean. There followed the first Provincial Synod in Lusaka a week later. The first confirmation in the Cathedral was in November before Oliver flew home for a short visit. This included a visit to St. Flannan Cathedral in Ireland and the honour of a lunch at Clarence House with the Queen Mother.

The whole family were able to be together over Christmas in London before Oliver confirmed Emma Wood his god daughter in All Saints, Kirby Underdale on 30th December.

We have already heard of the disappointment that Oliver was not an African, but there is another amusing story about Emma. One year, at the 4th of June Celebrations at Eton, John and 'Pip' were entertaining Richard and Diana for lunch at their home Heathfield in Sunninghill. Richard instructed Emma, who was arriving by train, to get out at Sunningdale station and ask a taxi driver to take her to Heathfield. This she did, and there was a party for the 4th June, in progress, but unfortunately it was at 'Sunningdale' and not 'Hill.' After half an hour of drinking wine, when, typically English, no one asked her who she was, she said "How is my Godfather Bishop Oliver?" It was only then that the penny dropped and she realised that she was at the wrong 4th June party. Richard and John were rung up and asked to rescue her from the neighbouring village.

OLIVER CROSSING THE RIVER ON THE WAY TO FIWILA

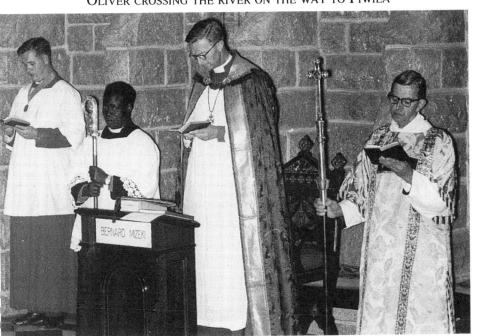

OLIVER ENTHRONED AS ARCHBISHOP OF CENTRAL AFRICA
IN SALISBURY (HARARE) CATHEDRAL

1963

David Whitfield was the Station Layman at Msoro Mission and now lives at Crackenthorpe in Cumbria. He has written of Oliver:

'Archbishop Oliver was the most approachable person that I've ever met. He was exactly the same with everyone, whether a Church dignitary or labourer. He seemed equally happy playing Scrabble with fellow clerics after dinner, to sitting on the ground having a tea break with a team of builders on a Mission Station. Bishop Oliver was so very much the right man for the job at the right time in the progress of the Church in Zambia - loving and being loved by everybody.

'With his sister Prudence he made a wonderful team and we looked forward to their visits to Msoro with pleasure, for apart from the spiritual help and their freely given friendship, Bishop Oliver was an absolute 'wow' playing Charades at Christmas time.

'I am sure you're aware that at times he was a little absent minded, hence when he borrowed Prudence's car (a Mini), because his own large one was being serviced, on his return home he forgot what he was driving and instead of driving into Prudence's smaller garage, he drove straight into the inspection pit of his own larger garage!

'Whilst conducting a Retreat at Lisomo, there was a silent lunch during which Bishop Oliver read to his captive audience (for their spiritual good) the most harrowing details of a medical operation, conducted under the most primitive conditions. If memory serves correctly, a few could not finish the meal and others collapsed with hysterical laughter!'

At the end of July Oliver flew to England on his way to New York and then on to Toronto. He was due to attend the Anglican Congress, which started with a Service on 13th August in the Maple Leaf Gardens. It was reported in *The*

Eagle in Lusaka that 'High-powered Conferences like the Anglican Congress are likely to resemble the love-life of elephants: nothing is done without a great amount of trumpeting: any achievement is at the highest level, and there is nothing to show for it for at least two years.'

The Archbishop of York referred to the interdependence of the Anglican Communion and that 'We have got a mutual responsibility for one another.' Then Oliver in his letter to the Diocese mentions the 'hope of help from new sources of prayer, men and money held out by the plans made in Canada.'

He also refers in his letter to the encouragement that can be found from the number of men he was due to ordain in the Cathedral on 8th December. There were to be eight Priests and four Deacons, who are listed in Appendix C. One Deacon was Clement H. Shaba, who is now Bishop of Central Zambia at Ndola and has lately written of Oliver:

'I first met Archbishop Oliver in the late fifties when he came to visit our church St. Philips in Matero, Lusaka. He impressed me as a Holy Father. His right hand man then Canon John Houghton, became Priest in charge of what was then called South Midlands which is West of Lusaka where I happen to come from (Mumbwa). Canon Houghton influenced me to join the Seminary of St. John's in Lusaka in 1962. I went for my interviews with Archbishop Oliver at Bishop's Lodge driving a big Caltex petrol tanker. Oliver was surprised to see this Big Tanker at his place. He laughed and took me into his office. He accepted me to join the Seminary. He was a man of prayer, so he prayed for me.

'I joined the Seminary on 27th January, 1962. Archbishop Oliver was a simple tall loved Father. Every end of the term, he called each of his candidates to his office at Bishop's Lodge to chat, encourage and pray for. In his office there was a bed and he used to sleep there. As the Seminary was very close to Bishop's Lodge, we used to see Oliver in the early morning before six saying his prayers walking around Bishop's Lodge with a prayer book in his hands.

'Oliver was a caring, loving Father. Without the love of Oliver, I do not think that I could have taken the church Ministry. Oliver ordained me and three others - Julius, Cuthbert and David as Deacons in 1963. After ordaining me to the Priesthood in 1965, he sent me to Luanshya as an assistant Priest. I thought this was a favour to me as all my other three friends were sent to the rural Mission Stations.

'I told Oliver of my problems with the Education of my children and he kindly paid for their fees so did Father Michael Wilson who was one of his best and kindest Priests. I worked under him in Luanshya.

'My wife became mentally sick while in Luanshya and good Oliver took all the care sending a Doctor from Lusaka to come and examine my wife. He did all he could and paid for the expenses. My children and I owe Oliver our lives for his Fatherly care. He appointed me Rural Dean of the Copperbelt when I was then in Mufulira.'

Prudence had been unable to fly out with Oliver, as she was due to have an operation, but she was able to join him by the end of November, so that she could help with the Diocesan Synod held in December. The ordinations took place at the end of the Synod, for all to take part.

On 22nd November he had noted with sadness the death of his Magdalen Tutor C.S. Lewis.

The Anglican Eagle of December also refers to a Mothers' Union meeting in the Eastern Province, which was addressed by Vera Hassall, who in 1953 described Oliver's travels in the Msoro area. She said 'men often accuse women of wanting the last word. Well perhaps they want it because they have something worth saying! This was certainly true of the Mother's Union meeting at Petauke after I had been speaking on the theme 'I am the light of the world.' 'Ye are the light of the world' a Mothers' Union member stood up to thank me for the visit adding "Our lamps will not go out." James Robertson has written of this period:

'In 1963 he released Archdeacon Kingsnorth to become General Secretary of U.M.C.A. and that move resulted in the fusion of S.P.G. and U.M.C.A. within U.S.P.G. in 1965. Oliver was to play his part in leading the diocese with its long tradition into accepting the fundamental changes of finance and planning that inevitably ensued. His own election as Archbishop of Central Africa in 1962 set the seal on the new maturity achieved within the Anglican Communion.

1964

At the end of March Father David S.S.F. the new Minister General of the Franciscans came out to visit Father Francis at Chipili mission. Together with Oliver they visited Fiwila Mission and were attracted by the work there among lepers, which is very much a Franciscan concern. Oliver hoped that eight men he knew might come forward to join S.S.F. at Fiwila, but it did not happen. However, Fathers Francis and Stephen with Brother Randall and a Tertiary Nurse Katherine Dolton who came out in 1965 moved to Fiwila. They had a primary school, a hospital and a Leprasorium to look after, Father Francis has written. There were three Catechists to train for the rural priesthood, which was continuing the valuable training of priests started at Chipili.

In April Prudence and Oliver were able to visit Jerusalem on their way to England for a brief visit. Then on 20th September he consecrated Filemon Mataka Bishop in the Cathedral. James Robertson has written:

'He had long been preparing for the division of the Diocese and to that end held many consultations about strategy. He eventually decided upon the prior step of appointing an indigenous priest as Suffragan Bishop and his choice was

243

Filemon Mataka who had been a priest for 20 years. His consecration took place just a month before Zambia became an independent nation in 1964.

On 4th October Oliver visited the Cathedral on Likoma Island in Nyasaland. On his return journey Bishop Donald Arden, who was later to take over as Archbishop, describes a slight hitch!

'One of my most vivid memories imprinted on my mind was soon after I came to Nyasaland (later Malawi) when Oliver was on a Visitation to the Diocese.

'We had been on Likoma Island and we were coming across to the mainland opposite in the middle of the western shore of the Lake, and we were on a thing called Betty Paul which was, in fact, a flat-bottomed Dutch canal barge. How on earth that ended up on Lake Malawi and how on earth anybody ever thought that a canal barge was a suitable vehicle to travel round Lake Malawi on I cannot imagine. But there she was; quite a sizeable boat, 40 or 50 feet long, and she was powered by a maize mill engine which Francis Bell, our most ingenious engineer had put in; I think during the war or at the end of the war, because it was impossible to get proper marine engines. So it was a maize mill engine, without a reverse gear. That was fine when you were going ahead; not so good when you had to go into reverse.

'The crew, of course, were very knowledgable about Betty Paul. They had been manoeuvring her all over the Lake for many years, but they hadn't actually been to this village for quite a number of years. There was a hitch-hiker, a Malawian on the boat who claimed to know the area well and said: "No, don't go in the usual way you go down by the river. Just turn straight in here - there's a gap in the sandbanks where you can go straight through." '

'We were about a mile off the coast, I suppose, and there's a long stretch of shallowish water with sandbanks parallel to the coast. So rather trustingly but a bit unbelievingly

244

we turned 94 points to starboard and headed straight for the coast. And about 100 - 200 yards out we struck the sandbank and stuck firmly in the middle of it. No chance of going out astern because we hadn't got a reverse gear. We tried to turn it, pushing the head round with oars and putting the engine full speed ahead, and so on. We got it more or less broadside on; she rocked like mad and then I think it buckled the propeller and twisted the rudder and goodness knows what, and there we were, a complete wreck, 100 yards from shore, a fairly brisk breeze blowing, not huge waves, but plenty of splash about - with a spare Archbishop on board and having to get him ashore. Nothing daunted, the Church Elders from the village stripped off everything, waded out and carried him ashore shoulder high, borne by six or eight nude Church Elders. It was a wonderful picture.

'I have the clearest memory of him as a person, and his humour and his fun; an extraordinary mixture of Franciscanism and English aristocracy mixed up together. He was a wonderful guest and a wonderful host. He spent occasional days in our house for Provincial Meetings; much more as a guest in his house when I went there to Lusaka.'

The Celebrations for the Independence of Northern Rhodesia took place on 24th October and the country became Zambia. Plans had already been made for the Diocese to change its name as well.

CHAPTER 22

ZAMBIA 1964

Canon John Weller is now in retirement in Birmingham. As Warden of St. John's Seminary next to Bishop's Lodge he saw a great deal of Oliver. He remembers:

'I moved to Lusaka with my family in April, 1964 and soon discovered how fortunate we were to have the Green-Wilikinsons as our neighbours. This was the year of Zambia's Independence, one consequence of which was that the Diocese which covered the whole country also changed its name. The brief signature + O.N.R. became the even briefer + O.Z., and the Archbishop was much amused to find himself sharing a name with a wizard.

'Even without the additional burden of being in charge of a Province which was deeply divided politically, the Archbishop's task as father-in-God of a Diocese roughly the size and shape of France and Spain together was an extremely demanding one. The Mission Stations were widely separated, and each in a different language area. Although there were now roads linking them, the Bishop was necessarily, like St. Paul, in journeyings oft. It was a matter of great satisfaction for him that the decision was made to divide the Diocese into three. Another major problem was that Zambia's Independence was soon followed by Rhodesia's unilateral declaration, which caused enormous tensions in the Diocese as well as in the Province. We were very fortunate to be led by an effective reconciler whose gentle nature enabled him to retain the confidence of people of different races.

'The Archbishop still found time to give help and guidance to the Seminary. He celebrated communion each week when he was in residence. When the continued existence

246

of the Seminary as a Provincial institution was threatened because Zimbabwean students could no longer obtain travel documents acceptable outside their country as a result of U.D.I, the Archbishop, Bishop Mataka and I went to see the Minister for Home Affairs and we were able to secure special arrangements.'

The Diocese of Matabeleland in Southern Rhodesia (Zimbabwe) was part of Oliver's Province. Kenneth Skelton was its Bishop at that time. He now lives in Sheffield and has written:

'I have been re-reading the Address I gave at Oliver's Memorial service in Westminster Abbey. It made me feel afresh the great affection I had for him. He was very appreciative of the gifts of his Suffragan Bishop, Filemon Mataka, the first African to be a Bishop in the Province. He also delighted in his eccentricities, like sucking on an empty pipe which he never smoked. There was always much innocent hilarity in their relationship.'

1965

James Robertson has written:

'Early in 1965 I had to tell Oliver of my intention to leave the Diocese on completing twenty years of service there. That June we said farewell, but met again in 1968 when he came to the Lambeth Conference.'

At the beginning of January Oliver had married Ray Phillips and Phyllis Hall; at the end of that month there was a Memorial Service for Sir Winston Churchill in the Cathedral. A second African, Josiah Mtekateka, was consecrated Bishop in May in Likoma Cathedral, Nyasaland (Malawi).

Rodney Hunter came as sub-Warden to the Seminary

at this time. He is still training priests, but now in rural surroundings, in Malawi and has written:

'I lived at Bishop's Lodge from 1965 until his death. Nearly every memory of Oliver includes Prudence. She was able to bring him out. Without her he might have been rather reserved. They were the most hospitable pair that could be imagined. Oliver was addicted to a certain genre of humourous books, which he delighted to share with his guests. Great mirth was derived from *the Good Loo Guide; Where to go in London* and even *Harold Wilson Bunkside Book*. He would read extracts to the assembled company and show round the pictures. 'He was an enthusiastic devotee of the newly independent Zambia. I think he was too optimistic with regard to the prospect of the immediate future. '

In August Haile Selassie of Ethiopia worshipped in the Cathedral. Two months later Oliver was able to bless the new Franciscan House at Fiwila. He was lunching at State House with the President and Sir Robert Tredgold when he first heard the news of the Unilateral Declaration of Independence (U.D.I) by Rhodesia.

1966

After the marriage of Cyril Mudford and Marjorie Bristow, Oliver left with Prudence for a longer visit to Palestine. They saw the Sea of Galilee and Mount Tabor and visited Nazareth before flying to Amman. Oliver then flew to New York and preached early in May in St. Paul's Cathedral, Detroit. He also addressed the Convention of New York District on 10th May. Before flying to Alaska for Whitsunday he went to the Harrisburg Convention in Williams Port. On 5th June he flew a Beechcraft plane on the way from Yakima.

248

to Pasco before confirming in St. Peter's church, Pomeroy, Washington.

On his way back to Zambia he was able to see Sir Harold Wolson, the Prime Minister, to discuss the situation in Africa. He then preached in Coventry Cathedral and St. Albans Abbey at their annual festival. These are some of his words: 'May I give you the text St. Luke 21, verse 26. "And when these things begin to come to pass, then look up and lift up your heads, for your redemption is drawing near."

'I live in a part of the world where the signs of which Jesus spoke are seen in abundance. There is much distress of nations with perplexity with men's hearts failing them for fear. In Central Africa we differ deeply in our beliefs as well as in the colour of our skins. Differences soon lead human nature into fear and fear leads to hatred. On both sides in Africa and in this country there is a regrettable tendency to maintain that one side is all good and the other is all bad. As Christians we are surely called to remember that all men are sinful and that we must be ready to forgive others. This will not solve our problems, but it will enable us to approach them in the right spirit.

'We must seek for God's will for Rhodesia and Central Africa, confident that He has a purpose for us now and in the future. I believe that the Europeans in Rhodesia were, and still are, deserving of special treatment compared to Europeans in other states in which African majority rule has been established. A high proportion of these people are farmers, committed to the land, many in the second or third generation of Rhodesia. They number about 250,000, four times as many as in my own country of Zambia, and have over many years maintained very good race relations in their country. Unfortunately, in November last a step was taken which was in my belief both morally wrong and politically unwise. The

Unilateral Declaration of Independence was a deliberate attempt to stop with force the growth of the African majority of well over three million people in attaining further political and social responsibilities in their country.

'What are we to do about this within the Body of Jesus Christ, the Church? First let me tell you what we have done by God's help last January. Our Province of Central Africa consists of four Dioceses, my own Zambia and the neighbouring Malawi, both situated in independent African states; Mashonaland covering Salisbury and the East of Rhodesia; Matabeleland covering Bulawayo, the West of Rhodesia and the state of Bechuanaland, soon to be free. We are almost the only free meeting place between these neighbours who differ so sharply in politics. Do please pray that we may continue to maintain a fruitful Christian fellowship, so that spiritual blood may continue to course through the limbs of Christ's Body. We can only do this in the power of God's love.'

At this time Oliver had his own personal worries. On Independence Day the previous October he had written to his brother:

'The trouble in Prudence's right hand is the first sign of Parkinson's Disease. We must be thankful that it is diagnosed. Prudence has taken this news wonderfully. It must be a horrible shock for her, but she carries on with all her gaiety and resolution. I am sure she is relieved that a diagnosis has been made.'

On 27th November Patrick Appleford was installed as Dean of the Cathedral to replace Alfred Webster-Smith who left Africa for family reasons. John Klyberg, later Bishop of Fulham, wrote at the 25th Anniversary of the Cathedral: 'I was at Fort Jameson (now Chipata) from 1963 - 1967. Oliver was one of my heroes. The Cathedral (of which Alfred Webster-Smith was the first Dean) is in these days the jewel in the crown of the Anglican Church in Zambia. It could never have been built without Oliver's vision and determination.' From 1977 - 1985 John Klyberg was the Dean and recently wrote of Oliver: 'He was about the most delightful person I have ever met. He thought well of people in a way that made us behave better than we would have done otherwise. I pray for him weekly and will never forget him.'

1967

Little is recorded in the Anniversary Book for this year. Oliver celebrated his birthday on 7th May in the Cathedral at the Diocesan Synod; and there was some mild trouble with the Government, possibly caused by a sermon preached by the Roman Catholic Archbishop Emmanuel Milingo at an ecumenical service in the Cathedral, when he attacked the Government's policy from an Anglican pulpit. In September the Cathedral received a Cross of Nails, the gift of Coventry Cathedral which Oliver had visited the year before. Four Priests were ordained in December. One of them was Francis Makambwe, recently installed as Vicar of St. Catherine's at Hatcham in South-East London.

1968

After having an operation to his foot in February Oliver returned to England in June for the Lambeth Conference, this time as an Archbishop. At the end of that month, on St. Peter's Day, he consecrated Paul Burrough Bishop of Mashonaland in Birmingham Cathedral. Paul has recently written:
'The Province was so large that we only occasionally met while I was one of his Bishops. He had telephoned me

LUSAKA CATHEDRAL STANDING ON THE RIDGEWAY ABOVE LUSAKA

OLIVER VISITS POPE PAUL VI,
ON HIS WAY BACK FROM THE LAMBETH CONFERENCE

from Salisbury (now Harare) in April to say that the committee of 21 Bishops, Priests and laity had chosen my name. After nine years in Birmingham it seemed the right time for a move. I said "Yes." I asked my Bess to put a kettle on for tea, saying that we were going to Salisbury. She said she liked the South of England and I explained that it was more south than that!

'In Africa Oliver and I were at some difference about the gift of money to Mugabe, which would end up in the purchase of arms. While opposed to the U.D.I. of Ian Smith I believed that armed infiltration of the country would be tragic and, in fact, it cost 30,000 lives by 1979.'

Paul was a rowing Blue at Oxford and was captured by the Japanese during the war. When peace came he was able to inform his captors that the war had ended. He was the better informed, thanks to a secret radio!

Another Bishop, Dr. Thomas Butler, Bishop of Leicester has written about that year, 1968:

'I went then as a young Priest to the Diocese of Zambia. I lectured in electronics at the University and laid the foundations of an Anglican chaplaincy. Oliver was an example of the very best sort of English public servant whilst being totally committed to the new nation of Zambia. One of his great desires was for the Cathedral to be thoroughly used by the Zambian people, but it remained stubbornly ex-patriot. Perhaps the local Zambians felt rather uncomfortable in its rather grand atmosphere. When his tragic death occurred in a car accident in the Eastern Province, his body was brought back to the Cathedral and was placed there overnight before the funeral service the following day, as was the Zambian custom. When I went to the Cathedral late at night I discovered it was full of Zambian people with their families. They had moved to be with their beloved Archbishop and I like to think that from that day on the Cathedral belonged thoroughly to

Zambia.'

While in England during the Lambeth Conference in 1968, Oliver visited the Prime Minister, Harold Wilson, with Kenneth Kaunda to discuss the situation in Africa. The Lambeth Conference began at Canterbury on 25th July and ended at St. Paul's Cathedral on 25th August. On his way back to Zambia Oliver had an audience at the Vatican with Pope Paul VI.

On a visit to John at Sunninghill before he left England he spoke to the Ascot District Christian Council on the subject of Ecumenism in Zambia. The guardian of the Franciscan Friary reported that 'between 80 and 100 people came. He was pleased by an evening in which he found everyone accepting one another.'

John Houghton explains in his book *Borrowed Time Extended* that the new United Church of Zambia (U.C.Z), formed in 1965, considered further union with the Anglican Church but 'recoiled from the prospect of yet more discussions so soon for yet another Union. It was also felt that the Europeans were leading the request for union and that nothing should happen until the Zambian grass roots of both Churches considered the matter once more a matter of urgency.'

1969

The division of the Diocese was announced in April. Oliver explained in the Diocesan leaflet that the other three Dioceses of the Province had similar plans. It would allow for more intimate fellowship in the vast areas and the election of Africans as Bishops would be likely at that time. To start with, two Dioceses were suggested in Zambia, but later it was changed to three. The birth of the new Dioceses was due in

January 1971.

Oliver reported in the leaflet that his niece, Penelope, would be visiting him in August during her first summer vacation from Kent University. At the end of July he told John that 'he had an excellent new secretary - she comes from Sunninghill!' Penelope had arrived. Not long before this he had heard the sad news that his elder sister, Deborah, had died. Much as he had tried, they had not been close friends.

CHAPTER 23

PENELOPE'S VISIT

Penelope's first letter to John and Pip ended: 'Life is all go here. The house is never empty and you never know who will turn up next.'

Oliver's report on 20th July was very cheerful: ' It is wonderful having Penelope with us - a real tonic in these difficult days. She is full of life and has already impressed so many people, European and African. Her views on race seem to be very sound. On 22nd we are due to go to the Northern Province for ten days of semi-holiday.'

Penelope wrote to her parents after they had left Lusaka: 'Luckily it is not very exhausting for Oliver as there are very few Anglicans up here. We spent one night at Serenje and the next at Kasama with the Matron of the hospital. While we were there the Roman Catholic Archbishop showed us round his new Cathedral. Mbala is quite a nice place, only twenty miles from the end of Lake Tanganyika. To-day Prue, Oliver and I went to see the highest waterfall in Africa, the Kalambo Falls (600 feet). It was lovely up there and we spent a lot of time watching Maribou Storks gliding round us. They are enormous - five feet - and very ugly except when in flight.

'The emptiness of the country comes over even more when travelling 600 miles by car. A lot of the road is now tarred, but the earth ones are good enough to maintain a steady 50 mph. All one can see on each side is bush and occasional gardens and mud huts.'

On 2nd August she wrote: 'We spent Sunday night at Kasama and then went to Shiwa Ngandu for three days. It is the stately home of Zambia, built in the 1920s and now inhabited by the daughter of the man who built it, and her

256

family. Although the house is not really very old it had the atmosphere of the 16th Century. In style it looks fairly Italian and has a lovely view over a lake. One morning a dead leopard was brought in. It had been shot in a trap. Apart from that I have not seen much game, except for a few monkeys.

'One day was spent at a cottage about 15 miles from the house, where there is a hot spring in which we bathed. Our last stop of one night was with Sir John Moffat who was Prime Minister for a time. We got back yesterday, having called at Fiwila on the way. It was interesting to see my first Mission and I must say all the Nuns and Brothers are incredibly nice.

'Next weekend there is the Lusaka Show. The Shiwa people have enrolled me to drag cattle round the ring and, as they usually win, it might be amusing.'

Penelope later reported that 'I only led a cow in the Grand Parade, which meant I had to stand in the ring for an hour while the Show was opened by Prince Dhlamini of Swaziland who made a speech for half an hour.'

'A very nice girl called Mercy, training to be a nurse in Kitwe, came to tea. For a Zambian woman she is very talkative and self-confident. The Friday before last Mrs. Smith, wife of Canon Smith, an old-timer here, died very suddenly. Prue and I had been to tea the day before. The funeral was on Monday morning.

'Prue and I set off that afternoon for Livingstone. We saw the Falls, magnificent with a rainbow that was nearly a full circle. On Wednesday we drove to the Chobe River Hotel in Botswana, crossing the Zambesi on an ancient ferry. The Hotel organised trips up the river and game-viewing in an open Landrover. There were beautiful birds on the river as well as hippos and crocs. The game trip was exciting as the man tried to frighten us as much as possible. We left Chobe on Friday and joined Oliver at Choma. Oliver and I then set off for Kitwe where there is a youth camp. I am meant to be teaching them English games.'

At the end of August Penelope reported to her parents that 'my plans for going to Dar-es-Salaam with Alan Mackintosh, a medical student, have now been abandoned. Oliver objected very strongly although he said he wouldn't stop me if you didn't mind me going. He obviously thought it would cause a scandal and reflect very adversely on what he believed. There is a Cathedral Fête on Saturday.' Penelope continued. 'I had hoped to go to St. Francis Hospital at Katete before going to Rhodesia but I don't think anyone can give me a lift out there.'

A few days later Oliver wrote again: 'We are enjoying tremendously having Penelope with us. She really does take a most intelligent and refreshing interest in everything and has been a real help over typing. I much enjoyed our weekend together when we went to Mindolo on the Copperbelt for a Youth Conference. Penelope was most brave and successful in teaching them games.

'We have recently been through a time of political turmoil' he added, 'but it really does look as if Dr. Kaunda has recovered his hold on the helm.'

Penelope resumed her letters on 6th September from Rhodesia: 'Prue and I are staying with a very nice friend of hers in Salisbury while Oliver is at Provincial Synod. Salisbury is a beautiful town, very English with gorgeous gardens. To-day we went to Bernard Mzeki College where Synod is being held. We saw the shrine, erected in honour of a catechist who was martyred there in 1896. The country is very beautiful at the moment as the new leaves are coming out. They are orange and brown, as the autumn in England. Rhodesia looks totally different to Zambia as everything is much more cultivated with farms all along the road instead of the open bush.

'With regard to the politics, it is very easy to criticise everything on emotional grounds, but it doesn't get you anywhere. It merely leaves one feeling hopeless and claustrophobic. Even people who don't support Smith are not prepared to plunge straight into majority rule for the Africans. Smith certainly seems to be aiming for segregation when he won't even allow black and white children to meet together for sports and competitions!'

Penelope returned to continue her studies in England. On Christmas Day Oliver broadcast a Christmas message. After speaking first of how we can seek and serve Jesus, he continued:

'We are also to seek Him in the common man - to seek Jesus in all those who are in need; for He has told us that if we do give help to the least of these, His brothers, we are helping Him, Himself. So at this time let us pray "Come to our hearts, Lord Jesus." Let us seek to welcome Him as His Holy Spirit comes to take possession of our lives. Let us seek to welcome Him in all who are in any need; the old and the sick. As we do this a joy will come into our lives, which will remain with us today and in all the days and years to come.'

1970

The Anglican Archbishops in Africa met in Lusaka on 14th February, and then at the end of April the Cathedral of the Holy Cross was Dedicated. Its building was complete and the necessary money had been raised. The 11th Diocesan Synod (the last before the Diocese was divided) was opened at the service of Dedication. After welcoming clergy and laity, as well as observers from the Roman Catholic Church and the United Church of Zambia, together with Ian Reeler, the partner of the architect, Dick Hope, who could not be there, Oliver spoke of the Christian response to the the challenge of communism and atheistic materialism.

He spoke of the present political challenge to Christian

259

faith and of the closer relations between Christians who worshipped God in different ways. He reported with joy the world wide connections which had been established with the Episcopal Church in the United States, the Church in Australia and the Sudan.

During his visit to England for the Lambeth Conference the year before, Oliver had given much thought how best to respond to President Kaunda's plea for the development of rural areas.

He had met in Ludlow Peter Bugg, a Priest with agricultural skills. He and his family came to Zambia in June 1967 and worked at Mpongwe Farmer Training Centre, 200 miles north of Lusaka. A few weeks before Oliver's death they stayed at Bishop's Lodge. He remembers well breakfast with Oliver when he treated the children as grown ups. Then on 9th August Peter Bugg and the family waved him off to his last visit to the Eastern Province.

Prudence had earlier returned to England to see a specialist and Oliver wrote to John on 2nd August, anxiously awaiting news of the effects of her drug, L. Dopa, and whether she would be allowed to return to Zambia.

Meanwhile, plans were being laid for the division of the Diocese into three parts; Northern Zambia would be the huge Luapola and Northern Province; Central Zambia based on Ndola; and Lusaka Diocese covering the South and Eastern Provinces with Filemon Mataka as its first Bishop. Oliver would take the central Diocese and a senior Priest humorously suggested that Oliver in future might sign himself Oliver Zamtan Railway [from Zambia to Tanzania]. Having made these plans, Oliver set out on a tour of the Eastern province to say farewell. After a farewell Mass and a walk to the river Luangwa at Chilingosi, he dedicated St. Andrew's Church at Chinkwamba.

CHAPTER 24

THE FATAL ACCIDENT

John Gore has described Oliver's last visit:
'The Eastern province was to be part of the new Diocese of Lusaka. Everywhere he went he was showered with gifts. After two weeks travelling with him, I said good-bye to him as he left St. Francis Hospital on his way back to Lusaka on 26th August. I was not at the hospital when he was brought back after the accident, but I returned to Katete as soon as the news reached Msoro and was there when his body was flown back to Lusaka. A Hercules of the Zambian Airforce came to the small airfield at Katete. Oliver's simple coffin was lifted into it and carried off to Lusaka. At the hospital I saw again the gifts that Oliver had been given by the folk in the villages. Later, I was immensely proud to be one of the coffin-bearers at the funeral in the Cathedral.

'I was back in Zambia in 1995, staying at St. Francis Hospital. I said a prayer at Oliver's memorial in St. Francis Chapel there, which Father George Hewitt had put into the floor in front of the Altar. It reads, in Chichewa,
ANALI MUNTU WABWINO
'HE WAS A GOOD MAN.'
'He was indeed. In another age he would have been a saint. He had a great influence on me and on so many others. May he rest in peace and rise in glory.'

John Houghton has described the car accident, which took place at Kawele, near Petauke, on the Great East Road:
'Taking Oliver back the 400 miles from Katete to Lusaka was a very steady African driver who had safely driven him on countless journeys. As his custom was, Oliver reached for his brief case, intending to work on papers he had brought with him. As he reached for his seat belt a tyre burst. Oliver

was flung out, hitting his head on a tree. They were only a few miles from Katete, so he was taken back to St. Francis Hospital and there he died.' The hospital was by then in the charge of his friend Dr. James Cairns and his wife Faith.

The family were later told that his injuries were such that he could not have carried on his work; so he was mercifully spared life as an invalid. Prudence would certainly have been with him in the car, if she had not been in England.

The shock caused by his death was also described by Bishop Shaba, who writes:

'When the news reached us on the Copperbelt, I fainted and fell down in Father Bakare's house at Mindola. I thought it was not possible for such a holy man to die like that. Oliver was a living Saint. He and his sister, Prudence, were symbols of love from God. That was Oliver, white in colour but true Zambian, loved and admired by all.'

Ray Philips was in England by then, and when he and Phyllis heard news of the accident, they were overcome by the loss. Ray adds 'it was truly a family feeling and one that I know we shared with Central Africa and all who knew him'. John Houghton has written in praise of Oliver and all he achieved in Zambia, and thought him 'much more than a great leader of the Anglican Church there - he was also prominent in the affairs of the nation. On a personal note' he added 'he was not only my Father-in-God but also a friend. I loved both his sense of fun and his sense of humour - the two are not necessarily the same. Above all I admired his gifts of wise leadership and sound judgement.'

Richard Holderness wrote of his last visit to Zambia 'when Diana came with me and relations between Zambia and Britain were obviously at a low. Oliver thought that K.K, as he generally referred in a friendly way to Kaunda, who greatly respected him, might not then have welcomed a Conservative British Minister (as I was at the time) on over-

262

friendly terms with his Bishop. So Oliver advised that it would be wiser for us to stay with the High Commissioner, Laurie Pumphrey, and his wife. We knew them well and were very fond of them. Sad though we were not to stay with Oliver and Prue, we were probably housed in greater luxury in the High Commission! We saw much of both Oliver and Prue on that visit, but this was the last chance we had to spend time with them. On board Bob and Hilaré's boat south of Norway in August, a telegram was sent to me to give them the news of Oliver's death in the road accident.

'I have often wondered' Richard added 'whether Oliver would have been happy to retire to England when the time came for him to leave Africa; and what work there would have interested him. None of us can know and perhaps about some things it is very foolish to try to guess.'

Prudence, on the point of flying out when she heard the news, was accompanied to Lusaka by John. Hilaré was still off Norway in their boat, which she could not leave Bob to bring home alone. Her son, Lisle, however, flew out in time for the funeral and was able to stay longer than John to help Prudence tidy up. Her diary records those late August days:

Aug. 24th Waiting to hear from Prof. Gillingham ref flying 29th, [would he allow her to return to Africa?]

Aug. 25th Hear from Prof G - can go [as] new drug in 6 months.

Aug. 26th Tea under apple trees. Treat five Green-Wilkinsons at Forresters. [She was staying with John and family at Sunninghill.]

Aug. 27th Tel. call at 9.30 a.m from Barlow saying O. died car smash Petauke [1.20 p.m 26th]; Joram O.K, Henry broken leg.

Aug. 28th Mass 9.30 All Saints, Ascot [Lumley's old parish. Freddie Lancaster, the Rector, kindly held a Requiem Mass for the family].

Aug. 29th J and I fly 8 - Robertsons see us off - bumpy. [Held up for three hours in Rome due to a storm].

Aug. 30th Barlow, Vera and Reg met us 12.45. Brother Desmond is staying. Hear how crash was caused by tyre burst.

Aug. 31st Lisle arrived 2.30. O's coffin brought to Cathedral 5.30. Many singing all night.

Sept. 1st Funeral 2.30. Kapwepwe, Pam and Arthur [Barlow] sit with us. O. cremated Ndola.

Kapwepwe, the Vice-President, was present because the President was in Addis Ababa. President Kaunda requested that a Memorial Service be held on 5th September so that he could give the Address. The Address at the funeral was given by Donald Arden, Bishop of Malawi. In it he referred to the bringing of the Brothers and Sisters of St. Francis to work in Zambia, the farewell to Oliver's many friends at St. Francis Hospital as the last act of his ministry and the prospect of his soon being laid to rest in the nearby Chapel of St. Francis. He also spoke of St. Francis' words as he came near to his death.

'It meant an immense amount to him' the Bishop said 'that your great President, Kenneth Kaunda, could write to him by his Christian name and as a personal friend. It meant a lot to him that he was a citizen of this country of Zambia.'

In his closing words he again drew attention to Oliver's attachment to St. Francis and spoke of him as 'a man and a lover of men; a shepherd and a lover of sheep; a Franciscan and a lover of Christ.'

'May he rest in peace.'

Father Francis S.S.F. has written: 'I was often taken aback by Oliver's personal humility. I was abashed at being asked by him for a Blessing, or his insistence on carrying my luggage.'

Kenneth Kaunda, the President, spoke at the Memorial Service of his friendship with Oliver and of the long evenings they spent together, both before and after Independence, discussing issues that affected his country. 'Oliver loved us in this country' he said. 'We shall miss him because we loved him. My pride is that his body rests in Zambia, the country he loved.'

James Robertson paid a further tribute to Oliver in the Diocesan leaflet, writing especially of his debt to Prudence. 'With her constant support he made his own home in Lusaka an example and inspiration to every family in the land. God has taken him to Himself in a very special way, but we all know that this is simply the climax of a taking that had already been accomplished in life.'

OLIVER'S COFFIN ESCORTED OUT OF THE CATHEDRAL, FOLLOWED BY JOHN, PRUDENCE AND HIS NEPHEW LISLE RYDER.

265

EPILOGUE

John returned to England after the Memorial Service while Prue and Lisle set about sorting out Bishop's Lodge and answering letters. They somehow found time to drive to Livingstone, see the Falls and call in at Mapanza on the way back. Before they left for London at the end of the month they attended an Ordination in the Cathedral, but were back in England in time for the Memorial Service in Westminster Abbey on 28th September.

Many years later John received a letter from Fanuel Isaiah Chiwawa explaining that the Anglican Christian congregation around Kawele decided to build a Chapel near the crash site in memory of the late Archbishop OLIVA. The Church was built of pole and mud construction with full permission of Senior Chief Kalindawalo of the Nsenga people of Petauke. Church services were conducted there every Sunday until it collapsed as a result of heavy rains in the wet season of 1992-93.

After this it was decided to build a permanent brick building, and fund-raising began. On 21st October 1995 Bishop John Osmers laid the Foundation Stone of the Church of St. Francis. Work is proceeding slowly, partly due to lack of funds, but work on the roof should be well under way by now.

After returning to London, Prudence lived for some time in Kensington, where she was visited by many old friends from Zambia. She had a companion to help her there before she had to move to a Nursing Home, near Oxford. This was not far from Bob and Hilaré, nor from Felicity and Ted, who were then living near Bicester. Both Hilaré and Felicity died not long after Prudence moved, but John and his wife, Pip, moved to West Ilsley, near Wantage and were able to pay regular visits to Freeland. She had many other visitors there - friends from her days in Zambia, like Celia Phillips, Peter Wyld and Bishop Paul Burrough and his wife, Bess, who was one of her favourites. Often, and sometimes unexpectedly, so John reports, a flash of Prudence's acute intelligence, humour and quickness would surprise her visitors, with some item that they had forgotten but she remembered.

James Robertson paid to Prue a loving and richly deserved tribute at her funeral after she died on the Feast of the Epiphany in 1990.

John, the last surviving member of that generation of the family, now presents the story of Oliver which he hopes many will like to read.

APPENDIX A   2nd.Bn. K.R.R.C.

MOVEMENT ORDER NO.2

Ref.Maps: EL HAMMAM)
          EL ALAMEIN) 1/100,000.

- - - - - - - - - - - - - - -

1. Information.   Enemy and own trps. dispositions to be seen on
                   map in Rear link.

2. Intention.   2 K.R.R.C. will move to Regulating Point on receipt
3. Method.   of order from 7 Motor Bde.
                  Route. From present position of Bn.H.Q. for half
                  a mile north along track marked with petrol tins
                  to start of Star Route. Thence along route marked
                  with stars to Regulating Point.
                  S.P. Present position of Bn.H.Q.
                  Time past S.P. As ordered later.
                  Order of March. C.Coy, Control, Lt.A.A.,B.Coy,A.Coy,
                  D Coy less trps,"S" Coy 2 R.B. less 5 trps,H.Q.
                  Coy with Light Recovery Vehicle.
                  Speed and Density.
                  By night . 6 M.I.H.   50 V.T.M.
                  By day   . 10 M.I.H.   20 V.T.M.
                  Movement. Wheeled vehicles will leave all route
                  marking lights or signs on their right. Tracked
                  vehicles will move beside and NOT on the route
                  .... except where routes cross
                  ....of C.Coy ...

4. Admini......................................

                  ....water will be consumed at ....
                  of half gallon per man per day ....further orders
                  Emergency Rations will be carried by each man.
                  Petrol. 15 miles of petrol will be carried by each
                  vehicle in addition to normal load in order to be
                  able to top up at regulating point.
                  Recovery. All crocks will be towed forward if possible
                  Exact location of any crocks which neither Coys nor
                  unit Light Recovery vehicle can tow forward will be
                  forwarded to this H.Q.

5. Intercommunication.
                  Listening watch from time of Order to move.
                  Wireless silence until broken by Bn. control.

In the field

23 Oct. 42.   Captain.
                                   The King's Royal Rifle Corps.
Distribution.   Adjutant 2nd Battalion.

All Coys.
"S" Coy 2 R.B. (MW)
Coy Lt. A.A.
Sig. O.
R.Q.
Page 5.

Churches Blessed, Consecrated or Dedicated
1952 to 1970.

1952	Nave of the Pro-Cathedral, Ndola
	St. Philip's Church, Luanshya
1953	St. Barnabas' Church, Chingola
	Cross of the Cathedral, Lusaka
	St. Francis Chapel, Katete
	St. Philip's Church, Matero
	St. Joseph's Church, Jumbe
	All Saints Church, Mutipula
1954	Chapel at Chalimbana
	St. John the Evangelist Church, Fort Roseberry
	Nave of the Church of African Martyrs, Ndola
1955	All Saints Chapel, Chipili
1956	St. Giles Church, Fiwila
	St. Peter's Church, Lusaka
	Church of St. Mary Magdalene, Katuta
	St. Stephen's Church, Chombaomba
	St. George's Church, Broken Hill
	St. Cyprian's Church, Mufulira
	St. James' Church, Buchi, Kitwe
1957	Church of St. Francis of Assisi, Mutwe-wa-Nkoko
	St. John's Church, New Mzenja
	Altar on the site of the Cathedral, Lusaka
1958	St. Andrew's Church, Elizabethville
	St. Nicholas Church, Kalulushi
	St. Anne's Church, Mazabuka
	St. Aidan's Church, Kalomo
1959	St. John's Church, Chingola
	St. Matthew's Church, Chibondo
	Chapel of St. Francis of Assisi of the Cathedral, Lusaka
	St. Mary's Church, Ciwali

1959	St. Matthew's Church, Lundu
(contd.)	St. Monica's Church, Luanshya
1960	St. Martin's Church, Monze
	Priory Buildings, Chipili
	St. Mary's Church, Mufulira
	St. Mary's Church, Shakashina
	St. Barnabas Church, Fort Jameson
	St. Nicholas Church, Katemo
	The new Pro-Cathedral, Ndola
	St. Philip the Deacon's Church (extension), Matero
1961	Christchurch, Fort Jameson
	St. Thomas Church, Petauke
	St. Mary Magdalene Church, Woodlands, Lusaka
	St. Matthew's Church, Kapopo
1962	Church of St. Laurence the Martyr, Chikupili
	St. Mark's Church, Sisuika
	St. Alban's Church, Solwezi
	St. Agnes Church, Chingola
	St. Bartholomew's Church, Nceka
	Church of St. Simon and St. Jude, Simambumba
1963	St. Francis Church, Mutwe-wa-Nkoka
	Church of St. Augustine of Hippo, Kakwelesa
	All Saints Chapel of the Cathedral, Lusaka
	Cross over the High Altar of the Cathedral, Lusaka
	(given by St. George's, Broken Hill)
	St. Clare's Church, Bancroft
	St. Mark's Church, Liteta
1964	St. Patrick's Church, Chifuba, Ndola
	Church of Bernard Mzeki, the Martyr, Mwanza
	St. Stephen's Church, Kalumba
	St. Mary's Church, Mkushi
	St. John's Church, Kabwe
1965	St. Mary's Church, Ngulusa

1965	Franciscan House, Fiwila
(contd.)	Holy Cross Church, Ngolwe
	St. Luke's Church, Mpinda
	St. Luke's Church, Mwanerupaya
	St. Mary's Church, Mkushi
1966	St. Augustine's Church, Serowe
	St. Peter's Church, Mulungwe
1968	Church of St. Mary the Virgin, Chinika
1969	St. Matthew's Church, Chibondo
1970	St. Paul's Church, Muchinda's Village, Mkushi
	All Saints Church, Chansa
	St. Andrew's Church, Chinkwamba

APPENDIX C

ORDINATION of PRIESTS and DEACONS 1953 to 1966

1953   Christopher Kaoma

1955   Francis Lester Msokosela

1956   Francis Lester Msokosela

1957   Vincent Chilombe: James Njamu: Julius Chinise

1958   Emilius Nalumpa: Boniface Katebe

1959   Vincent Chilombe: James Njamu: Julius Chinise

1960   Emilius Nalumpa: Boniface Katebe

1963   Sebastian Bakare: Birinius Haundu:
        Christopher Manga: Henry Nkonga:
        Emmanuel Chimbelu: Domenico Muwana:
        Dunstan Kalungushi: Verrall Johnson:
        David Banda: Cuthbert Lambeta:
        Julius Mwengwe: Clement Hlanya

1965   David Banda: Cuthbert Lambeta:
        Julius Mwengwe: Clement Hlanya

1966   James Hoyle: George Bennett: Peter Armstrong

1967   Joseph Mbula: Francis Makambwe: Stephen Mumba:
        Nathan Mwanza

1968   Tom Cripps: Alfred Chilombo
        Joseph Njama

1970   Brother Aidan S.S.F
        (Priest in Charge, Church of the Holy Name, Fiwila)

272

APPENDIX D

PRIESTS INSTITUTED or INSTALLED 1955 to 1966

1955   Bernhard Higgins, Rector of Livingstone

1956   Howard Gribble, Mufulira

1957   Frederick Sillett, Rector of St. George's, Luanshya

1959   Peter Blake, Mufulira
        Canon Alfred Webster-Smith, All Saints, Lusaka

1962   Canon Alfred Webster-Smith, Dean of the Cathedral

1966   Patrick Appleford, Dean of Lusaka

APPENDIX E.

My dear people,

When a body ceases to breathe the life has gone out of it - when we cease to pray the life has gone from our souls. So long as we are struggling on in prayer, however poor it may be, our hearts and minds are open to God and He will renew His power within us. Now in Lent there is an opportunity for us to think about our prayer. How regular are we in praying day by day? Are we really seeking God in our prayer? Are we growing stronger in our Christian life through prayer?

There are many different ways of praying, though the object of all prayer is the glory of God. It might well be that you would find new interest in your prayer through reading a book about it during this Lent. Prayer should always be both simple and personal, but we can learn much about it from the experience of our fellow Christians. There is in particular one type of prayer, which helps us to grow in friendship with God and which is strongly recommended to us by those most experienced in prayer. It goes beyond the stage of asking for things, beyond the necessity of using words with our lips. In this prayer we dwell in heart and mind upon God revealed to us in Jesus Christ and so grow in friendship and understanding with Him as did His Disciples. This prayer is often called Mental Prayer or Meditation.

To practice this prayer all that is essential is to give the time to prayer, to read a passage from the Bible and to dwell in heart and mind upon the truths revealed in the passage. But many find help from using some more definite method to train our minds which wander so easily. I will therefore outline to you one of many possible ways of mental prayer, a way that I have long found useful for myself. You need to have at least a quarter of an hour. Half an hour would be better if possible and would seem all too short. If you haven't fifteen minutes each day I am sure you can make that time on certain days, if you think this prayer is worthwhile. First kneel down and remember the presence of God, be still and know that God is awaiting you. After a few minutes ask God the Holy Spirit to come to help you by using the hymn *Come, Holy Ghost, our souls inspire*, or the Collect for Whitsun. Then read from the Bible a passage which you have previously chosen, sitting or kneeling as is most helpful to you. Let us suppose that you have chosen the story of Our Lord's Agony in the Garden of Gethsemane. Then follow Our Lord's own teaching in using the first three petitions of His own prayer - *Hallowed be Thy name.* Think in wondering adoration of God's love revealed in Jesus praying to His Father before His death for us. Make full use of your imagination as God comes before you in majesty and love in the scene in the Garden. *Thy Kingdom come.* Think of the failure of the Disciples in their prayer that night and of our own frequent failures in prayer - ask to be forgiven failure and sin which so easily besets us. Pray that the Holy Spirit may drive the evil out of us and may reign in our hearts and minds. *Thy will be done, in earth as it is in heaven.* Our time in prayer with God is drawing to a close, but let us go back to our life in the world determined to live a little nearer to the ways of Heaven. Offer your whole self to God, that He may use you as a part of His Body, the Church. It will help to avoid disappointment and vagueness if you take one particular action which you can offer to God as your resolution. It may be something suggested in your prayer and it need not be something new. Finally thank God for your time spent with Him and sum up your whole prayer by saying the Lord's Prayer straight through. Whether by this way or another I do hope tshat we may grow in friendship with God this Lent by prayer.

INDEX

COMPILED BY THE AUTHOR